THE SHADOW OF THE GUILLOTINE

Representation of that Instrument of French refinement in Assassination the GUILLOTINE
Gentlemen of the Phalanx" & other well wishers to the King & Constitution of Great Britain.
by their devo
The Assassins of the King
Whither, – O whither shall my Blood ascend for Justice! – my Throne is seized on by my Murderers; my Brothers are driven
into exile; – my unhappy Wife & innocent Infants are shut up in the horrors of a Dungeon; while Robbers & Assassins are sheathing
their Daggers in the bowels of my Country! – Ah! ruined, desolated Country! dearest object of my heart! whose misery was to me the
sharpest pang in death; what will become of thee! – O Britons! vicegerents of eternal Justice, arbiters of the world! look
down from that height of power to which you are raised, & behold me here! – deprived of Life & of Kingdom, see where
I lie pillow, festering in my own Blood! which flies to your august tribunal for Justice! – By your affection for your own
Wives & Children – rescue mine; – by your love for your Country, by the blessings of that true Liberty which you possess; by the
virtues which adorn the British Crown – by all that is Sacred, & all that is dear to you – revenge the blood of a Monarch most
undeservedly butchered, – and rescue the Kingdom of France from being the prey of Violence, Usurpation & Cruelty.
Pub. Feb. 16th 1793. by H. Humphrey No. 18. Old Bond Street
The Blood of the Murdered crying for Vengeance.
J. Gy. des. et fect.

THE SHADOW OF THE GUILLOTINE

Britain and the French Revolution

DAVID BINDMAN

WITH CONTRIBUTIONS BY

AILEEN DAWSON

AND

MARK JONES

PUBLISHED FOR THE TRUSTEES OF THE BRITISH MUSEUM
BY BRITISH MUSEUM PUBLICATIONS

The Trustees of the British Museum
acknowledge with gratitude the generosity of
Musée de la Révolution Française (Vizille)
in sponsoring the colour plates for this book.

Published by British Museum Publications Ltd
46 Bloomsbury Street, London WC1B 3QQ

British Library Cataloguing in Publication data
Bindman, David, *1940–*
The shadow of the guillotine: Britain and the French Revolution
1. English visual arts. Influence on the French Revolution 1789–1799
I. Title II. Dawson, Aileen III. Jones, Mark, *1951–* IV. British Museum
709'.42

ISBN 0-7141-1637-8

Designed by Harry Green

Set in 11/13pt Baskerville by
Rowland Phototypesetting Ltd,
Bury St Edmunds, Suffolk,
and printed by
St Edmundsbury Press Ltd,
Bury St Edmunds, Suffolk

Front cover 87a Anon., *The Hopes of the Party! or the Darling Children of Democracy!*, aquatint, coloured, published 28 February 1798 by W. Holland.

Back cover 206p Thomas Spence, *Tree of Liberty*, copper token, *c.* 1795.

Frontispiece 111, James Gillray, *The Blood of the Murdered Crying out for Vengeance*, etching, coloured, published 16 February 1793 by H. Humphrey.

Contents

Foreword

The events of 1789 in France were so remarkable in themselves and so momentous in their consequences that they must be commemorated in Britain in their bicentennial year. It is equally clear that the British Museum, an institution that was already thirty-six years old at that time, was the appropriate place in which to hold it. On the other hand, there was no point in trying to mount a historical narrative of a type that would need access to the resources of the great French museums and libraries, which would themselves be committed to their own exhibitions.

We therefore welcomed Professor Bindman's proposal that we should approach the Revolution through the eyes of its contemporary British onlookers. These reactions ranged from sympathy or amusement to horror and revulsion as the Revolution pursued its course. But the material assembled shows that the response went far deeper than mere observation, and that the issues raised by the Revolution fundamentally affected British politics. The responses were, therefore, equally determined by the political position of each participant.

It was always intended that the exhibition should concentrate on the response in the visual arts. The visitor will find only glancing allusions to the great literary figures of the day; but this is an area which is already relatively well known. The same could not be said of the objects here catalogued. To locate these has involved considerable research in museums and libraries in Britain and abroad. The results have exceeded our most sanguine expectations, and we are confident that the resulting catalogue will be a major contribution both to French Revolutionary studies and to the wider investigation of the links between the visual arts and the societies that have produced them.

The compilation of this exhibition has depended on the ready co-operation of many lenders, to all of whom I would like to express the Museum's thanks. Most particularly I would single out Madame Tussaud's, whose contribution has included some of the most dramatic items. We are also grateful to Professor Brewer for writing the Historical Introduction. Finally I must thank David Bindman himself for the enormous effort he has made on our behalf. He has been ably assisted by two members of the staff of the Museum, Aileen Dawson and Mark Jones, who have respectively written the entries on the ceramics and the medals included in the exhibition. The liaison with the Department of Prints and Drawings, from which the majority of the exhibits are drawn, has been in the hands of Antony Griffiths, and the administration of the loans has been capably handled – as always – by Janice Reading.

Sir David Wilson
Director, British Museum

Acknowledgements

I should like to record my gratitude to everybody in the British Museum who has made working on this catalogue a pleasure from beginning to end, especially Frances Dunkels, her team in the Print Room and Janice Reading, and also Antony Griffiths, Aileen Dawson in the Department of Medieval and Later Antiquities and Mark Jones in the Department of Coins and Medals. A great many people have suggested objects I would not otherwise have known about and have helped in innumerable ways. I would like to express particular thanks to the following: Susan Adams, David Alexander, Brian Allen, Terence Allott, Martin Angerer, Malcolm Baker, Stella Beddoe, Geoffrey Bindman, Steven Blake, Philippe Bordes, John Brewer, David Blayney Brown, Julius and Barbara Bryant, Lionel Burman, Stephen Calloway, Frances Carey, Linda Colley, Undine Concannon, Grace Dempsey, Diana Dethloff, Stephen Deuchar, John Dinwiddie, Robert Douwma, Bill Drummond, Ann Eatwell, Andrew Edmunds, Caroline Elam, Ann Forsdyke, Ruth Fine, Celina Fox, John Gage, Kenneth Garlick, Richard Godfrey, Sir Ernst Gombrich, Miranda Goodby, Catherine Gordon, Richard Gray, Michael Jaffé, Joyce Jayes, Ralph Hyde, Anthony Kilroy, Lionel Lambourne, John Leighton, Keir McGuinness, John Mackrell, John Mallet, John May, Lynn Miller, Tim Miller, Janie Munro, Tessa Murdoch, Patrick Noon, Leonée Ormond, Nick Penny, Julia Poole, Stephen Price, Ben Read, Aileen Ribiero, Gaye Blake Roberts, Hugh Roberts, Janie Roberts, Duncan Robinson, John Rowlands, Judy Rudoe, Sydney Sabin, Katie Scott, David Scrase, Jacob Simon, Jeremy Smith, Michael Snodin, Richard Spencer, Lindsay Stainton, Neil Stratford, John Sunderland, Joan Sussler, Patrick Sweeney, Rosemary Treble, Philip Ward-Jackson, Anthony Wells-Cole, Helen Weston, Reginald Williams, Christopher Wilson, Timothy Wilson, Andrew Wilton, Christopher Wood, Pamela Wood, Richard Wrigley.

Special thanks are also due to my friend and colleague Tom Gretton who read the manuscript, Louise Simson who helped to track down many of the most elusive objects, Deborah Wakeling, the editor at British Museum Publications, and as ever Frances Carey.

Preface

The starting-point for the idea of this exhibition was a review by Roy Porter in *The London Review of Books*, 20 March 1986, in which he complained that satirical prints had been too often used 'as visual documentation for a political narrative, rather like a Georgian version of the Bayeux Tapestry', and that we must 'analyse these prints not just as "evidence" but as "art", with its own conventions for expressing moral messages'. It is easy to imagine a French Revolution exhibition along the lines deplored by Porter, with the major events represented by prints and paintings, regardless of their conventions of representation and the attitudes of their producers. Another possibility, in which the works in the exhibition are chosen for their artistic quality rather than for their historical interest seems equally unsatisfactory. The aim of the present exhibition has been to avoid both extremes and, more positively, to look at the British response to the French Revolution in the light of the visual culture of the period. This has led to an emphasis on the variety of the visual material: no arbitrary barriers have been set up between art and non-art, or one medium and another, so the exhibition contains not only paintings but among other things domestic pottery and trade tokens. They are all, however, in one way or another, public works, designed for general consumption, and completely private objects like working manuscripts or printed books without illustrations that make no visual point have been excluded. Such a range of objects, often highly partisan in their intentions, inevitably raises the question of the persuasive power of images, not only in their own time but also in ours. If our first thought of the French Revolution is of a guillotine rather than a cap of liberty, then a partial version of events has triumphed despite all the attempts of historians to give a more balanced view.

From a more practical standpoint the theme of the British response to the French Revolution has also presented an opportunity to show some of the extraordinary resources of the British Museum, not only in the Department of Prints and Drawings but also in the Departments of Medieval and Later Antiquities and Coins and Medals. Yet the very richness of the collections also means a superabundance of material from which to choose, and the selection of objects has required rigorous self-denial on the part of the organiser. It would have been very easy to have included 1,000 objects rather than 300, or to have restricted the scope of the exhibition. As far as possible all types of object produced in the period are represented, but some, like the caricatures, may stand in each case for dozens of other designs, while the Staffordshire mugs, though a fairly full representation of types presently known, are only samples of what was probably an immense production. An event like the publication of Burke's *Reflections on the Revolution in France* in 1790 provoked at least a dozen separate caricatures of which only one has been represented in the exhibition; in other cases the print itself may have been issued in an exceptionally large run with the explicit purpose of reaching a national audience. On the other hand, the small size of trade tokens has allowed an almost complete representation of the radical variety produced in the 1790s.

The French Revolution is defined here in terms of the period from the fall of the Bastille on 14 July 1789 to Napoleon's *coup d'état* of 9–10 December 1799 (18–19 Brumaire, l'an VIII). This means that the Thermidor government and the Directory, which followed the fall of Robespierre in July 1794, are regarded, as they tend to be by recent historians, as just as much part of the Revolution as the Terror of 1793–4. Objects of the mid-Victorian period which refer to events within that ten-year period have been brought in to the retrospective section at the end of the exhibition. British observers tended to focus almost exclusively upon events in Paris, and the concern of many present-day historians with the effects of the Revolution in the French provinces is not generally reflected in the objects produced, though there are exceptions.

The exhibition also makes no claim to be comprehensive in terms of Britain. Birmingham, Somerset and Staffordshire play an important part in the story, but London was the chief centre of production for almost all the prints, paintings and trade tokens in the exhibition. It was assumed that Scotland and Ireland would have their own commemorations of the Revolution and so they have not been brought within the compass of the exhibition, and there is also an exhibition in the British Library of manuscript and printed material relating to the French Revolution.

Finally, the point needs to be made that the selection has been made as much on visual as on purely historical grounds: if one were to be rigorously historical, the exhibition would have to contain a great many portraits and images from periodicals, which were the chief means of giving the British public an actual picture of events in France. I have tried in every case to choose objects with some visual impact or resonance; not all of them are pleasant to look at, but I would hope that none are dull.

David Bindman
Westfield College, University of London

'This monstrous tragi-comic scene': British reactions to the French Revolution

Madness and revolution

In 1796 the proceedings of the House of Commons were rudely interrupted by an agitated and vociferous Welsh tea-broker, James Tilly Matthews. His disruption was prompted by a burning desire to expose a dastardly French plot against the British state. For Matthews believed that he had discovered a plan by Britain's revolutionary enemies to employ 'magnetic spies' using 'animal magnetism' to mesmerise the British into 'surrendering to the French every secret of the British government . . . republicanising Great Britain and Ireland, and particularly . . . disorganising the British navy, to create such a confusion therein, as to admit the French armaments to move without danger'.[1] Using the potent and invisible powers of suggestion, employing their special knowledge of the scientific work of Dr Mesmer, the French, Matthews thought, would gain control of the nation's will, reducing Britain's leaders, armies and navies to mere marionettes, unknowingly manipulated in accordance with the revolutionaries' wishes.

Matthews's expostulation failed in its attempt to convince the political nation that its leaders had been seduced by France. This sanguinity was not a sign of scepticism about the theories of mesmerism – which continued to enjoy a vogue in England well into the nineteenth century – but of incredulity at the suggestion that members of the current ministry, especially William Pitt and Lord Liverpool, were in league with England's oldest foe. The idea was unanimously discounted and Matthews seen as deluded, possibly deranged. Brought before the Privy Council, he was declared insane and clapped into Bethlem, the lunatic asylum.

The hapless tea-broker was never to be freed. During the years of his protracted confinement he was often the victim of grandiose and contradictory delusions, at one minute becoming an all-powerful despot, the 'Arch-Grand-Arch-Emperor Supreme' lording it over the likes of George III and Louis XVI, at other times degenerating into a totally impotent creature, subject to tortures more terrible than any devised in a bastille. Yet, whether the perpetrator or victim of tyranny, Matthews never lost his antipathy towards monarchical authority and its minions. This ensured his continued incarceration. Advocating the extermination of George III, his government, and most European kings, Matthews was unlikely to be released by the politicians who, mindful of their own safety, had placed him under lock and key. In 1815, the year in which the French revolutionary bogey was laid to rest, Matthews died in Fox's London House Asylum in Hackney.[2]

James Tilly Matthews's tale is the sad story of a paranoid and deeply disturbed man. The tea-broker had the dubious distinction of being classified as a lunatic both by the revolutionary regime in Paris (where he was locked up between 1793 and 1796) and by Pitt's government in London. But Matthews's response to the astonishing events in France was less idiosyncratic than might appear. His only peculiarity was to embody, in schizophrenic fashion, both the radical and conservative British reactions to the French Revolution. To a republicanism that outstripped the antimonarchical irreverence of Tom Paine he added a conservative paranoia even greater than that of Edmund Burke. Matthews's misfortunes also highlight two other enduring English responses to the French Revolution: the association of madness with revolutionary fervour and the mixture of fear and exhilaration – what contemporaries described as the 'terrible of the sublime' – provoked by the expression of unconstrained revolutionary power.

Revolutionary politics

Matthews and his fellow Britons were frightened and excited by the ferocious, energetic, restless revolutionary politics that emerged in France after 1789, a politics that at once seemed to turn the world upside down and to offer infinite possibilities, both good and bad. The crisis of the *ancien régime* radically redrew the boundaries of the French political universe. No longer confined to courtly aristocrats and the salons of the intelligentsia, it burst its confines to encircle the artisan and peasant, the café, the club and the street. Hundreds of journals were launched, articles poured from the press; the boulevards resounded to revolutionary songs and ballads; bourgeois and sans-culottes set up associations in which the hard dogma of revolutionary politics was forged in the intense heat of political debate. At a stroke the French acquired a political culture which resembled that which the English had developed over a century or more.

France was awash with politics. They ebbed and flowed in the nation's new institutions – the National Assembly, the Convention, the Committee of Public Safety and the Commune of Paris – and saturated the social order. No aspect of everyday life was too mundane to escape the flood. Revolutionary politics had its language, rhetoric and slogans; its own gestures, forms of deportment and costume – including hairstyles; its own imagery, symbols and iconography; its distinctive temples, ceremonies and festivals. The Revolution even produced its own timetable, a calendar which began with the Revolution and was divided into ten-day weeks.

Some of this revolutionary political culture had its roots in the past, drawing on the familiar stock of classical allusion or the icongraphy found in emblem books. Yet even here there were new departures, a break with tradition which can be seen in some of the Revolution's most powerful symbols. During the Revolution the classical female figure of liberty – a familiar symbol in British politics – was portrayed not only as tranquil, passive and sedentary but, with short dress and spear or pike in hand, as an active and energetic proponent of the principle she embodied. In similar fashion and thanks largely to the efforts of the revolutionary painter Jacques-Louis David, the figure of Hercules ceased to represent the power of kings, becoming a symbol of the strength and unity of the French people. No longer resting in classical, Farnese-like repose, Hercules was even portrayed in the mien and guise of a revolutionary sans-culotte.[3]

The leitmotif of revolutionary political culture, even when its idioms were familiar, was radical change not continuity. 'To be truly Republican', exclaimed one revolutionary manifesto, 'each citizen must experience and bring about in himself a revolution equal to the one that has changed France. There is nothing, absolutely nothing in common between the slave of a tyrant and the inhabitant of a free state; the customs of the latter, his principles, his sentiments, his action, all must be new'.[4]

Edmund Burke, that most ferocious critic of French revolutionary politics, was right: 1789 was not 1688; the French Revolution was not the 'Glorious Revolution' in France. While at the end of the seventeenth century the English had fiddled with the tangled skein of history, in the final decade of the eighteenth the French used the sword of reason to cut the Gordian knot. Of course there were important continuities which crossed the revolutionary divide, and the old order was less moribund and more reformist than it was portrayed in retrospect. But revolutionary ideology was utterly committed to the idea that 1789 marked a sharp caesura with the past. The sclerotic ogre of the *ancien régime*, its arteries blocked by privilege, vision blinded by secrecy, reason distorted by superstition, temper destroyed by outbreaks of autocratic rage, and its body wracked by the disease of social divisiveness, was one of the most potent images created by revolutionary politics. The French Revolution was not just the midwife of a new and youthful type of politics; it also brought the *ancien régime* into being.

Revolutionary politics was both demonstration and proof of a new social and cultural order. To prove that a total break had been made with the past it had to appear everywhere: its symbols to be ubiquitous; its rituals and ceremonies perspicuous and public. For the ardent revolutionary the Revolution must not only happen; it had to be seen to occur, its images and messages inscribed again and again on revolutionary participants and observers alike. This visual quality provided artists with unparalleled opportunities: it gave the painter a number of subjects which distilled the essence of revolutionary conflict, the engraver the opportunity to record or, more usually, invent history, and the visual satirist the chance to deploy a wonderful graphic repertoire which included old symbols and new devices. When the controversy over the French Revolution was joined in England, the caricaturist and the engraver were among its most vigorous participants.

First reactions

The first English responses to the French Revolution were generally favourable, though even those who agreed in welcoming France's political upheaval did so for different reasons and with conflicting analyses of what was happening across the Channel. Some government ministers were simply glad that France's military might and diplomatic influence would be curbed by her domestic turmoil. (Their pleasure proved misplaced: revolutionary France showed herself capable of combining both internal discord and external military triumph.) Most of the Whig Opposition, which had close links with liberal aristocratic opinion in France, welcomed 1789 as a new 'Glorious Revolution' destined to plant the firm flower of English politics in Gallic soil. Radicals, on the other hand, saw events in France not as imitative of England but as an international phenomenon. Looking to events in North America as well as in Europe, they viewed the Revolution as the most recent example of the progressive overthrow of privilege and superstition, the advent of a political world governed by popular sovereignty.

At its inception the Revolution bolstered the forces in favour of radicalism and reform in England. It was used to corroborate the critical analyses of Church and State by the likes of Joseph Priestley, Tom Paine, John Horne Tooke, Thomas Spence and Richard Price; it inspired the political, literary and aesthetic works of William Blake, William Godwin and Mary Wollstonecraft; and it encouraged the revival of old political associations such as the Society for Constitutional Information as well as the foundation of new societies, most notably the London Corresponding Society, devoted to political education and reform.

The aims, extent and social composition of the radical supporters of the French Revolution in Britain have long been a matter of debate among historians. On some matters there can, however, be little doubt. Radicals seem to have had a political rather than social agenda. They aimed to achieve political equality and the removal of privilege through institutional reform, though they did not, with the notable exception of Thomas Spence, usually advocate the abolition of private property. Radicals also emphasised popular sovereignty and natural rights, even when they claimed to be ardent proponents of the British constitution rather than republicans. Most were committed to achieving peaceful reform through the powers of persuasion – hence their emphasis on the press and political education – though there were always some radicals willing to contemplate violence to accomplish their ends. Members of the professions, manufacturers and middle-class intellectuals, as well as artisans and those of the labouring classes, all supported the radical cause. Dissenters – Protestants who were not members of the Church of England – and non-believers were also prominent. The social mix of radicals varied in different parts of the country. In Norwich middle-class dissenters provided radical leadership; in Sheffield support was more demotic.[5]

Between 1788 and 1792 Britain saw the most sustained radical and reformist activity since the civil wars of the seventeenth century: a radical newspaper press flourished as never before; radical clubs and associations were set up in nearly thirty English towns, as well as in Scotland and Ireland; and the astonishing success of Thomas Paine's *The Rights of Man*, published in two parts in 1791–2, ensured the unprecedented exposure of radical political ideas. William Pitt's government may have exaggerated the extent of republican ideas and the threat of insurrection but it was rightly apprehensive about the reformist initiatives which challenged the prevailing conventions of parliamentary politics.

But in the early days of the Revolution English support for change in France was not confined to radicals or reformers. A more general sympathy was expressed for what was seen as the justifiable overthrow of the overweening and arbitrary power which every Englishman knew to be characteristic of the French state. Such sentiment is exemplified by the English accounts – both verbal and visual – of the storming of the Bastille. Above all, English graphic art strongly underscored the revolutionary representation of the Bastille as the embodiment of the *ancien régime*: the struggle for its capture was portrayed as heroic, the proportions of the fortress exaggerated to enhance its menace, and its interior depicted, most notably in Gillray's engraving of Northcote's painting (no. 24), as an oubliette with prostrate skeletons, shackled prisoners and infernal machines of torture. As David Bindman points out, these images owe much to the sensational memoirs of those, such as Simon Linguet, who were incarcerated in the Bastille; they are also informed by a sensibility shaped by Piranesi, 'Gothic' literature and the aesthetic of the sublime.

Nevertheless, such representations of the fall of the Bastille were readily accepted in England because they accorded with long-standing ideas about the absence of French liberty and the enormities of French justice. At the fall of the Bastille French revolutionary politics and English stereotypes of France converged. Both glossed over many awkward facts: the paucity of prisoners, most of whom were sexual offenders and lunatics, in the fortress (if it had been stormed a

24 James Northcote, engraved by James Gillray, *Le triomphe de la Liberté en l'élargissement de la Bastille, dédié à la Nation Francoise*, engraving, published 12 July 1790. British Museum, Smith Collection. See also p. 92.

few weeks earlier, the Marquis de Sade would have been one of those liberated); its comfort when compared with many eighteenth-century gaols; the declining use of *lettres de cachet* to imprison offenders; and the aim of the assault which had been not to free prisoners but to capture gunpowder. Each helped make the storming of the Bastille the most important moment in the early years of the Revolution. In both English and French written accounts of the storming of the Bastille the fall of the fortress and of the *ancien régime* are virtually indistinguishable. For commentators of both nationalities 14 July 1789 was the essential revolutionary moment.

The years before 1792 marked an era of optimism in England about the Revolution. The future seemed bright, the atmosphere so heady as to produce euphoria. Such heady enthusiasm is personified in the young Wordsworth, exemplified by the pro-revolutionary iconography of Thomas Spence and perfectly captured in Samuel Romilly's lyrical celebration in 1790:

Who, indeed, that deserves the name of an Englishman, can have preserved a cold and deadly indifference, when he found a nation, which had been for ages enslaved, rousing on a sudden from their ignominious lethargy, breaking asunder their bonds, and, with an unanimity which has no example in history, demanding a free constitution: when he viewed all the fortresses of tyranny destroyed; when he saw the dungeons of the state thrown open, and the prisons of superstition unlocked?[6]

The conservative response

If, in the early days of the Revolution, there was widespread sympathy for its aims, there was one figure whose intractable opposition to the French Revolution stood out. The bespectacled, loquacious Edmund Burke, defender of political parties, friend of the American colonists, critic of England's policy towards Ireland and scourge of the Governor-General of India, Warren Hastings, was the first, the foremost and the most influential of the critics of the French Revolution. Almost all of the most important conservative perceptions of the Revolution were first formulated by Burke. He composed the score which others revised and embellished. Burke recognised the events in France as a new sort of revolution. He predicted its violence, energy and absence of constraint, condemned its conduct as a violation of nature, castigated its rejection of prescription and convention, branded its politics as the madness of reason, identified the sources of its attraction to English sensibilities, and took as one of his most potent images the predicament of the French royal family. Every one of these themes was to recur in subsequent polemics against the politics of revolutionary France.[7] Burke set the agenda for the debate about the French Revolution. It must not be forgotten that many of the great radical works of the 1790s, including Paine's *The Rights of Man* and Mary Wollstonecraft's *A Vindication of the Rights of Men*, as well as the popular tracts *Hog's Wash* and *Pig's Meat*, were written in response to Burke's scathing attack, *Reflections on the Revolution in France* (1790).

For all its vision and passion Burke's early and vehement denunciation of the Revolution has to be seen in the more mundane light of his career in British politics. By 1789 Burke's political prospects, if not in total darkness, were certainly in partial eclipse. His mentor, the frail and sickly Marquis of Rockingham, had died of influenza in 1783. His influence on other Whig political leaders, notably the raffish set which surrounded Charles James Fox and the Prince of Wales, had fallen into precipitous decline, and his obsessive hounding of Warren Hastings, impeached for his conduct in India, had given him the reputation for a vindictiveness which verged on mania. Indeed, during the late 1780s and early 90s the dark cloud of madness which had engulfed James Tilly Matthews threatened the genius of Edmund Burke. Burke's parliamentary histrionics and the vehemence with which he defended his views and denounced his critics led many MPs to believe that he had become unhinged.

Burke's wrath – expressed with an astonishing eloquence fuelled by bitterness and anger – was directed as much at English radical Dissenters who advocated popular sovereignty and at their aristocratic sympathisers, whom he believed to have abandoned the true principles of 'aristocracy', as it was towards members of the French National Assembly.[8] The first objects of Burke's venom in his *Reflections on the Revolution in France* were Richard Price, unitarian advocate of the accountability of kings, and Earl Stanhope, a Whig aristocrat with strong radical sympathies. This antipathy is not hard to explain. Radical Dissenters, of similar social (though very different religious) background to Burke, threatened to replace him as the intellectual leader of the Whig Party; aristocratic reformers had rejected his opposition to parliamentary reform for nearly a decade. For Burke the French Revolution was a new issue in an old political battle.

48 Anon., *The Knight of the Woful Countenance*, etching, coloured, published 15 November 1790. British Museum. See also p. 107.

The same can be said about the overall British reaction to the French Revolution. For, though the Revolution was, as Burke himself emphasised, an unprecedented event, and though it had novel consequences in Britain, its image and effects were constantly refracted through the twin lenses of British history and British politics. If, at the outset, the Revolution was viewed in the light of Britain's 'Glorious Revolution' of 1688, the events of 1792–3 – the Paris Insurrection, the September Massacres, the abolition of monarchy, the Edict of Fraternity, the execution of the French king and queen and the advent of the Terror – raised another spectre, that of Britain's seventeenth-century regicidal regime; and in the context of British politics these moves towards a sanguinary republicanism shifted the balance of forces away from supporters of the Revolution. Early sympathisers such as Samuel Romilly and Arthur Young turned against the Revolution; the Whig parliamentary opposition to the government of the younger Pitt fell into hopeless disarray; frightened men of property hastened to support both Crown and Government, and peaceful reformers struggled to preserve a distinction between their aspirations and events in France. Most notable of all, the government, convinced that sedition and insurrection were at hand, mobilised popular support in a concerted attempt to stamp out radical sympathies in Britain.

Pitt's so-called 'Reign of Terror' was a feeble creature compared with the furies unleashed in France. (The real British Terror occurred in Ireland, where over 30,000 died in the Rebellion of 1798 and its aftermath. This was a far greater number than perished during the Terror in France.) In many ways the government's tactics were no different from those of earlier eighteenth-century English regimes. The suspension of Habeas Corpus, the imprisonment of incautious radicals for uttering 'Seditious Words', the subsidisation of a sympathetic press, the development of a network of spies, the use of loyalist groups to terrorise dissidents and the repeated imprisonment of printers and journalists to prevent their publishing were all tactics used by earlier Whig governments against their Jacobite (and sometimes Tory) critics. Sir Robert Walpole would have been fully familiar with most of the younger Pitt's ploys.

But if the tactics used by the government and its supporters were not novel, the extent and scope of the suppression of radicalism were without precedent. In many towns Church and King Clubs and Loyalist Associations (of which the most important was the Association for Preserving Liberty and Property against Republicans and Levellers which met at the Crown and Anchor in London) were active in the systematic intimidation of radicals and their sympathisers. Meeting regularly in local taverns – the mugs and vessels with loyalist toasts and slogans (see, for example, no. 57) were almost certainly made for members of these fraternities – they sallied forth to interrogate local people about their political sympathies, and to force innkeepers to swear that they would not allow 'seditious meetings' on their premises. Regiments of volunteers, raised by public subscription and manned chiefly by the propertied classes, acted as a domestic military police. This crusade against 'sedition' in the countryside and provincial towns was co-ordinated by government officials at the recently created Home Office.

The scope of the propaganda campaign against English Jacobins and reformers was also new. In order to counteract the influence of Tom Paine's *The Rights of Man* which, as Hannah More complained, was being read in cottages, workshops, mines and coalpits, the government and its allies were forced to produce popular loyalist literature, some of it in the vernacular, aimed at the humblest classes. The Crown and Anchor Society not only produced the widely disseminated print, *The Contrast*, based on Rowlandson's design (see no. 72) but also distributed over fifty penny tracts at the end of 1792. In Manchester local loyalists gave out 10,000 copies of their loyalist address as well as 6,000 copies of loyal political pamphlets. Yet such efforts were dwarfed by those of Hannah More, who followed her deeply conservative *Village Politics* of 1792 by a series of Cheap Repository Tracts (no. 209) which sold nearly two million copies by 1798.[9]

The conservtive reaction was marked both by failure and success. The government was unable to convict the leading radicals of treason – brilliant lawyers and independent jurors thwarted their efforts – though it had greater success in its prosecutions for seditious libel. Harassment by magistrates and loyalist associations drove some radicals to despair, political quietism or exile; others it drove into the very revolutionary politics of insurrection which it aimed to prevent. The repressive legislation that reached the statute-book in 1795 (the Treasonable Practices Act and the Seditious Meetings Act) spoke to a parliamentary determination to crush dissidence even at the expense of Englishmen's liberties, but its bark was much greater than its bite. These notorious Two Acts were rarely used to prosecute radicals.

The conservative propaganda campaign undoubtedly had more long-term effects. Whatever its impact on the popular audience to which much of its printed and graphic material was directed, it certainly succeeded in altering the terms of political debate within the property-owning classes. As Romilly was to comment, the French Revolution created 'among the higher orders . . . a horror of every kind of innovation'.[10] Total loyalty to King and Constitution was required; any sort of criticism became tainted with the odour of insurrection. As a result, the limits of legitimate political discussion were severely contracted.

Conservative strategies

An extremely partial, deliberately exaggerated and deeply hostile depiction of the French Revolution was an essential part of the English conservative counter-attack against British radicals and reformers. Political commentators and caricaturists used a variety of means to tar their domestic enemies with the brush of French revolutionary politics. Techniques were crude though effective. Loyalist prints regularly 'Frenchified' Opposition politicians, dressing them as sans-culottes or identifying them with individual French Jacobins (see, for example, no. 149). This tactic of 'proletarianising' genteel politicians who flirted with reform or the lower classes was not new. Before the Revolution the leader of the parliamentary Opposition, Charles James Fox, had often been portrayed as an unkempt and uncouth plebeian – as a beggar, a knife-grinder, butcher, pugilist and blacksmith.[11] But after 1789 he and his allies were depicted as both vulgar *and* French. Not only did their plebeian appearance imply their support for the collapse of social distinctions, for social as well as political equality, but they were also identified as traitorous supporters of England's oldest enemy. Gillray took this theme to its logical conclusion. In his 1795 print *Patriotic Regeneration* (no. 189) he portrays Fox and his friends as the instigators of an oppressive and bloody regime, forcing French revolutionary politics on the English public.

At first sight the concentration of the political prints on the parliamentary Opposition – who may have been reformers but certainly were not republicans – seems a trifle odd. Where are the real radicals and revolutionaries in this conservative demonology? Tom Paine, of course, was caricatured as the radical staymaker and tailor. He also appears on the gallows, portrayed in his last moments or dangling from a gibbet (see nos 54–5). Such prints and engravings were a lasting visual reminder of the numerous ritual executions of Paine's effigy which were enacted in towns and villages all over the country in 1792 and 1793. But the caricature of individual English Jacobins is conspicuous by its absence. When throngs of reformers and revolutionaries, whether French or British, are depicted, they appear as a grotesque, undifferentiated mass. Only the tradesmen's tools – the barber's comb, the butcher's steel – give them much identity.

This is no coincidence. For the radical world depicted by its opponents is beyond that of civil society, public order or personal decorum. It is an inferno. As Burke put it in 1794: 'The condition of France at this moment was so frightful and horrible, that if a painter wished to portray a description of hell, he could not find

London Pub: Decr 20 1792 by S Fores N3 Piccadilly who has again opened his Exhibition Room to which he has added several Hundred Old & new Subjec
Ca Ira, Ca Ira, Ca Ira,
God Save Great George our King
IC
A RIGHT-HONORABLE alias a Sans Culotte
How Happy could I be with Either
Were I but the Chief of the Throng.
But Do—n it as I can get Neither
I'll take either Part of the Song.

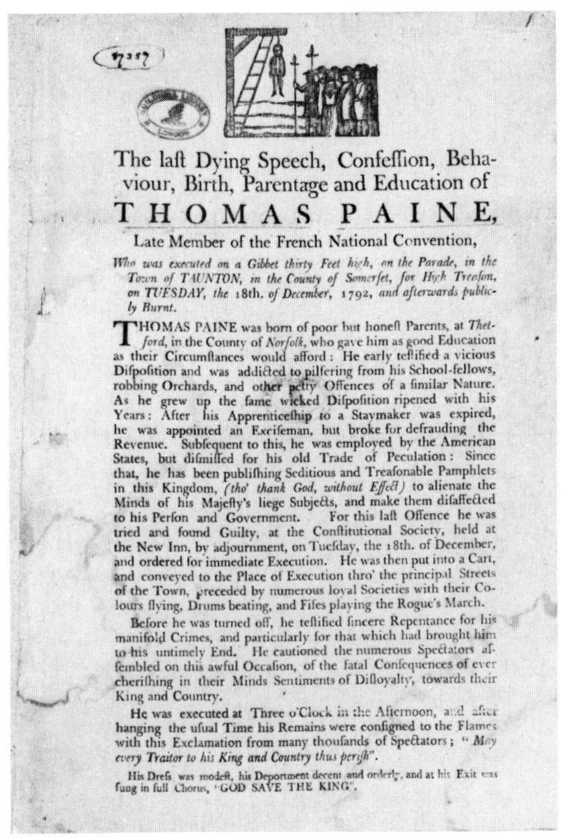

The laſt Dying Speech, Confeſſion, Behaviour, Birth, Parentage and Education of

THOMAS PAINE,

Late Member of the French National Convention,

Who was executed on a Gibbet thirty Feet high, on the Parade, in the Town of TAUNTON, in the County of Somerſet, for High Treaſon, on TUESDAY, the 18th. *of December,* 1792, *and afterwards publicly Burnt.*

THOMAS PAINE was born of poor but honeſt Parents, at *Thetford*, in the County of *Norfolk*, who gave him as good Education as their Circumſtances would afford: He early teſtified a vicious Diſpoſition and was addicted to pilfering from his School-fellows, robbing Orchards, and other petty Offences of a ſimilar Nature. As he grew up the ſame wicked Diſpoſition ripened with his Years: After his Apprenticeſhip to a Staymaker was expired, he was appointed an Exciſeman, but broke for defrauding the Revenue. Subſequent to this, he was employed by the American States, but diſmiſſed for his old Trade of Peculation: Since that, he has been publiſhing Seditious and Treaſonable Pamphlets in this Kingdom, *(tho' thank God, without Effect)* to alienate the Minds of his Majeſty's liege Subjects, and make them diſaffected to his Perſon and Government. For this laſt Offence he was tried and found Guilty, at the Conſtitutional Society, held at the New Inn, by adjournment, on Tueſday, the 18th. of December, and ordered for immediate Execution. He was then put into a Cart, and conveyed to the Place of Execution thro' the principal Streets of the Town, preceded by numerous loyal Societies with their Colours flying, Drums beating, and Fifes playing the Rogue's March.

Before he was turned off, he teſtified ſincere Repentance for his manifold Crimes, and particularly for that which had brought him to his untimely End. He cautioned the numerous Spectators aſſembled on this awful Occaſion, of the fatal Conſequences of ever cheriſhing in their Minds Sentiments of Diſloyalty, towards their King and Country.

He was executed at Three o'Clock in the Afternoon, and after hanging the uſual Time his Remains were conſigned to the Flames with this Exclamation from many thouſands of Spectators; "*May every Traitor to his King and Country thus periſh*".

His Dreſs was modeſt, his Deportment decent and orderly, and at his Exit was ſung in full Chorus, "GOD SAVE THE KING".

55 Anon., *The last Dying Speech, Confession, Behaviour, Birth, Parentage and Education of Thomas Paine*, broadside, late 1792. Guildhall Library. See also p. 110.

so terrible a model, or a subject so pregnant with horror, and fit for his purpose.'[12] In France, as a print of 1792 put it, 'Hell broke loose' (no. 47). The absence of constraints on the darker side of human nature, a result of the revolutionaries' infatuation with equality and intoxication with reason, unleashed the forces of darkness. Revolutionaries lost their humanity: they became diabolical or mad, behaving like savages or wild beasts in a state of nature.

Parliamentary commentators, graphic artists and the authors of popular conservative literature all pressed home this theme. Job Nott, the Birmingham buckle-maker, urged his readers to avoid the French 'while ruled by such bloody minded barbarians . . . why they are worse than the Antipoads that kill'd and chop'd our brave sailor Captain Cook to pieces . . . they cut out Gentlemen's hearts, and squeezed the blood into wine and drank it'.[13] Hannah More condemned the French by association: 'I'd sooner go to the Negroes to get learning, or to the Turks to get religion, than to the French for freedom and happiness.'[14] Time and again commentators returned to the theme of cannibalism, of a nation consuming itself, and to the rending and violation of human flesh, the tearing apart of the body politic by crazed and feral revolutionaries.

In English prints the predominant symbol of the Revolution is the guillotine. It appears not only as subject-matter, as in depictions of the execution of the king, but as part of France's new revolutionary iconography, replacing the cap of liberty at the feast of reason (see no. 147). The guillotine becomes the symbol of philosophy run mad. A scientific device originally designed to alleviate suffering, it is transformed by the madness of revolution into the instrument of judicial

Fig. 1 Isaac Cruikshank, *A Right-Honorable alias a Sans Culotte* (Charles James Fox), etching, coloured, published 20 December 1792. British Museum.

murder, providing the rational and technical means for mass execution. It hangs, like the sword of Damocles, over the entire French nation.

This nightmare world, summoned up by Burke, luridly described in popular pamphlets and graphically portrayed by Gillray, is grotesque. It deviates from the natural order, breaking down the categories which distinguish masters from men, men from women, and human from animal form. In counter-revolutionary propaganda the Jacobins are often women, simian creatures or wolves. Paris women are depicted as the most ferocious and bloodthirsty revolutionaries (for example, *Philosophy Run Mad*, no. 77). Their conduct proves that the times are out of joint, that authority has collapsed and family life been destroyed. Medea, the murderer of her brother; Pandora, who loosed chaos on the world; the Furies: these are the prototypes of revolutionary women.

The cumulative effect of the avalanche of counter-revolutionary propaganda published in England during the 1790s was to convince many English men and women that perpetual chaos prevailed across the Channel. There was little sense of the fluctuating state of revolutionary politics, even less idea of the ebb and flow of revolutionary violence. In their place was a strong conviction, expressed even by those who were sympathetic to the aims of the Revolution, that the enormities of the *ancien régime* and the violence of counter-revolutionary forces in France and Europe had plunged the French nation into a political frenzy. Generations of harsh repression and lack of experience in the ways of politics were deemed a combustible combination, exploding into violence. The Terror was therefore considered not as an aberration but as a natural consequence of French politics. It would have been surprising to see it end. Thus, when a peace mission led by the Earl of Malmesbury went to France in 1796, its members were astonished to find an orderly and peaceful nation. They had expected to see a landscape depicted by James Gillray. What they found more closely resembled the work of George Morland.

Opponents of the French Revolution were primarily concerned to place the events in France in their darkest light; but they also wished to repair some of the authority swept away by the Revolution. Above all, they wanted to recreate or reinforce a hierarchical social order based on the family. Hannah More's *Village Politics* is as much about authority in the household as in the nation: 'the woman is below her husband, and the children are below their mother, and the servant is below his master'.[15]

This patriarchal image of good order and domestic felicity is closely connected in counter-revolutionary rhetoric to the fate of the father of the French people and the head of the first family in France, Louis XVI. Prior to the Revolution Louis's domestic history had been somewhat chequered. He had great difficulty consummating his marriage to the young Austrian Princess, Marie Antoinette, and only timely help from a surgeon sent by Joseph II enabled Louis to become the father of more than his people. The conduct of his wife, who flirted outrageously at the court, appeared in public in 'undress' and deliberately cultivated a 'natural' and informal manner, shocked stuffier members of the royal court, led to accusations that Louis was unable to control her, and rumours that he was a cuckold. Pornographic works circulated in Paris accusing Marie Antoinette of adultery, lesbianism and child abuse. Prior to the Revolution the king appeared no more master of his own household than of an increasingly restive nation.

Louis's lack of authority and Marie Antoinette's notoriety make Burke's

95 Mather Brown, engraved by P. W. Tomkins, *The final interview of Louis the Sixteenth*, engraving, published 1 January 1795. British Museum. See also p. 132.

famous defence of the French queen all the more remarkable. Though it exposed him to much ridicule, not least from Tom Paine, Burke's impassioned denunciation of the mob's violation of the queen's bedchamber was the opening salvo in the counter-revolutionary campaign to conserve the ideal of a royal family based on patriarchal authority. In 1792–3 numerous depictions of Louis's separation from his family reinforced the impression of a united family rent asunder (see, for example, no. 95) They also reminded Englishmen of Charles I's final meeting with his two youngest children before his execution in 1649. Louis's last words, 'I forgive my enemies, I Die Innocent', as reported in prints like *The Martyrdom* (no. 106), were also reminiscent of Charles's final statement on the scaffold at Whitehall. Louis's association with Charles lent him some of the English king's reputation as a devoted and doting parent. Both monarchs, by dwelling on the fate of their nations, also fulfilled in their final hours their allotted role as father of the people.

If Louis acquired a new authority as head of his family, Marie Antoinette's rehabilitation was even more remarkable than that of her husband. Portrayed as a wife and mother torn first from her husband and then from her son, she is translated from court voluptuary to the symbol of virtuous motherhood in several prints which focus on the moment at her trial when she scornfully dismisses the accusation that she has abused her children (see nos 133–5). In William Hamilton's painting of her last hours she walks to her execution like Joan of Arc, a symbol of legitimist France. On the scaffold she calls for peace in her distracted country and for mercy for her orphans: at the last she thinks of her natural and her political children – the royal family and the French nation.

It is not surprising, then, that William Hamilton's depiction of the royal family reunited in heaven should be called the *Apotheosis* (no. 142). For it marks the re-creation not only of a domestic order – which we have good reason to suppose never existed – but of a kind of authority on which the *ancien régime* rested. The return of family decorum and social harmony is in marked contrast to the milieu of Gillray's family of sans-culottes. His famous print, *Un petit Souper a la Parisienne – or – A Family of Sans-Culotts refreshing after the fatigues of the day* (no. 81), shows what a revolutionary family is like. Mothers, fathers and children are oblivious of each other, consumed by manic revolutionary energy. Gorging themselves with the flesh of their victims, they represent the new domestic and civil order, one devoted to the destruction of human kind.

Conclusion

Supporters of the Revolution in France saw it as an event of universal significance: the triumph of the Feast of Reason, the successful assertion of the Rights of Man. But opponents of the Revolution in England saw it as peculiarly French, a demonstration of the inherent weakness of a society raised to submit to arbitrary power. The sins of the *ancien régime* were visited on France's young revolutionaries who were deemed incapable of throwing off a political tradition that first nurtured and then worshipped unconstrained power. The Committee of Public Safety was just the absolutist monarchy in another guise. Revolutionary politics may have rejected much of the *ancien régime* but it had retained its essence.

This counter-revolutionary analysis, which some reformers came to share, had the great advantage from a conservative point of view of placing the Revolution in the context of England's long-standing antipathy towards France. It cemented the alliance between chauvinism and conservatism, making the advocacy of change unpatriotic and foreign.

The Revolution failed to eliminate the old stereotypes of the French as either craven and duplicitous subordinates or effete, vicious and arbitrary wielders of power. Nor could it dispel the cliché that Frenchmen were impoverished and emaciated, forced or gulled into eating soup, snails and garlic. On the contrary, these figures of contempt provided an important contrast with the conservative stereotypes of John Bull and his England: the mad, starved Jacobin counterpoints the well-fed, contented and devotedly patriotic John Bull; a barren and blasted landscape makes England's fertile fields seem all the more attractive.

The effectiveness of this propaganda meant that radicals and reformers found their association with France, especially the France of Burke, the political prints and Hannah More, to be more and more of a liability. Though English Jacobins cropped their hair in the French manner, called each other 'Citizen', and retained close connections with allies in France, they failed to construct revolutionary politics in the French manner. Only Thomas Spence seems to have adhered wholeheartedly to the French iconographical tradition. The most radical sympathisers with the revolutionaries across the Channel were driven underground, unable to give public expression to their brand of revolutionary politics. The reformers who remained visible reverted to distinctively *English* constitutional ideas rather than adhering to the universal appeal of reason.

The effectiveness of the counter-revolutionary case was both symptom and cause of the determination of the English propertied classes to defend the *status quo*. There was no revolt of the nobles in England. On the contrary, the events of the 1790s both in France and England frightened patricians who had flirted with reform into the legitimist camp. Radicals failed to convince those with power at both a local and national level that their view of the Revolution should prevail. The conservatives, especially Burke, set the agenda. If 1789 therefore saw the birth of the republican tradition that flourishes in France today, it also helped reinforce the prudent monarchism that still prevails in Britain.

John Brewer
Director, William Andrews Clark Memorial Library
University of California, Los Angeles

Introduction

Attitudes to revolution

British responses to the French Revolution in the period 1789–99 were almost entirely determined by the precise phase of the Revolution in which they were expressed. From a general agreement in Britain after the fall of the Bastille that the French Revolution was either a good thing or at least of little direct concern, a process of polarisation began with the publication of Edmund Burke's *Reflections on the Revolution in France* in November 1790. This was exacerbated by the publication of the first part of Tom Paine's *The Rights of Man* in February 1791, and especially by the second part in February 1792. By late 1792 and early 1793 with the September Massacres and the execution of Louis XVI the gulf between 'Democrats' and 'Loyalists' in Britain became unbridgeable. By 1794 enthusiasm, even firmly renounced, for the earlier and more hopeful phase of the Revolution could be construed by loyalists as complicity in the bloodier aspects of the Terror, while the judicial assault on radical publications in 1792 and especially in late 1795 with the 'Gagging Acts' could be seen by radicals as evidence of 'Pitt's Reign of Terror'. Rhetoric became ever more extreme: the Whig Opposition led by the liberal gentleman Charles James Fox could be routinely depicted in newspapers and caricature as bloodthirsty sans-culottes avid to lead the mob in universal head-chopping.

No response could remain static as 'the Revolutionary Power Toss[ed] like a ship at anchor, rocked by storms'.[1] Observers in England had to absorb successively reports of murderous disorder in Paris and elsewhere from mid-1792 onwards, the execution of the King and Queen of France and of prominent members of the aristocracy, as well as of political leaders like the Girondins, some of whom had friends in London. Even so what stirred up most feeling was the fear of loyalists, and to some degree of 'constitutional' radicals, that the common people of Britain might be led by the ideas of Paine to hold the British constitution in contempt. Furthermore, from February 1793 Britain and France were at war, and the latter proved a formidable enemy despite the supposedly debilitating destruction of the social order under the Revolution.

For all the forthright and often hysterical denunciations which marked the debate between sympathisers and enemies of the Revolution, ambiguities lay at the heart of all British attitudes: even the most conservative upholder of tradition could not easily contemplate the restoration of the Bourbon dynasty or the system of despotism which was presumed to have survived in France until the fall of the Bastille. Equally, radicals could hardly look complacently on the incessant use of the guillotine in the months before Robespierre's fall. The fall of the Bastille could give satisfaction to traditional upholders of the constitution, for it could be interpreted as a recognition of the supremacy of the British model, a choice of

'British liberty' over 'French despotism', though Burke vehemently denied this. The fall of the French monarchy also meant the humbling of a traditional enemy and retribution for Louis XVI's support of the American revolutionaries. For those directing British foreign policy internal discord in France had the advantage of rendering French power in the world indecisive and therefore ineffective. Burke in his *Reflections* of 1790 raged furiously against 'democratic' France, but not even he denied the ultimate right of a people to depose a tyrant.

The loss of sympathy among the educated classes in Britain for the French Revolution came in the years 1791–2 not as a direct consequence of Burke's *Reflections*, which was much ridiculed at first; nor was it primarily a response to the humiliation of the French king. The main fear was that the 'levelling' tendencies of the Revolution might spread to Britain, as it became clear that the British constitutional model was not going to prevail in France. The perceived danger was that the lower orders, under the malign influence of Paine's *The Rights of Man*, especially part II published in February 1792, might begin to see themselves as the 'people' whose sovereignty could prevail over the king's. Lord Auckland's satisfaction at 'the disjointed and inefficient Government' in France, which he believed to be 'the best security to the permanence of our prosperity',[2] gave way from 1793 onwards to a fear, largely manufactured by loyalist groups and tacitly supported by the government, that the Jacobin Republic would rouse the British masses to revolution through the agency of treacherous intellectuals, under the protection of the French. The painter Joseph Farington's Diary, which gives a detailed account of responses to the events in France from July 1793 onwards, shows that many in high positions were genuinely fearful of the revolutionary intentions of the common people, though Farington himself claimed at the time of the agitation over the Sedition Bill in November 1795 that 'the English were not a people who wd. soon be moved to violent acts, they had too general a sense of the advantages they derive to put everything at risk'.[3]

To a large extent, then, the story of the British response to the French Revolution is about British rather than French politics, and there seems to have been little curiosity outside the governing circles about events in France which did not impinge directly upon Britain. The issue of the Civil Constitution of the French Clergy and the nationalisation of church property in the years 1790–2, which drew a great number of French satirical prints and attracted the wrath of Burke, was scarcely noted by British caricaturists, while there is very little consciousness that the Revolution was taking place anywhere else but Paris. For obvious reasons less news came through during the Terror, but this left French Royalists in London free to propagate their often highly coloured version of events. After the fall of Robespierre in July 1794 'Authority in France/Put on a milder face',[4] but for the British government it remained a matter of policy, particularly with the resurgence of radical discontent in the desperate economic situation of 1794–5, to encourage the fiction that the Terror represented the natural condition of French society. In the years after 1794 the possibility of a French invasion conditioned all responses, and though in October 1795 Farington noted that violence was not as general in France as 'we in England have supposed',[5] this was not the common understanding of matters. With the acts against sedition and public meetings of November 1795 radicalism was largely driven underground in England, but not without some protest from caricaturists like Richard Newton and Isaac Cruikshank.[6] At the same time loyalists, again with government support, sought to encourage a robust patriotism, and visual imagery of all kinds, as always, played a major part.

If we turn now to those who had sought parliamentary reform from long before 1789, we can see with hindsight that despite their enthusiasm for the French Revolution it was a disaster for the cause of reform. Parliamentary reform was associated by their opponents with French 'levelling', and a split developed from 1792 onwards between those reformers who saw the British Constitution, if properly observed, as a guarantee of rights for the unfranchised, and those who followed Thomas Paine in believing it to be good for 'courtiers, placemen, pensioners, borough-holders, and the leaders of the parties . . . [and] a bad Constitution for at least ninety-nine parts of the nation out of a hundred'.[7] As perceptions of the situation in France became more confused under the Republic inaugurated in September 1792, radical sympathisers like Mary Wollstonecraft, though remaining sympathetic to the Revolution, began to argue that the French Revolution was not necessarily the best model for others: 'the French were in some respects the most unqualified of any people in Europe to undertake the important work in which they are embarked',[8] because they had been infected by the habits of mind engendered by the *ancien régime* rather than the traditions of British liberty. The London Corresponding Society also argued, in the face of bad news from France, that the granting of demands for reform in England would be a way of avoiding the spread of the discontents which had erupted so tragically in France.[9]

The harsh economic conditions in England in 1795–5 saw not only a resurgence of radicalism but the emergence of a different kind of radical. If British radicals of 1789 were often close in spirit to their Girondin counterparts across the Channel in being highly educated, broadly humanitarian and convinced of the perfectibility of man and the power of reason to appeal to the inherited sense of justice of the nation, the radicals of 1794 tended to be nearer the sans-culottes in social background and ideas.[10] Though their belief in violent revolution was much exaggerated, radicals like John Thelwall, who came to prominence in 1794, were inclined to boast of being sans-culottes to dissociate themselves from the constitutional reformers of the Whig Opposition.[11] They were encouraged rather than repelled by mass discontent among the labouring classes, and were not afraid of a prison sentence. Publishers of caricatures, like other small manufacturers, tended to lose their initial sympathy with the Revolution by mid-1792, and this is reflected in the anti-French direction of the caricatures they commissioned. There are interesting exceptions, however. Gillray had evidently been convinced by Burke's strictures on the Revolution by December 1790 (no. 49), while the publisher William Holland, for whom Richard Newton worked, proclaimed his radical sympathies at least through 1794. Painters, where they were radical, were usually liberal reformist in sentiment, and so there are few paintings or prints which are in tune with the radicalism of the later 1790s, though this may have as much to do with prudence as with the renunciation of radical principles.

The makers of images

Almost all the main events of the French Revolution were given visual form in low-quality engravings within weeks of their occurrence. The *Gentleman's Magazine* often accompanied articles on the Revolution with prints of dramatic events, especially executions, and some were apparently published independently, occa-

MASSACRE OF THE FRENCH KING!

VIEW OF La Guillotine; OR THE MODERN Beheading Machine, AT PARIS.

By which the unfortunate LOUIS XVI. (late King of France) suffered on the Scaffold, January 21st, 1793.

Decree of the National Convention of the 15th, 17th, 19th, and 20th of January, 1793.

ARTICLE I.

THE National Convention declares Louis Capet, last King of the French, guilty of a conspiracy against the Liberty of the Nation, and of a crime against the general safety of the State.

II. The National Convention declares, that Louis Capet shall undergo the punishment of Death.

III. The National Convention declares, that the act of Louis Capet, brought to the bar by his Counsel, and termed an Appeal to the Nation on the Sentence passed against him in the Convention, is null; and forbids every person from giving it authority, on pain of being prosecuted, and punished as guilty of a crime against the general safety of the Republic.

IV. The Temporal Executive Council shall notify the present Decree, within the Day, to Louis Capet, and shall take the necessary measures of police and safety to secure its execution within *twenty-four hours*, reckoning from the notification, and shall render an account of the whole to the National Convention immediately after its execution.

Report of the Council who communicated the Decree to LOUIS.

The Executive Council was convoked and assembled at a very early hour this morning, in order to consult on the execution of a decree relative to Louis Capet.

The Council then sent for the Mayor of Paris, the Commandant General, the President, and the Accusateur Public of the Criminal Tribunal: After having consulted with these constituted authorities, the Minister of Justice, the President of the Executive Council, a Member of the Council, the Secretary of the Council, and two Members of the Department repaired to the Tower in the Temple.

At two o'clock they were conducted before Louis, to whom the Minister of Justice, as President of the Executive Council, spoke as follows:

Louis, the Executive Council hath charged us to notify to you the Extracts of the *Proces-Verbal* of the National Convention of the 15th, 17th, and 19th of the present month: the Secretary will now read them.—[On this the Secretary of the Executive Council read the three above Articles.]

Louis then observed, that he had something to say; on which he took out the following requisition, written with, and signed by his own hand.

"I demand a delay of three days, in order to enable me to appear in the presence of Almighty God; and the better to effect this, I request leave to call to my aid the Ex-Bishop of Fermont, who lodges at No. 483, *Rue de Bacq.*

"I demand that his person be protected from all manner of insult, in order that he may be enabled to deliver himself up without fear to the work of charity which he is about to be employed in, with respect to me.

"I demand to be freed from the perpetual inspection which the General Council of the Commons has made use of towards me for some time past.

"I demand, that during this interval, I may be permitted to see my Family, without any witness, every time that I solicit this permission.

"I desire that the National Convention may deliberate immediately about the fate of my Family, and that they may be permitted to retire wherever they please.

"I recommend all the persons who were attached to me to the care and protection of the Nation. There are many of them who have expended the whole of their fortunes in order to purchase their places, and must consequently be in great distress.

"Among my pensioners are a great number of old men, and of poor people burthened with large families, who have not any thing to subsist on but the allowance which I paid them.

"*Given at the Tower in the Temple,*
January 20, 1793.
(Signed) "LOUIS."

The Convention having heard the Report of the Minister decrees,

That the *respite* demanded by Louis *shall not be granted.*

That the vigilance of the Municipality shall be continued in the chamber adjoining that of Louis. Respecting the other points, the Convention passes to the order of the day, considering that the Committee of Legislation is competent thereto.

ORDERS FOR THE DAY.

January 20, 1793.—Second Year of the Republic.

The Provisional Executive Council, after deliberating on the measures to be taken, in order to execute the decrees of the National Convention of the 15th, 17th, 19th and 20th of January, 1793, has ordered as follows:

I. That the Execution of the Judgment of Louis Capet shall take place to-morrow, Monday the 21st.

II. The place of Execution shall be *La Place de la Revolution, ci-devant Louis XV.* between the Pedestal and the Elysian Fields.

III. Louis Capet shall leave the Temple by eight o'clock in the morning, and the Execution shall take place at noon.

IV. Commissaries from the department of Paris, Commissaries from the Municipality, and two Members of the *Tribunal Criminel*, shall assist at the Execution. The Secretary of the Tribunal shall draw up the *proces-verbal*; and the said Commissaries and Members of the Tribunal, immediately after the Execution, shall render an account of it to the Council, who will remain in permanent during the whole day.

V. Louis Capet shall pass by the *Boulevards* to the Place of Execution.

By the Executive Provisional Council,

ROLAND, CLAVIERE, | MONGE, LEBRUN, | GARAT, PACHE.

By order of the Council,
GRONVILLE, Secretary.

On which the Period of his Fate, and the Day of Execution, took Place, and was as follows:

At six o'clock in the morning he took his last farewel of the Queen and Royal Family, and was with them some time; the parting was affecting to the last degree; the distress of the Queen passed all description. He left the Temple agreeable to the Instructions from the Provincial Council, at eight o'clock, at which time the mournful procession set out from the Temple. The Royal Victim sat in the Mayor's Carriage, with his Confessor by his side, praying very fervently, and two Captains of National Light Horse on the front seat. The carriage was drawn by two black horses, preceded by the Mayor, General Santerre, and other Municipal Officers. One squadron of horse, with trumpeters and kettle-drums, led the van of this melancholy convoy; three heavy pieces of ordnance, with proper impliments, and cannoneers, with lighted matches, went before the vehicle, which was escorted on both sides by a treble row of troopers.

The train moved on with a slow pace from the Temple to the *Boulevards*, which was planted with cannon, and beset with National Guards, drums beating, trumpets sounding, and colours flying. The *Guillotine* † was erected in the middle of the square, directly facing the gate of the garden of the *Tuileries*, between the Pedestal on which the Grand-father of Louis was standing, before the 10th of August, and the avenues which lead to the groves, called the *Elysian Fields*. The trotting and neighing of horses, the shrill sound of the trumpet, and the continual beating of drums, pierced the ears of every beholder, and heightened the terrors of the awful scene.

The scaffold was high and conspicuous, and the houses surrounding the place of Execution were full of women, who looked through the windows. The very slates which covered the roofs were raised for the curious and interested to peep through.

The King alighted from the carriage at twenty minutes past ten. His hair was dressed in curls, his beard shaved; he wore a clean shirt and stock, a white waistcoat, black florentine silk breeches, black silk stockings, and his shoes were tied with black silk strings. At the foot of the scaffold he threw off his coat himself, and finding some difficulty in unbuckling his stock, he calmly thanked a by-stander, who assisted him.—His hair was then cut off, when he took leave of his confessor, who shed a thousand tears on this mournful occasion; but roused the King with these animating expressions: "Farewell Louis! *ascend the Scaffold and go to heaven.*"—He then ascended the steps of the scaffold with heroic assurance, and every feature of his majestic countenance bespoke the calm serenity of conscious innocence, and the heroic fortitude of a Christian. Having walked half round the horrid preparations, he then beckoned with his hand to be heard; the noise of the warlike instruments ceased for a moment; but soon after a thousand voices vociferated, with detestable ferocity, "*No speeches! No harangues!*" The unfortunate Monarch wrung his hands—lifted them up towards heaven—and with agony in his eye and gesture, exclaimed, distinctly enough to be heard by those persons who were next to the scaffold, "*To thee, O God, do I commend my soul! I forgive my enemies! I die innocent!*"

He was then seized by the Executioners, dressed in black, who directly laid him upon his belly on the bench, and lifted up the upper part of the board which was to receive his neck, adjusted to his head properly, then shut the board and pulled the string which is fastened to the peg at the top of the machine, which lifted up a latch, and down came the axe; [See the annexed plate.] the head was off in a moment, and fell into a basket which was ready to receive it; the executioner took it out by the hair, to show the populace, and then put it into another basket along with the body.—The final part of his execution was exactly twenty-two minutes past ten.

After his head was cut off, the *Sans Culottes* and *Jacobines* waved their hats in the air, exclaiming, *Vive la Nation! Vive la Republique!* The music struck up *Ca Ira*, and the body was immediately removed in a black coffin.—The procession returned to the Temple in full gallop, and the sworn Deputies went to make their report.

DESCRIPTION OF LA GUILLOTINE.

This destructive instrument is in the form of a Painter's Easel; about ten or twelve feet high. At two feet from the bottom is a cross bar, on which the head is placed, in a circular opening, to contain the neck, in the form of the English pillory, which is kept down by another placed above. In the inner edge of the frame are grooves, on the top of which is placed a sharp axe, with a heavy weight of lead suspended to the top by cords through a block, and which axe is kept up by being fastened to a peg, about four feet from the bottom of the machine, which the executioner taking out, the axe falls and beheads the criminal.

He is first tied to a plank of about eighteen inches broad, and an inch thick, standing upright, fastened with cords about the arms, body, and legs; this plank is about four feet long, and comes almost up to the chin; the executioner then lays him on his belly on the bench, lifts up the upper part of the board which receives his neck, adjusts his head, then shuts the board, and pulls the string fastened to the peg at the top of the machine, which lifts up a catch. The axe falls down, and the head, which is off in a moment, is received in a basket ready for that purpose, as is the body in another basket. This preparation was omitted in the Execution of this unfortunate Monarch, he being immediately placed at length under the machine.

Louis made a will, in which he asked pardon of God, for having sanctioned the Decree upon the Civil Constitution of the Clergy, although this sanction was extorted by violence; and was contrary to his solemn protest.

In this testament, Louis acknowledges his having freely accepted all the other parts of the Constitution; and having neglected nothing to remove from his dominions the scourge of War, and prevent the invasion of the Prussians.

In a previous Decree made by the National Convention, the place for putting their inhuman sentence into execution was to have been the Carousel, fronting the Palace of the Tuileries. This was changed by the Ministers, to whom all the arrangements were confided, to the Place de la Revolution, heretofore the Place Louis XV.

This City yesterday resembled an immense Camp; the Sections and Federates were marching and counter-marching through the different districts;—they had their watch word;—they wheeled round wherever one corps met the other. They carried with them upwards of 153 pieces of heavy artillery, and it made a most imposing spectacle. They were constantly in motion, and could not stand still five minutes.

During the exhibition of this horrid scene, all Paris was in consternation.

The Commissaries of the Temple found in the King's desk some gold coin, to the amount of about 3000 livres. It was done up in rouleaus, and on them was written, "to M. Malasherbes." This grateful bequest of the deceased Monarch was not complied with—the money was deposited in the Secretary's Office.

The following Anecdotes shew that for some Time he had been expecting his Fate.

Louis saw his last moment approaching with coolness and tranquillity. It is long since he resolved to sacrifice life, if we may judge from the two following anecdotes.

Two years ago, M. de Liancourt representing to Louis, that the modifications and the *veto* which he opposed to certain Decrees might be dangerous—"What can they do?" replied Louis, "They will put me to death—well, I shall obtain an immortal for a mortal crown."

The other Anecdote is more recent, and proves, like the former, that Louis never feared death.—On the day that Deseze made his defence in the Convention, Malasherbes, in a conversation which he had with Louis in the evening, wished to prepare him for the event by hinting that his defence might not be attended with the desired effect, and that the issue of the trial was uncertain. "I understand you," replied Louis; "but my resolution is already taken. I see, without fear, my last hour approaching; and I shall lay my head on the block without uneasiness. You will perhaps be surprised when I tell you that my wife and my sister think exactly as I do."

The last requests of the unfortunate Louis breathes the soul of magnanimity, and a mind enlightened with the finest ideas of human virtue. He appears not to be that man which his enemies reported.—His heart was sound, his head was clear, and he would have reigned with glory, had he but possessed those faults which his assassins laid to his charge.—His mind possessed the suggestions of wisdom; and even in his last moments, when the spirit of life was winged for another world, his lips gave utterance to them, and he spoke with firmness and resignation.

Thus has ended the life of Louis XVI. after a period of four years detention; during which he experienced from his subjects every species of ignominy and cruelty which a people could inflict on the most sanguinary tyrant.—Louis XVI. who was proclaimed at the commencement of his reign, The Friend of the People; and by the Constituent Assembly, The Restorer of their Liberties.—Louis, who but a few years since was the most powerful monarch in Europe, has at last perished on a scaffold. Neither his own natural goodness of heart—his desire to procure the happiness of his subjects—nor that ancient love which the French entertained for their monarch, has been sufficient to save him from this Cruel Sacrifice.

† A more particular account of this machine may be seen in TWISS's TRIP to PARIS, lately published.

London: Printed at the Minerva Office, for WILLIAM LANE, Leadenhall-Street, and sold Wholesale at One Guinea per Hundred.

And Retail by every Bookseller, Stationer, &c. in England, Scotland and Ireland.

PRICE THREE-PENCE.

Where may be had an exact and authenticated Copy of his Will, Price One-Penny.

102 Anon., *Massacre of the French King!*, broadsheet, published early 1793. British Museum. See also p. 134.

sionally in broadsheet form. William Lane produced the first visual report of the execution of Louis xvi by simply altering the title of an already published woodcut illustrating Dr Guillotin's new humane method of execution to *Massacre of the French King!* (no. 102), leaving the design unaltered. Even so this undramatic image was widely popular and was adapted for use on a wide range of objects.

Visual artists, like many others of the artisan and professional classes, were likely to have been moved by enthusiasm for such events as the fall of the Bastille or to have felt a surge of pity for the French royal family, but their decision to produce images of such subjects would initially depend upon their own area of specialisation and their sense of the market for them. The events of the Revolution might offer scope for extending their range of subject-matter, or the type of image they produced habitually might specifically preclude any direct reference to political events. Despite the immense numbers of prints of all kinds of events in France produced in 1789–99, many well-known British artists, some passionately involved in the Revolution, avoided direct reference to it in their work.

Painters who did attempt large-scale interpretations were either, like Johan Zoffany, who began to paint a series of three pictures of revolutionary atrocities in 1794, at a difficult period of their career when they needed a popular success,[12] or the kind of artist who felt no sense of conflict in working within the conditions of a market economy: ever in search of a popular audience, prepared to work in more than one genre, and with an ingratiating skill in handling. Their names – James Northcote, Henry Singleton, Charles Benazech, William Hamilton, Mather Brown – are not likely to be familiar to non-specialists. There are no paintings of French Revolution subjects by Benjamin West, the President of the Royal Academy from 1792 onwards, nor by John Singleton Copley, both of whom were famous for heroic interpretations of contemporary events. Most strikingly, the artists who were most notorious in their day for their sympathy with the French Revolution, such as Henry Fuseli, James Barry, George Romney or William Blake, did not depict the actual events of the Revolution, though their work of the period was fundamentally conditioned by it.

This avoidance was partly due to the influence upon painters of traditional academic theory, which was restated in its most recent form by Sir Joshua Reynolds in his Discourses as President of the Royal Academy from 1768 until 1792. He argued that the serious artist should, in depicting scenes from the Bible, mythology, great literature and the most momentous events of history, bring before his public ideal examples of heroic conduct.[13] In practice few artists paid more than lip-service to such high ideals and those that did were often the ones, like James Barry and William Blake, who were more bitterly critical of Reynolds himself and, as it happens, most sympathetic towards the French Revolution.[14] By the 1790s the depiction of contemporary rather than fictional or distant events in an heroic and antique manner had become commonplace for military and naval victories, on the grounds that Britain's military success demonstrated that the times were at last propitious for true heroism to flourish as it had in antiquity. The growing strength of the idea of patriotism thus reinforced a language of hyperbole which crossed easily from contemporary life to the world of the mythological heroes of the past.[15]

In practice also the demand for high-minded paintings was challenged by a growing and predominantly middle-class demand for decorative paintings and prints of 'common nature', by artists like Francis Wheatley and George Morland,[16] who depicted ordinary, if idealised, people exhibiting recognisable feelings in a rustic context. In such works the association between virtuous conduct and contentment in the lives of the rural poor was emphasised. The sorrows of life, like the parting of a soldier or sailor from his sweetheart, may be alluded to but always in the context of constant love, though such sentimentality was an easy target for the more cynical satirists like Gillray and Rowlandson.[17] In the present context it can seem a short step from a painting by Wheatley of a virtuous but modest family in a cottage to one of the French royal family adapting bravely to the privations of imprisonment, or from a soldier's farewell to his sweetheart to Louis XVI's farewell to his family on the eve of his execution. By the 1790s the distinction between contemporary history and sentimental genre was hardly an operative one except in the minds of writers on art, and Louis XVI was represented as expressing in varying degrees emotions thought appropriate to either 'high' or 'low' genres: the sadness of familial loss, antique resolution in his parting, or a Christian faith in the life beyond.

The fragility of such distinctions of genre can also be illustrated in James Northcote's painting, known only from Gillray's engraving, *Le triomphe de la Liberté en l'élargissement de la Bastille, dédié à la Nation* of 1790 (no. 24). Despite the epic implications of its subject, our sympathies are openly enlisted on behalf of the dead whose horrific fate is depicted, and of the living represented by the old man supported reverently by the youthful *vainqueurs*. Gillray's engraving of the painting was not conceived as a separate work but was originally paired with a scene of the philanthropist Howard liberating prisoners, under the title *The Triumph of Benevolence*,[18] a classic 'sentimental' subject. In Singleton's painting of *The Destruction of the Bastile*, published in 1792 (no. 21), the emphasis is upon the rich humanity and pathos of the attackers who display feeling and pity as well as determination. The association between sentiment and history, however, is not an uneasy one, for the Revolution itself is represented as a supreme triumph of sentiment.

By the 1790s the growth of the print market was such that many artists painted directly for reproduction.[19] Topicality could be as important to the painter as to the political caricaturist, and the drama of the imprisonment of Louis XVI and his family, followed by the execution of the king and queen, brought forth a number of paintings which were immediately published in print form. The passionate sympathy expressed for the French royal family was entirely in tune with the hagiographic tone of contemporary reports of their fortitude in the face of death and loss, and the artists who produced them must have had hopes of popular success and profit. Such apparent opportunism was probably frowned upon by the more idealistic members of the Royal Academy, and something of the professional cynicism with which such pictures might have been regarded by some Academicians is expressed in Gillray's tasteless caricature of *Louis XVI taking leave of his Wife & Family* of 20 March 1793 (no. 96), which, according to the artist's disingenuous inscription, was 'an exact Copy of an infamous French Print, which has lately appeared in Paris, among numberless others, intended to bring the Conduct of their late Monarch in his last moments, into Contempt & Ridicule'. In fact it is clearly meant to be a satire of the vogue for tearful representations of the last days of the French king by Charles Benazech (no. 92), Mather Brown and others, and it is no coincidence that Gillray – himself a Royal Academician *manqué*[20] – should have been so censorious of their works.

While topicality could be problematic for academic painting, it was of the essence for caricature. Though a handful of caricaturists like Gillray and Rowlandson were household names, the majority were amateurs who might occasionally hire a professional to produce their design in printed form. From the outbreak of the French Revolution a number of print publishers, like William

92 Charles Benazech, engraved by L. Schiavonetti, *The Last Interview between Lewis the Sixteenth and his Disconsolate Family*, engraving, published 10 March 1794. British Museum, Lucas Collection. See also p. 131.

Holland and S. W. Fores, were eager to exploit the sensational events taking place on the other side of the Channel and had hopes of exporting them to Paris.[21] Even so the production of caricatures tended to depend more on domestic than foreign events, and a speech by Charles James Fox or Edmund Burke upon the affairs of the French nation was more likely to attract their attention than the events themselves. The extraordinary number of prints provoked by the publication of Burke's *Reflections on the Revolution in France* in 1790 was more a consequence of the notoriety of Burke in party political life than of a concern for French politics. The innumerable caricatures of Fox as a sans-culotte reveal a revulsion against French plebeian revolutionaries, but their main purpose was to undermine the air of antique virtue with which Fox's supporters tried to surround him. Where the French, and in particular the sans-culottes, are caricatured unsympathetically the intended targets are invariably British sympathisers, potential and actual, of the Revolution, and many were commissioned by such anti-Jacobin organisations as John Reeves's Association for Preserving Liberty and Property against Republicans and Levellers, known as the Crown and Anchor Society, founded in November 1792 (see p. 117).

The services of caricaturists could often be bought by interested politicians, and Gillray was especially involved in quasi-government campaigns against radicalism. Throughout the period of the French Revolution British caricature tended with some exceptions to be pro-government and, despite the fears of nervous officials in 1794–5, 'seditious' pro-French caricature appears to have had little

96 James Gillray, *Louis XVI taking leave of his Wife & Family*, etching, coloured, published 20 March 1793. Andrew Edmunds. See also p. 132.

substantive existence.[22] One exception was the publisher William Holland who was imprisoned in Newgate for publishing seditious books in 1793, and was depicted there among a group of notorious radicals by his chief caricaturist Richard Newton (no. 194). There is no reason to doubt Gillray's sincere involvement in the anti-radical campaign, though government supporters never found him easy to handle.[23] Like most other caricaturists he tended broadly to go along with the views of London commercial interests. He initially rejoiced at the fall of the French aristocracy (see no. 18), but he seems to have been greatly stirred by the attack on Dr Price in Burke's *Reflections*, and his first attacks on radical sympathisers with the Revolution date from as early as December 1790 (no. 49). At the same time Gillray and others reserved the right to satirise Pitt, particularly over taxation to finance the war against France, and to ridicule the king: indeed, Gillray was required to desist from such disrespect by the terms of the pension awarded to him in 1797.[24] Caricaturists also tended to be hostile towards the moves against sedition of June 1792 and November 1795, for they had much to lose from the close attentions of the government.

The great anti-radical campaigns, beginning with the 'Church and King' movement in 1791, encouraged the spread of anti-French Revolution images even to transfer-printed pottery and other 'popular' media, though most were evidently made after the outbreak of war with the French Republic in February 1793. Images on Staffordshire jugs and pots tend to show either the last farewell or the execution of Louis XVI, or contrasting images of England and France deriving from well-known caricatures by Gillray and Rowlandson. The image-type whose progress can be most easily traced is *The Contrast*, which first appeared in a version etched by Rowlandson, dated prominently 1792 (no. 71). It depicts in emblematic form the opposed faces of a fictive medal, in which Britain is represented by a figure of Britannia with liberty cap, Magna Carta and balances, suggesting true liberty under the law, with the ship as an emblem of trade. France, on the other hand, is represented by Eris or Discordia who rampages with trident bearing a head and two hearts over a decapitated body, while an aristocrat hangs from a lantern.

According to a contemporary, Sarah Sophia Banks, who gave an impression of the print to the British Museum, it was 'Designed by Lord George Murray. Sent by him to the Crown & Anchor from whence they have been distributed & likewise sold by Mrs Humphrey in Bond St'. In fact this account is not quite correct for it was a slightly smaller copy, dated equally prominently 1793 (no. 72), with a publication date of 1 January 1793, which was widely distributed. It has on it not only the price of individual impressions (3*d*. plain, 6*d*. coloured) but also a heavily subsidised price for distribution of £1. 1*s*. 0*d*. per hundred plain and £2. 2*s*. 0*d*. coloured. The print would have been distributed through Reeves's network across the country and placed in the hands of working men along with such broadsheets as *A Pennyworth of Truth*.[25] The distribution of such material was proposed at a meeting at the Crown and Anchor on 24 November 1792 where Reeves claimed the principal aims of the Association for Preserving Liberty and Property were 'by circulating cheap books and papers,[to] endeavour to undeceive those poor people who have been misled by the infusion of opinions dangerous to their own welfare and that of the State'.[26]

The Crown and Anchor may have been involved in the production of a very cheap broadside version of *The Contrast* with patriotic songs beneath (no. 74), but it is impossible to know at present whether the appearance of the design on a pottery mug or any other object was the result of a direct intervention from the society or the act of a friendly manufacturer. What is clear, however, is the direction of the process from the top to the bottom of society, and other examples suggest that manufacturers of pottery almost invariably borrowed such designs from metropolitan prototypes. There are also examples of medals like those of William Mossop or Mainwaring (no. 100), which offer cruder, and one assumes cheaper, lamentations on the death of Louis XVI and his family, and there was an immense production of anti-Paine medals probably dating mainly from after 1793. Groups of radical tokens and medals were also produced by members of the London Corresponding Society to celebrate the release of the accused at the Treason Trials of 1794 (no. 195) and also by the radical author Thomas Spence in the following years (nos 205–6).

The works considered so far were all directed principally towards a domestic market, but before mid 1792 there was also a potential market in France itself. Several caricatures dating from 1789 to 1791 contain captions in French as does Gillray's engraving after Northcote's *Le triomphe de la Liberté en l'élargissement de la*

Bastille (no. 24), and there is plenty of evidence later of the spread even of anti-French prints to France. The most notable attempt at export was Josiah Wedgwood's production of decorative medallions incorporating revolutionary motifs in the years 1789–91. Wedgwood was sympathetic to the Revolution in its early years, as were many manufacturers of Dissenting background, and his interest in exporting to France was evidenced earlier by his successful promotion of the Anglo-French Trade Treaty of 1786 (no. 11). By the time the Revolution broke out he had already made agreements to supply shops in France, and he seems by the summer of 1790 to have had ready a set of jasper ware medallions of the first revolutionary leaders (still including Louis XVI; see, for example, no. 37), and a whole range of allegorical medallions (no. 36). The initiative for these medallions seems to have originated from Wedgwood's son, also called Josiah, who had prepared designs for some of them before the end of July 1789.

Josiah Wedgwood's own mixture of commercial opportunism and sympathy for the first phase of the Revolution was shared by Matthew Boulton who supplied money medals from French designs as a form of currency (no. 35), while another Birmingham manufacturer supplied commode handles with revolutionary slogans (no. 32). When the Revolution became problematic in England in 1792, some manufacturers, though not Wedgwood, changed to producing anti-revolutionary objects, with the hope perhaps of establishing their loyalty and appealing to the large colonies of *émigrés* throughout Europe. Prints designed by Charles Benazech seem to have been copied for the French Royalists based in Coblentz, and they may well have circulated in France in the Directory period.[27] Furthermore, *émigré* circles in London also produced their own anti-revolutionary images. A number of *émigré* artists, professional and amateur, were involved in works of propaganda, and the engraver Francesco Bartolozzi sometimes produced prints from their designs (see no. 140).

The extent and diversity of the types of image produced in England and especially in London in the revolutionary period suggest a widespread belief in the efficacy of images as a means of persuasion, especially of the uneducated. Though some caricatures, especially those designed by gentleman amateurs, attempt a certain philosophical complexity (see no. 77), on the whole the tendency is towards the simplification of ideas. The diversity of media does not reflect a comparable diversity of viewpoint. On the contrary, as the example of *The Contrast* shows, this diversity opened up an unexpected range of different circumstances in which the same sorts of images could be absorbed. It must have been in the minds of the Crown and Anchor Society for the people of England to have the evil consequences of revolution and their debt to their king and the established order reinforced at every turn. Such images ideally would have joined popular moralising prints on the walls of every tavern, adorned the mugs from which each labourer would drink, while for the educated classes they might decorate such everyday objects as kerchiefs and enamel boxes.

It is also clear that such images were not produced spontaneously by the operation of popular feeling, though some anti-Paine demonstrations certainly had the character of street theatre (see nos 54–6).[28] In practice the greater part of all imagery, whether pro- or anti-revolutionary, emanated from London manufacturers or their equivalents in provincial towns, and there was an input of visual ideas from such gentlemen as Lord George Murray, Sir John Dalrymple, and the circle around George Canning.[29] Pitt and his government were not averse to direct intervention in anti-Jacobin campaigns, and others like Dalrymple voiced suspicions of the loyalties of manufacturers, but there is no reason to suppose that they needed to give more than encouragement and occasional financial assistance to the promotion of views that would have come naturally to those producing the images in the first place.

The legend of the Bastille

The surrender of the Bastille was invariably perceived in Britain as a decisive event in the history not only of France but of the world. In eighteenth-century France the prison of the Bastille had been identified by the *philosophes* as a symbol of despotism, and an expression of the arbitrary power of the French monarch who had the power to incarcerate anyone there indefinitely by means of a *lettre de cachet*. The fact that so many writers had spent short periods in the Bastille in the first half of the eighteenth century created an aura of glamour around it, which was reinforced by the promotion of tales of its legendary inhabitants, like the Man in the Iron Mask, and dramatised accounts of its horrors by former prisoners, such as Simon Linguet and the 'Chevalier' Latude.[30] Ironically Louis XVI did all that he could to defuse its reputation by no longer issuing *lettres de cachet* for political offences, reserving them for intervention in intractable family problems, and improving conditions to the point that the Bastille was by European standards a model prison.[31] By the time it fell on 14 July 1789 there were only seven prisoners and none were there for political crimes. The notorious rat-infested cells were no longer used, and prisoners were unmanacled. Despite these improvements the Bastille's massive presence in the artisan quarter of Saint-Antoine and its reputation for impregnability made the fact that it should fall before the assault of citizens of Paris a sign to the populace of the immense power of popular opinion and the king's lack of divine powers. The besiegers were so convinced that the cells were filled with groaning prisoners that they desperately pushed into every corner of the vast edifice, and tales of secret cells, still containing their victims, remained part of folklore long after the Bastille was razed to the ground.

Two themes dominate the first visual representations of the fall of the Bastille in France and in England: the collapse of the edifice of despotism before the will of the people, and the liberation of the innocent from their manacles. Virtually all representations of the events of 14 July 1789 depend upon the contrast between the seemingly impregnable immensity of the Bastille and the varied humanity of its besiegers. This can be seen in the many French popular representations and in the famous Andrieu medal,[32] and also in the 'eyewitness' depiction in a coloured aquatint by Charles Benazech, published in London on 20 November 1789 (no. 13). In fact Benazech was almost certainly not in Paris at the time, and its credibility is further undermined by its derivation from French popular images, which it follows in combining the entry of the besiegers across the drawbridge with the later arrest of Governer Delaunay by two citizens.

English caricaturists immediately saw the possibilities in the fall of the Bastille. The first to depict it seems to have been the engagingly naïve William Dent whose *Revolution, or Johnny Bull in France* of 25 July (no. 17) represents the most complacent British view of the Revolution, that the French have realised that the British way is best: Marie Antoinette is tossed aloft before her supplicating husband by 'Johnny Bull', who has 'Tiers Etat' on his horns and 'Orleans' on his collar, while soldiers, their bodies made up of joints of beef and plum puddings, with pints of porter on their heads, sing of the 'Roast Beef of Old England' they will now be able to enjoy in liberty. Gillray, ironically in view of his later attitudes, contrasts the new French liberty, in which Necker is carried in triumph by the people from the ruins of the Bastille, with the oppression suffered by the British people under the yoke of Pitt (no. 18). In the autumn of 1789 two London theatres had set up rival performances, recreating the fall of the Bastille on stage (no. 20), and jugs with transfer-printed designs appeared shortly afterwards. Wedgwood produced for export, though probably not until the next year, a pair of medallions showing the fall and the demolition of the Bastille. However, the storming itself seems to have been the subject of only one painting in the heroic style, Henry Singleton's *Attack on the Bastille* published in 1792 (no. 21).

The British attitude to the Bastille as a symbol of despotism had a long history in the eighteenth century. It had initially been defined by Laurence Sterne in *A Sentimental Journey* of 1768, in which Yorick meditates upon the possibility of being confined to the Bastille for debt. At first he makes light of it, seeing it simply as a place of confinement, from which the prisoner 'comes out a better and wiser man than he went in'. The interruption of his reverie by a starling in a cage repeating endlessly the words 'I can't get out' forces upon him a realisation of the true pain of slavery. He imagines himself in the position of a single captive: 'I beheld his body half wasted away with long expectation and confinement, and felt what kind of sickness of the heart it was which arises from hope deferr'd. Upon looking nearer I saw him pale and feverish: in thirty years the western breeze had not once fann'd his blood.'[33] The captive lies manacled in the cell, notching up the days of his captivity, and looking hopelessly towards the door which he knows will not open.

Sterne's image was a deeply affecting one, and it was painted on more than one occasion by Joseph Wright of Derby (no. 22). Though Sterne's captive was held in the Bastille, no specific association was made between his loss of liberty and France itself: Sterne's captive is a universal figure. In Cowper's *The Task* of 1783, on the other hand, the Bastille has now become a symbol of *French* despotism, from which England is still mercifully free:

> Then shame to manhood, and opprorious more
> To France than all her losses and defeats,
> Old or later date, by sea or land,
> Her house of bondage, worse than that of old
> Which God avenged on Pharaoh – the Bastille.
> Ye horrid towers, the abode of broken hearts;
> Ye dungeons, and ye cages of despair,
> That monarchs have supplied from age to age
> With music, such as suits their sovereign ears,
> The sighs and groans of miserable men!
> There's not an English heart that would not leap
> To hear that ye were fallen at last; to know
> That e'en our enemies, so oft employ'd
> In forging chains for us, themselves were free.[34]

The Bastille's position as a symbol of despotism was further reinforced by the publication in England in several editions of Simon Linguet's fanciful *Mémoires sur la Bastille*, which first appeared in 1783, and by the time of its fall the word

22 Joseph Wright of Derby, engraved by T. Ryder, *The Captive* (from Sterne), stipple engraving, published 1 October 1786. British Museum, Lucas Collection. See also p. 91.

'bastille' was established in common English parlance for any form of arbitrary and cruel confinement. After the fall the demolition of the building itself was put in the hands of 'Citizen' Palloy who, calling himself 'Entrepreneur de la démolition de la Bastille', set out to exploit the legendary potential of the Bastille in every way possible.[35] The demolition was constructed as an event of equal significance to the fall, being made to symbolise the irreversibility of the new epoch of liberty. Stones from the Bastille were sent out to all *départements*, massive keys were presented to notable persons (see no. 226), bones found in the building were reburied in a mortuary chapel as those of martyrs, and medals were produced supposedly from manacles found in the dungeons.[36]

Even so a problem was created by the unromantic reality of the Bastille's last days and its mere seven inhabitants on 14 July 1789. As none of these prisoners in any way fitted the stereotype of the true victim of despotism necessary to sustain the legend, the journalist Jean-Louis Carra published before the end of 1789 a pamphlet containing an account of another prisoner liberated from the Bastille, who appeared on none of the lists, apparently dying shortly after his release. He was called the Comte de Lorges, and he was, according to the pamphlet, 'a prisoner in the Bastille for thirty-two years, from the time of Damiens [who had made an assault on Louis xv's life in 1757] until his release on the 14th July 1789'.[37] He was described as 'an old man whose beard descended to his waist, made venerable by his sufferings and the length of his captivity'. He had fallen foul of Madame de Pompadour by complaining of corruption at court and had been sent to prison, like Sterne's captive, for an indefinite period and would have

Fig. 2 Anon., French, *Déliverance de M. le Comte de Lorges*, etching and aquatint, *c.* 1789–90. Bibliothèque Nationale, Paris.

died there but for the fall of the Bastille. According to Carra the old man died soon after his liberation, honoured by a grateful nation.

The Comte de Lorges, though he did not actually exist, was not so much a fabrication as a conflation of many of the stories which gathered round the Bastille in the eighteenth century. Physically at least the Comte bore a resemblance to one of the last prisoners of the Bastille, the aged and insane Frenchman from an Irish Jacobite family, Whyte de Melville, who also had a long white beard and venerable air.[38] Indeed, a contemporary French print by L. Carpantier (no. 23) shows such a figure being escorted from the Bastille on the day of its liberation, and it is not clear whether it shows Whyte or the Comte de Lorges. The Comte does not appear in all the early histories of the Bastille but he was frequently shown in French popular images, usually at the moment of liberation, greeting his liberators though still manacled and surrounded by vermin.[39]

The story of the Comte de Lorges may well owe something to Sterne's description of the captive: even the length of captivity is almost the same. In any case the Comte was rapidly absorbed into the British picture of the liberation of the Bastille. He can be identified as the noble white-bearded figure escorted by his liberators in Gillray's engraving after Northcote's *Le triomphe de la Liberté en l'élargissement de la Bastille* of 1790 (no. 24), where he is virtually the lone survivor of this horrific scene for many of the prisoners have long been reduced to skeletons. The tender care with which the Comte is treated by the young invaders of the Bastille, and their horror at what they see, are signs of hope that despotism will never be allowed to return.

This hellish vision of the inside of the Bastille, which bore absolutely no relation to reality, was given an apocalyptic force in the poem by William Blake entitled *The French Revolution*, the first section of which appeared under the imprint of the radical publisher Joseph Johnson in 1791.[40] Here the fall of the Bastille is seen as nothing less than the dawn of human awakening 'from slumbers of five thousand years'. Delaunay, the vacillating governor of the Bastille, is depicted as 'panting over the prisoners like a wolf gorg'd', and these prisoners number such unfortunates as 'a man chain'd hand and foot, round his neck an iron band, bound to the impregnable wall'. The Man in the Iron Mask is also there, his mask hiding 'the lineaments of ancient kings'. The type of the Comte de Lorges is divided between two prisoners; one, kept in 'the tower nam'd Order', is 'an Old Man, whose white beard covered the stone floor like weeds On margin of the sea', and the other, in the Tower of God, is 'a man Mad, with chains loose, which he dragg'd up and down; fed with hopes year by year, he pined/For liberty . . . He was confined/For a letter of advice to a King'.

The Comte's role as exemplary prisoner of despotism lived on also in more popular British accounts of the Bastille, and his longest-lasting incarnation was as part of the display of Madame Tussaud's waxworks which was set up in Paris under the direction of her uncle Curtius before the Revolution. It appears that a wax of the Comte's head was brought over from France by Madame Tussaud in 1802, and a figure showing him in captivity was displayed in the famous waxworks display in Baker Street until 1968. He was shown in a barred cell, held by chains purportedly from the Bastille itself, surrounded by stuffed rats. The account of the display in the 1803 Tussaud catalogue draws in legends associated with other famous prisoners of the Bastille, and at certain times in the nineteenth century the Comte seems to have shared his cell, somewhat anachronistically, with the Man in the Iron Mask, and even with the unfortunate Calas, with whom the Comte was occasionally confused. The existence of the Comte must have attracted some scepticism, for in the 1820 Tussaud catalogue Madame Tussaud made the astonishing claim that she had actually met the Comte: 'The existence of this unfortunate man in the Bastille, has by some been doubted. Madame Tussaud is a living witness of his being taken out of that prison, on the 14th July, 1789. Madame T. was then residing in the house of her uncle [Curtius] . . . The Count was brought to the house, but his chains had been taken off.'[41] In her *Memoirs and Reminiscences* of 1838 it is claimed that 'the Comte de Lorge . . . was brought to Madame Tussaud, that she might take a cast from his face, which she completed, and still possesses amongst her collection'. The wax head survives to this day in the collection of Madame Tussaud's waxworks and is displayed in the present exhibition (no. 25).

The Comte does not appear in Carlyle's *The French Revolution*, though the author does quote a touching letter from an earlier prisoner found in the archives of the Bastille. In fact the Comte seems to have been a useful touchstone of the seriousness of accounts of the French Revolution: scrupulous historians would omit all mention of him, while those seeking to dramatise the events would tend to bring him to the fore. The figure of the Comte in Madame Tussaud's establishment in Baker Street was familiar to Dickens who described a visit to the 'Chamber of Horrors':

237 (*below right*) H. L. Browne (Phiz), illustration on title-page to *A Tale of Two Cities*, Charles Dickens, 1859. Victoria and Albert Museum. See also p. 218.

> Let the visitor enter the very terrible apartment at a swift pace and without pausing for an instant. . . . Let him thoroughly master all the circumstances of the Count of Lorge's imprisonment, the serge dress, the rats, the brown loaf – let him hasten up the steps of the guillotine and saturate his mind with the blood upon the decapitated heads of the sufferers in the French revolution – this done the worst is over.[42]

25 (*above*) Madame Tussaud, wax model of head of Comte de Lorges. Madame Tussaud's, London. See also p. 92.

The story of the Comte must also lie partly behind the character in *A Tale of Two Cities* of Dr Manette who was imprisoned in the Bastille for eighteen years, becoming deranged, until he was 'recalled to life' by the devotion of his daughter. Manette's period in the Bastille was one of unimaginable suffering and he is shown in an illustration by H. K. Browne as a pathetic, manacled and bearded figure seated abjectly in his cell (no. 237).

The ghastly display at Madame Tussaud's kept alive the idea of the horrors which existed in the *ancien régime* alongside the grislier relics of the Terror, and in *A Tale of Two Cities* a balance is maintained, and a causal connection strongly implied, between the injustices of the *ancien régime* and the excesses of the Terror. Madame Tussaud, though a staunch Royalist, at least in later life, pictures the Bastille as containing 'engines for putting to torture those unhappy persons whom the cruelty or jealousy of despotism had determined to destroy. An iron cage, about twelve tons in weight, was found with a skeleton of a man in it, who had probably lingered out a great part of his days in that horrid situation'.[43] The fact that such a travestied version of the Bastille should continue to hold sway even among Royalists is another indication of the power of images to influence perceptions to the point that they become part of the common assumptions of the age.

Old and new stereotypes

Contemporary British responses to the fall of the Bastille, even where they were sympathetic to the Revolution, were still strongly influenced by tendentiously simplified conceptions of France. British caricaturists entered the age of revolution with an armoury of well-established stereotypes of the French dating from Hogarth and even back to the seventeenth century, and reinforced by the state of war and commercial rivalry which predominated throughout most of the eighteenth century. Even so, as Gerald Newman has argued, satire tended to be directed not so much against the French themselves as against those English gentlemen who were enthralled by French sophistication, and paid it the compliment of imitation in manners and patronage.[44]

The two nations were invariably stereotyped in British caricature in terms of a contrast between the plain-speaking, manly and prosperous Englishman and the lean, foppish and effeminate Frenchman. In the various versions of the type of print known as *The Contrast*, which date back in one form or another at least to the 1740s, food expresses the essential difference: 'Frogs & soup meagre, is with the Frenchman fine/But Englishmen, still boast, the fam'd Surloin.' The supposed desire of the French to invade England is explained in countless caricatures by their envy of the 'Roast Beef of Old England'. Frenchmen are divided into either skinny snuff-taking, elaborately coiffed and affected aristocrats, or equally skinny lower orders, notorious for their insolence to British travellers. The thinness common to both classes makes the point that all Frenchmen are really brothers, and that the pretentions of the French aristocracy to breeding and elegance conceal their essential vulgarity and that of their English imitators. The only fat people in France, we are led to believe, are the *poissardes*, the fishwives of the north coast of France, who were often employed to carry visitors ashore, and the clergy, who are depicted through the traditional stereotype of the greedy and lustful monk, dominating the simple-minded by superstition, expressed through devotional images on the walls of inns and other public places.

In the first two or three years the French Revolution did not appear to demand a new satirical vocabulary. F. C. Byron's *Breakfast at Breteuil* of 1790–1 (no. 3) shows a characteristically confused comic scene, derived from Bunbury, in an inn on the way to Paris. France appeared unchanged by the 'First Year of Liberty', even to the dim-witted postilion in oversize boots. Only the revolutionary cockade on his hat and the picture of the fall of the Bastille above the mantelpiece give hints of what has happened. Even Gillray's celebrated *French Liberty. British Slavery* of December 1792 (no. 84), hardly goes beyond the crude contrasts of his 1779 satire, *Politeness* (no. 2). A fat John Bull eats roast beef and the scrawny Frenchman frogs

2 James Gillray, *Politeness*, etching, coloured, published 1779. British Museum. See also p. 81.

and onions, but John Bull is also a figure of ridicule, complaining of taxes while gorging himself to obesity. The Frenchman remains a ragged and mean figure still enslaved by hunger despite his new freedom, and the sword lying on the floor on top of a violin may suggest that he is to be taken as an aristocrat fallen on hard times rather than a member of the servant class.

The formal abolition of rank in France meant that the aristocrat could qualify as a figure of pity as well as derision, but the old comic stereotype shows some tenacity even as the Revolution progressed. The officer who arrests Louis XVI in the caricature by Nixon published by Fores in 1791 *Le Gourmand, Heavy Birds Fly Slow* (no. 40) is a bewigged fop who bows obsequiously to his king, and even the most brutish sans-culotte can exhibit the false *politesse* of the French aristocrat. In Rowlandson's *Reform Advised* of 8 January 1793 (no. 79) the sans-culottes who terrorise John Bull enjoying 'The blessed effects of a good constitution', a table groaning with roast beef, plum pudding and porter, are bewigged and speak graciously, 'My Honble Friend speaks my sentiments'. Only after worming their way into the Englishman's confidence do they don the *bonnet rouge* and belabour him with clubs. Such imagery reflects the perception, largely lost or deliberately forgotten as the Revolution progressed, that many of the most ardent revolutionaries were not plebeian but aristocratic or middle class. Caricatures of English revolutionary sympathisers, however, sometimes make an association between

40 John Nixon, etched by J. C., *Le Gourmand, Heavy Birds Fly Slow, Delay Breeds Danger. A Scene at Varennes June 21, 1791*, etching, coloured, 1791. British Museum. See also p. 102.

fashionability and a taste for 'dangerous' ideas. In a design for the 1793 edition of Gay's *Fables* (no. 60) 'The Monkey who had seen the World' is shown as a Frenchified fop, with a long pigtail, flaunting a copy of Paine's *The Rights of Man*, and in an anonymous print of November 1796, *A Gentleman of Moderate Income making himself decent to dine out* (no. 61), a portrait of Tom Paine is displayed prominently on the wall.

The rise to prominence in Paris of the sans-culottes from mid-1792 onwards, and their implication in the bloodier phases of the Revolution, inevitably encouraged the evolution of a revised stereotype of the French lower classes. Sympathetic prints of sans-culottes published in France in the period show a modest couple of plain manners and dress who counter all forms of aristocratic affection with unpretentious directness (no. 80). Indeed, their ideals are scarcely different from John Bull, though without the latter's greed and peevishness. Sometimes they are depicted as small craftsmen, other times as independent men of the mountains who breathe in the air of liberty. From the point of view of the British establishment, however, their intervention in public affairs represented the collapse of authority and the substitution of mob rule for constitutional government. The sans-culottes, not always fairly, were identified completely with the atrocities committed in the name of the Revolution, beginning with the September Massacres of 1792 and reaching an apogee in the Terror of 1793–4.

Though the sans-culottes are presented in British caricature as uniquely and essentially French, the typological origins of their representation, with a few refinements, are to be found in contemporary perceptions of the London rather than the Paris mob, which tended to act by collective coercion of the Assembly and Convention rather than like a mob in the British sense. The chilly righteousness of Robespierre and the prosecutor Fouquier-Tinville seems to have been perceived at the time in England only by the unusually well-informed, though it became commonplace to remark on it in the nineteenth century. The type of the sans-culotte motivated by envy and blood-lust can be traced back to the British experience of urban violence in the eighteenth century, and especially in the Gordon Riots of 1780.[45]

The Gordon Riots started as an anti-Catholic protest but quickly degenerated into attacks on Catholic houses and businesses, and on Newgate and other prisons with enormous destruction to property. Contemporaries observed that the riots were essentially leaderless, though many thought that they were encouraged by politicians who could thereby show the government's incompetence in the face of anarchy. Despite the destruction the Gordon Riots were usually perceived as a temporary breakdown of authority and not as an uprising, though, of course, a baleful sign of the times.[46] Without the restraint of authority the mob, it was assumed, would inevitably seek to satisfy their base desires in theft, drunkenness and envious destruction. Francis Wheatley's painting, known only from an engraving by Heath, of *The Riot in Broad Street, 7 June 1780* (no. 4) contrasts the mob as a disorderly rabble, looting, drinking and destroying, with the disciplined ranks of the gentlemen of the City of London militia who restore order with courage and humanity. In accordance with the predominant Whig ideology, anarchic behaviour was all that could be expected of the common people if they were left to their own devices, and it was up to the gentlemen of England to act according to a broad vision of society and impose restraint upon them.

The French mob accordingly are depicted by British caricaturists as seeking only the basest physical pleasures and motivated by envy, either of the luxury of French aristocratic life or of John Bull's roast beef. In Gillray's *Un petit Souper a la Parisienne* of September 1792 (no. 81) a family of *septembriseurs*, now identified as sans-culottes, mimic the feasting of John Bull, but this time with human flesh rather than roast beef. They are dressed in rags but without trousers, though in other respects the main figure corresponds to the starving Frenchman in Gillray's *French Liberty. British Slavery* (no. 84). The lack of trousers is a mischievously incorrect translation of 'sans-culotte', and it also symbolises a lack of civilised restraint and propriety. In Richard Newton's *A Party of the Sans Culotte Army marching to the Frontiers* of October 1792 (no. 82a) great play is made of the inconveniences of their exposed anatomy. One sans-culotte carries what appear to be surgical instruments in a pair of gigantic boots of the kind worn by the postilions encountered by British travellers to France.

Understandably after the events in Paris of late 1792 and early 1793 the humour becomes less good-natured, though was not necessarily absent, and an ironical sense of French fashion still surfaces at times. Both Isaac Cruikshank and Gillray made 'fashion plates' of hideously attired sans-culottes under the titles of *A Republican Beau and Belle* (no. 148). With the execution of Louis XVI the guillotine established itself as an attribute of the sans-culotte, and in caricature its triumph is seen entirely as a consequence of the seizure of power by the common people. The role of former aristocrats and professional men in administering the Terror

82a Richard Newton, *A Party of the Sans Culotte Army marching to the Frontiers*, etching, coloured, published 1 October 1792. British Museum. See also p. 124.

seems again to have been little considered, for the print publishers and caricaturists, most of whom had by late 1792 become loyalist, were concerned to show that the logical consequence of revolution was total anarchy. Robespierre, in fact, does not figure largely in British popular prints or caricatures, and Danton and other revolutionary leaders hardly at all. However, the fact that Louis XVI's cousin, the Duke of Orleans, or Philippe Egalité, who had been a friend of the Prince of Wales and frequent visitor to England, had voted for the king's execution, is recorded in Isaac Cruikshank's print *The Martyr of Equality* (no. 109) where he is shown on the scaffold holding the king's head triumphantly; he also appears in Zoffany's painting of *Women and Sans-Culottes dancing on the corpses of the Swiss Guards* (Stadtmuseum, Regensburg) of 1794,[47] in a nonchalant pose derived from his portrait by Reynolds, apparently shrugging off the ghastly consequences of his own attitudes.

The vision of the French Republic presented by the caricaturists in the years 1793–4 as in increasing thrall to popular revolution fitted the British government's ostensible view that peace with a republican government in France was inconceivable, though it is now known that Pitt never lost the hope of a peace treaty.[48] Furthermore, if the French government could be labelled as nothing more than cutthroats, then it cast suspicion over the Whig Opposition, under Charles James Fox, who argued for a less aggressive attitude towards the French. One motif tried out by several caricaturists was the vertical division of Fox into two halves – one side gentleman and other sans-culotte. James Sayers in the series *Illustrious Heads designed for a new History* of May 1794 (no. 149), identifies the Whig Opposition with leaders of the French government so that Fox becomes Robespierre, the Duke of Grafton, who had supported a motion for peace with France, is identified with his fellow-aristocrat Philippe Egalité, while a paper *bonnet rouge* was issued with the set to be placed at will upon their heads.

By 1793 the image of the sans-culotte had become nothing less than a sign to identify British opponents to government policy. Its universality as an icon also indicates an ignorance of what was actually going on in France, though this was understandable in the state of war between the two countries. Richard Newton's drawing and print of *Desmoulins in Prison* of June 1795 (nos 151a,b) refers to the touching correspondence between Desmoulins and his wife Lucille shortly before the former's execution on the orders of Robespierre.[49] Desmoulins is watched in the drawing by a grotesque plebeian gaoler, his face contorted in hatred of the elegant and aristocratic youth looking longingly towards the outside world through the bars of his cell. Desmoulins ought to have been, however, a scarcely less detestable figure in England than Philippe Egalité. He had voted for the death of the king and though an 'indulgent' had vilified the hapless Girondins in his journal before they were sent to the guillotine.

The person of the king

The execution of Louis XVI on 21 January 1793 was perceived in Britain as a momentous event, with a particular resonance in a country whose parliament had executed their own king in the previous century. In British caricatures published before his deposition in late 1792 Louis appears as a figure of ineffectual absurdity and gross appetites, while Marie Antoinette was usually depicted as more malevolent, even as a Messalina. Until about the middle of 1792 it was still possible in England to treat Louis as ridiculous; in the caricature *Le Gourmand, Heavy Birds Fly Slow* (no. 40) his capture at Varennes is attributed to his gluttony which makes him too slow to avoid his pursuers. Implicit comparisons were also made between Louis and his equally ungainly English counterpart George III, and when he was finally deposed in August 1792 the event was seen by more than one caricaturist through the panicky reaction of George III and Queen Charlotte who feared that Louis's fate might set an example to their own subjects (no. 47). Louis's execution, however, could not be treated as a laughing matter, and several caricaturists attempted to depict it seriously, though only Gillray can be said to have avoided bathos. Since the fall of the Bastille the complex progress of the Revolution had offered few potential subjects to British artists except in caricature. The death of Louis XVI and others of his family in 1793 created an opportunity for serious painters to find subjects of tragic events and noble conduct in their sufferings.

149 J. Sayers, *Illustrious Heads designed for a new History of Republicanism in French & English dedicated to the Opposition*, volume of etchings, published 12 May 1794. British Museum, Banks Collection. See also pp. 158-9.

From the beginning artists of all kinds saw Louis's death as an act of martyrdom, and this was fostered by the testimony of the Irish priest, the Abbé Edgeworth, who ministered to the king on the scaffold. According to the Abbé the king behaved with impeccable dignity in his last moments and faced death with true Christian resignation. When the king protested at having his hands bound, the Abbé was supposed to have remarked: 'Sire, in this new outrage I see one last resemblance between Your Majesty and the god who is about to be your reward', to which the king replied, 'Surely it needs nothing less than His example to make me submit to such an insult'. Louis's last words were those of Christian forgiveness: 'I die innocent of all the crimes with which I am charged. I forgive those who are guilty of my death, and I pray God that the blood which you are about to shed may never be required of France.' It was also claimed, though the Abbé later denied it, that at the moment of death he had exclaimed: 'Louis, son of St Louis, ascend to heaven.'[50]

The Abbé Edgeworth's account, even before it was published in his name and despite mutually inconsistent versions, became the basis for the many representations of the execution which came out within weeks of the event. Isaac Cruikshank's print (no. 106) shows Louis on the scaffold declaiming heavenwards the words, 'I Forgive my Enemies, I Die Innocent'. His declaration of forgiveness to the French people is also taken up by Richard Newton (no. 112), with the king's plea that 'I wish my death may be useful to the French people'. Gillray, on the other hand, in *The Blood of the Murdered crying out for Vengeance* of 16 February (no. 111) sees the execution as a triumph of the forces of disorder, and in an astonishing biblical image the blood of the martyr warns Britain of its duty of vengeance and its need to reimpose order upon France.

Once the shock had died down the subject of the actual execution lost favour with painters, though it lived on in transfer-printed pots, usually derived from Lane's broadside (no. 102) and other popular sources. The one widely distributed heroic rendering of Louis's last moments on the scaffold was Charles Benazech's full-size engraving (no. 103), first published in February 1795, from a painting dated 1793.[51] Benazech was a pupil of Greuze who had settled in London before the Revolution but mixed in *émigré* circles in London.[52] He was well known to Danloux, who wrote scathingly in his journal of his inferior painting technique but approvingly of his informed view of the London painting scene.[53] Benazech's print was undoubtedly extremely popular: it was engraved twice in England between 1794 and 1797 and copied ceaselessly in other countries.

It is puzzling at first that such an obviously heroic subject should have been avoided by other painters working in England, but the answer may lie partly in the strongly Catholic slant given to the story of Louis's end by the Abbé Edgeworth. Given the latent anti-Catholicism of late eighteenth-century England, Edgeworth's account might have seemed to dwell uncomfortably upon the way Louis took on the mantle of Christ and of his royal predecessor Saint Louis in forgiving his enemies. The first edition of Benazech's design, engraved by L. Schiavonetti in 1794, conspicuously avoids the issue in its caption: 'The Calm and Collected Behaviour of Lewis the Sixteenth on Parting from His Confessor Edgeworth the moment before a period was put to his existence on the 21 of January 1793', while the 'Historical Account' issued at the time of its republication in 1797 also avoids the associations of martyrdom by emphasising the king's concern for his servants. Edgeworth's words about Saint Louis are quoted in the 1797 edition, but all other references to Louis's Christ-like behaviour are avoided.

Such apparent sensitivity in England to the claim that Louis had died like a good Catholic is not surprising little more than twenty years after the Gordon Riots, but the issue seems to go beyond simple anti-Catholicism. To accept Louis XVI's claims to martyrdom was also to accept the divine attributes of his kingship. Louis XVI, and the same may be said of Charles I before him, had been executed not because of his personal qualities or lack of them but in order to exorcise the mystical nature of royal authority and lineage which still clung to the Bourbon dynasty.[54] To accept that Louis was king by divine right would have been unacceptable in England, even to those most horrified by the enormity of his execution. Burke rests his own concept of the monarchy upon the Revolution Settlement of 1688, and the British constitutional monarchy was contrasted favourably by all but Painite radicals with the pitiful results of French despotism. Loyalist claims for monarchy were increasingly constructed in the revolutionary period around such ideas of George III as 'Father to his People', the cornerstone of the constitutional arch, or the guarantor of British social stability and cohesiveness, none of which attributed to him divine sanction or powers.[55]

By comparison with the uncomfortable issues raised by the execution scene such often-treated subjects as Louis XVI's farewell to his family emphasised the humanity of the French royal family, and enabled their Jacobin tormentors to be depicted in the starkness of their cruelty, though sometimes they are seen doing

3

37,38

Pub March 20th 1793, by J. Aitken
Castle Street Leicester Fields
LOUIS XVI. taking leave of his Wife & Family.
NB: The above is an exact Copy of an infamous French Print, which has lately appeared in Paris, among numberless others, intended to bring the Conduct of their late Monarch in his last moments, into Contempt & Ridicule; – It is now Copied & publish'd, in order to hold up a Nation of unfeeling Assassins to that detestation which every true Englishman must feel for Wretches, who can sport with the sufferings of the unfortunate.
LIBERTE

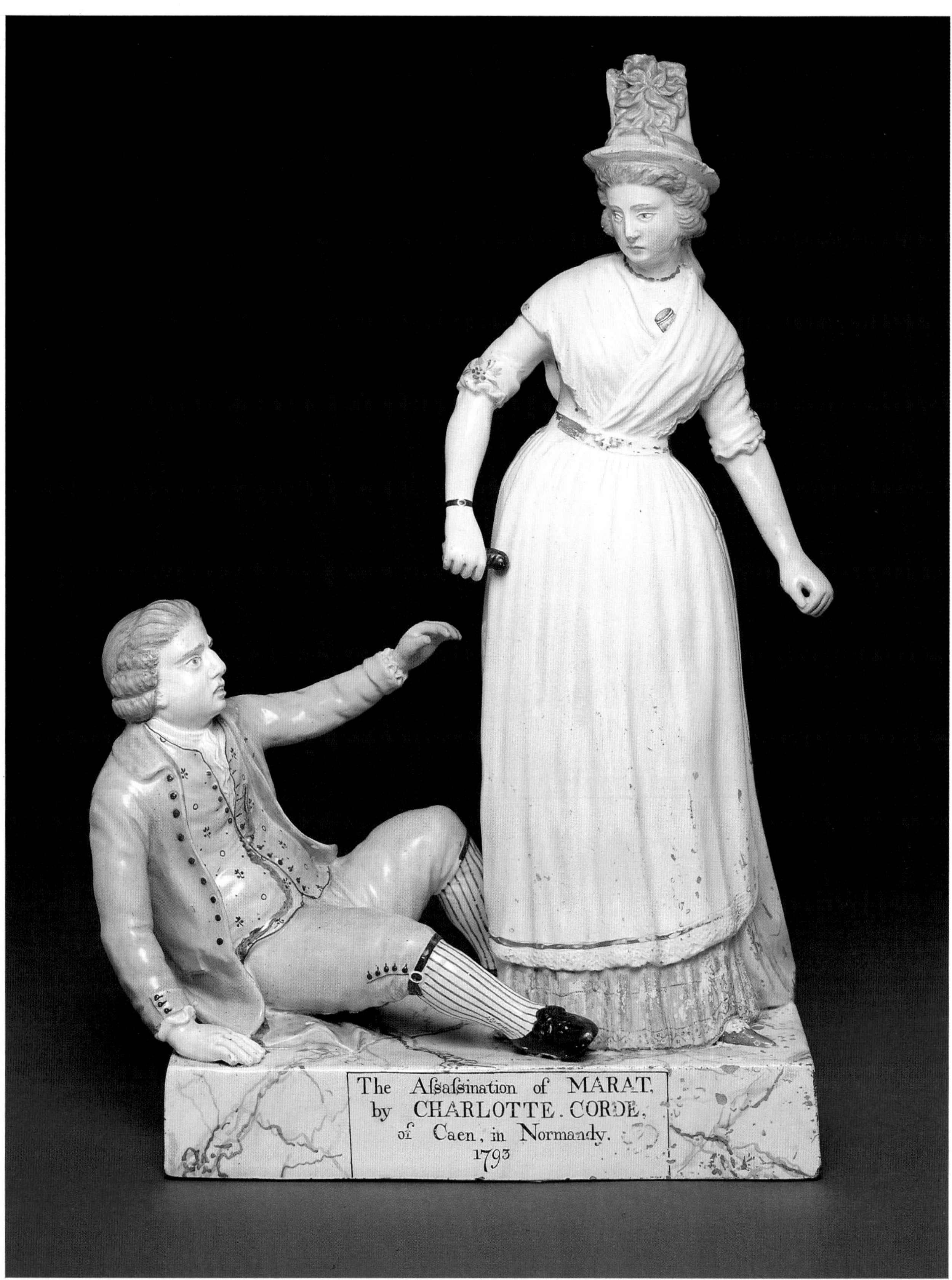
The Aſsaſsination of MARAT,
by CHARLOTTE . CORDE,
of Caen, in Normandy.
1793

131

Drawn by D. Pellegrini
Engraved and Aquatinta by L. Schiavonetti
The DAUPHIN taken from his MOTHER
The Committee of Public safety, by order of the National Convention, issued July 1793, a mandate, directing the seperation of the Dauphin from his Mother; The Commissioners on duty notified this order to the Queen and desired her to conform to it, the unfortunate Mother distracted with grief, held her beloved son clasped in her arms, unwilling to resign what could alone enable her to support her melancholy existence, but at length submitted to the fatal decree.
Le DAUPHIN enlevé à sa MERE
Le Comité de sureté publique de la Convention Nationale ayant rendu le 1. Juillet 1793, un decret qui ordonne, que le Dauphin sera separé de sa Mere, les Commissaires en exercice viennent le notifier a la Reine, et la somment de s'y conformer. Cette Mere infortunée que sa douleur égare retient pendant long-tems pressé contre son coeur, et baigné de ses larmes ce fils cheri dont la presence pouvait seul lui faire supporter ses malheurs, et sa penible existence, mais enfin le laisse enlever de ses bras.
Pub.d as the Act directs March. 1794, by Colnaghi & Co. (late Torre's) No. 132 Pall Mall London.

151a

161

London Pubd by W. Holland, Oxford Street Nov. 1799.
The Corsican Crocodile dissolving the Council of Frogs!!! 18th Brumaire i.e. 9 November

103 Charles Benazech, engraved by A. Cardon, *Louis the 16th with his Confessor Edgeworth ascending the fatal Steps*, engraving, published 1 March 1797. Lent by Her Majesty the Queen. See also pp. 134–5.

their job with reluctance. In the many depictions of the subject Louis XVI shows exceptional heroism in the face of adversity, but, it appears, not so much because of his royal blood as because of his personal courage and sense of honour. He does, it is true, often show paternal feeling for his country and in some prints is described as going to his death to preserve his nation's dignity; but his regeneration at the end of his life as a family man redeemed him from his previous association with the notoriously formal and sybaritic life of the French court, and from the dynastic imperatives of the Bourbons which involved active enmity towards Britain.

In the light of such considerations the popularity in Britain in the later 1790s of the subject of Louis XVI's farewell to his family becomes more understandable. It is as a man of feeling and not as a king that Louis suffers the agony of parting from his loved ones: the killing of the king is treated as an offence not against kingship but against humanity. It is interesting, therefore, that Charles Benazech was the only artist of the time positively to emphasise Louis's Catholic piety in his parting from his family. In his version (no. 92) the king looks not towards his grieving

94 M. Bovi after D. Pellegrini, *The King's Departure from his Disconsolate Family*, engraving, published 1 January 1794. British Museum, Lucas Collection. See also p. 132.

family but towards a crucifix before a window, suggesting his devotion to Christ and the imminent liberation of his soul. The Abbé Edgeworth supplicates the king as if the latter were Jesus himself, and the grouping of the family under Marie Antoinette's outstretched arms suggests a Lamentation with the queen in the attitude of the Virgin Mary. It is also interesting that Gillray in his satirical print of the subject, *Louis XVI taking leave of his Wife & Family* of 20 March 1793 (no. 96), should appear to single out Benazech's version for ridicule by crudely imitating Marie Antoinette's attitude in the latter's design and characterising Edgeworth as a demonic monk waving a crucifix.

In Mather Brown's rendering of the scene the grouping of the royal family also resembles a Lamentation, but the analogy between Louis and Jesus appears to be nothing more than a 'pathos formula',[56] which intensifies the spectator's sense of the tragedy of Louis's fate. Other artists used pictorial traditions of a more secular kind, though this did not necessarily preclude a reference to the idea of martyrdom: in the Domenico Pellegrini version, entitled *The King's Departure from his Disconsolate Family*, published 1 January 1794 (no. 94), the inscription beneath the print tells us that the king 'alone seems superior to the horror and despair that surrounds him, and tears himself from every endearing tye with the fortitude of a

Martyr'. However, he is actually depicted as an antique hero, a Hector parting from his affectionate family for a higher purpose, a man of action who rises above the emotions which touch him deeply and to which lesser mortals would surrender. The more popular depictions of the subject tend to dwell entirely on the human pathos of the parting. The transfer-printed mug produced by Fletcher and Co. even implies that Louis was at least partly responsible for his own fate: 'Farewell Queen, Children, Sister, Louis cries/Abate your grief & dry those streaming eyes./And O! my Son if e'er the Crown you wear./Think of my fate & steer your course with care.' The two medals by Küchler and Mossop or Mainwaring make a neat contrast with each other: Küchler's royal family have a sense of regal elegance, while in the other version they look as if they are engaged in a domestic quarrel.

Such subjects as Louis XVI's farewell and others which represent the aftermath of his death make much of the unity of the royal family: in such adversity the differences between Louis and Marie Antoinette, which had been the subject of persistent rumour in the years before the Revolution, have been transcended. Images of Marie Antoinette's last days emphasise her womanly qualities, not as a queen but as a grieving wife and devoted mother. Pellegrini depicts her at the moment when she was accused at her trial of the unnatural act of incest with the eight-year-old Dauphin, to which she answers: 'If I have not answered you it is because Nature refuses to answer such an incrimination made to a Mother but appeal to all mothers who may be found here present.' In the same series in *The Royal Family of France*[57] the bereaved family is depicted three days after Louis's execution in mourning. The Dauphin behaves like an ordinary little boy while Marie Antoinette 'is too much absorbed by Grief to attend to what passes'. There are two popular versions both apparently by Pellegrini of another tragic incident, *The Dauphin taken from his Mother* in July 1793 (no. 133): 'the unfortunate Mother distracted with grief, held her beloved son clasped in her arms, unwilling to resign what could alone enable her to support her melancholy existence'.

Despite the cruelty of the Dauphin's fate and the pathos of his end at the age of ten in the prison of the Temple, he features remarkably little apart from his family in British prints of the period. One reason must surely be that the Dauphin's existence kept open for Britain the painful possibility of the full recovery of the Bourbon dynasty, while his death gave credibility to the claims of the self-proclaimed Louis XVIII. Apart from the occasional documentary print and medal (nos 141–2) the only subject pictures to bring his fate to the fore seem to have been William Hamilton's *The Apotheosis of the Dauphin*, engraved in 1799 (no. 142), and Domenico Pellegrini's *L'heureuse Réunion*, engraved by Schiavonetti and published in 1800,[58] which emphasise the ordinary human feelings of joy in the Dauphin's reunion with his dead parents in heaven. For Royalist *émigrés*, on the other hand, the Dauphin was the repository of all their hopes, and this is expressed in a print designed by Caroline de Rigny entitled *Il ne leur reste, que l'espérance* of 1796.[59]

The ways in which the fate of the French royal family was represented were also conditioned by British perceptions of their own royal family. Indeed, the very notion of a 'royal family' seems to come to the fore at this time. The 1790s, as Linda Colley has argued,[60] saw a remarkable increase in the prestige of George III. The increasing loss of direct royal influence on affairs had led to a separation between the government and the king, so that in effect Pitt could be unpopular without its necessarily affecting the esteem in which George III was held. The

IL NE LEUR RESTE,
QUE L'ESPERANCE

Fig. 3 Caroline de Rigny, engraved by F. Bartolozzi, *Il ne leur reste, que l'espérance*, engraving, 1796. British Museum.

effect of the French Revolution and the fate of the Bourbons had in themselves reinforced the position of the monarchy as a symbol of resistance to Jacobinism, and George III's prosperous and orderly reign, his personal respectability and large family had made it easy to attach to him the role of 'Father to his People'. Extravagant and even religious language and ceremonial were often associated with the king's role in the 1790s, but they were balanced by the idea that George had earned the love of his people by his own attributes and essential ordinariness – brilliantly satirised by Gillray in the print *Affability* (no. 211) – rather than by virtue of the blood royal.[61]

Most representations of the French royal family emphasise Louis's domesticity and at the same time a love for his country which transcends even that for his own family. As the frequently printed broadside *The Will of Louis XVI* (no. 119) proclaims, he accepted death for his country but also *from* his country; in rejecting traditional absolutism he submitted to the people's will, and the pathos of his

212 R. Livesay, engraved by J. Murphy, *The Introduction of HRH the Duchess of York to the Royal Family*, mezzotint, published 4 June 1793. Lent by Her Majesty the Queen. See also p. 205.

death lay in the fact that he had been *unjustly* condemned. One may see in the sentimental depictions of the last days of the French royal family a kind of reversal of the felicity of the British royal family. In Richard Livesay's mezzotint, dated 4 June 1793, of *The Introduction of HRH the Duchess of York to the Royal Family* (no. 212), the British royal family are celebrated as united and gracious, rejoicing in the devotion of their countrymen, so cruelly denied to their counterparts across the water. Yet there is also a certain irony in such an emphasis upon the ordinary humanity of royalty, both French and English. In a sense it represents a victory for the French regicides, who had as one of their principal aims the elimination of the 'superstitions' which inevitably surround a monarchy and lead it into despotism.[62]

The visual culture of radicalism

The years 1793–5 saw the almost complete disappearance in caricature and painting of imagery which could be construed as sympathetic to the French Revolution. Pitt could still be attacked by caricaturists for taxing the nation to keep the war with France going and for the acts against sedition of late 1795, but even publishers like William Holland backed away from anything that smacked of sedition. Though constitutional reformers had tended to withdraw in the aftermath of the events of 1792–3, the establishment of the Republic in France in September 1792 and the successes of the reformed French army encouraged in England a renewed artisan radicalism which looked to brotherhood with the French sans-culottes and the eventual establishment of a British republic.[63]

In a way these artisan radicals were as much a threat to the Opposition Whigs as they were to the government, though at first they had been joined in their enthusiasm for the French Revolution. The London Corresponding Society founded in January 1792 and the Society for Constitutional Information revived in 1790 were by definition concerned with the spreading of information in support of their aims of universal manhood suffrage, annual elections and the redistribution of parliamentary seats. Both societies produced periodicals and pamphlets in abundance, and the works of Paine were widely distributed by them, but before 1794 they did not employ visual imagery as part of their enterprise, despite being regular targets for the scurrilities of caricaturists. One reason was probably the belief of their most prominent members, until the Treason Trials of 1794 put many of them in the dock on capital charges, in the persuasive power of reason and the inevitable triumph of Enlightenment.[64] They might have felt, therefore, that caricature would have harmed their image of seriousness and respectability.

It was only with the Treason Trials of 1794 that the LCS began to employ visual imagery to spread its ideas and consolidate the loyalty of members. A few medals and simulated trade tokens, often of high quality, were produced under its auspices or by its members to celebrate the acquittal first of Daniel Eaton in March 1794, then of Thomas Hardy, Horne Tooke and the others in November of the same year. Many of these medals and tokens list the names of all the jurors: at Eaton's trial silver impressions were given to each of them, for their refusal to convict was seen as representing the triumph of the people over the government and the restoration of the prisoners' rights as 'Free Born Englishmen'. In the high-relief medal of Hardy, Tooke and Thelwall (no. 195a), the three defendants at the November 1794 Treason Trials are shown in overlapping profiles on one side with their counsel Gibbs and Erskine on the other, and the names of the jurors for each defendant encircling them. A medal dedicated to Thomas Hardy (no. 195e) shows a heavenly hand carrying the scales of justice over an elaborately worked image of the Tower of London. In addition to these a widely distributed token produced for the LCS in 1795 (no. 195i) makes a call for unity in the face of threat, by showing a Greek philosopher demonstrating how easily one stick may be broken but how difficult it is to break a bundle. On the reverse a dove with an olive branch flies up surrounded by the slogan 'united for a reform of parliament'.

195 Treason Trial medals, 1794. British Museum. See also pp. 192–3.

From about 1794, and perhaps a little earlier, there are indications of the

195a
195b
195c
195d
195e
195f
195g
195h
HORNE TOOKE ESQ.
195i
LONDON CORRESPONDING SOCIETY
1795

growth of a distinctive and more obviously popular iconography, deriving from the language used by such pamphleteers as Daniel Eaton and Thomas Spence, who were members of the LCS but on the more radical fringe.[65] A striking example is a jug in the Brighton Museum (no. 53), which has a full-length transfer-printed portrait of Paine on one side and a caricature of Burke on the other, showing him as a gentleman riding upon a pig and addressing other pigs condescendingly: 'Ye pigs who never went to college,/You must not pass for pigs of knowledge'. Pigs were adopted as an emblem of 'the people', for they refer to Burke's notorious remark in *Reflections on the Revolution in France* about the fate of learning under the Revolution: 'Along with its natural protectors and guardians, learning will be cast into the mire, and trodden down under the hoofs of a swinish multitude.'[66] Henceforward the image of the people as swine was adopted ironically by radicals and occasionally by others. Daniel Eaton associated himself with the emblem of the cock (no. 195b), which might suggest the 'Crow of Liberty', and perhaps also revolutionary France – the shop sign of his printer's shop was 'The Cock and Swine'! – but he may have thought of it as having a more sinister meaning. In a medal of 1795 (no. 195g) he commemorated another acquittal on a charge of sedition by a token with his own head on the obverse, and on the reverse a design of a cock presiding over pigs in a sty, captioned 'printer to the majesty of the people'. The cock here seems to refer to Louis XVI, and by implication to George III, for Daniel Eaton was arrested for printing in his *Politics for the People, or Hog's Wash* the parable of the gamecock, 'a haughty sanguinary tyrant of the farm yard', who was beheaded by its owner.[67]

This kind of radical iconography was developed most fully by the Newcastle pamphleteer Thomas Spence,[68] who arrived in London in 1792. Like Eaton he was on the more radical wing of the LCS; a 'violent democrat', in the words of an informer, with 'levelling' tendencies that worried the more moderate executive.[69] The LCS had consistently disclaimed 'that visionary Equality of Property, the practical assertion of which would desolate the world and replunge it into the darkest and wildest barbarism',[70] but Spence had been an agrarian Utopian since the 1770s, arguing passionately for the division of property on parochial lines. Such ideas had been developed in his early years in Newcastle before he came to London, and he had already produced pamphlets and a number of tokens with crude hand-punched slogans, cut by his friend Thomas Bewick (no. 205). In March 1793 he started a shop under the sign 'The Hive of Liberty' where he first began to issue tokens and set up as a dealer, issuing a catalogue in 1795. Some of the tokens were given away to purchasers of his periodical *A Pennyworth of Pig's Meat; or lessons from the Swinish Multitude*, but others were sold to potential

205 Countermarked coins. British Museum. See also p. 198.

sympathisers, and also to collectors who would have provided a source of income. Spence seems to have been the designer of the tokens, leaving Charles James to sink the dies.

Thematically, Spence's tokens often follow his pamphlets and broadsides, and many of them show a commitment to revolution on the French republican model and a knowledge of French revolutionary imagery. The obverse of the token *Before the Revolution* (no. 206i) shows a skeletal figure in a Bastille-like prison, and the reverse, *After the Revolution*, a figure seated at a laden table drinking porter, while three figures dance under the shade of a tree. Spence does not always pair his scenes consistently, and sometimes this idyllic scene backs one ironically titled *British Liberty Displayed* (no. 206k) of a well-dressed man assaulted by a villain with a stick. In another token liberty is represented by a jolly group of four men dancing around a *Tree of Liberty* (no. 206p), which reveals itself as a pole surmounted by the head of Pitt. Animal imagery also plays a part; the cock of liberty and France is seen on the back of the British lion, and the cat is used on more than one occasion as a symbol of liberty. In the farthing token advertising *Pig's Meat* (no. 206f) the obverse shows a cat with the surrounding inscription 'in society live free like me', while in another token a cat on one side ('I among slaves enjoy my freedom') is paired with a dog on the other ('much gratitude brings servitude'). On one medal of a beautiful pastoral scene, clearly derived from a vignette by his Newcastle friend Thomas Bewick, a snail appears to stand for the aspirations of the people ('a snail may put out his horn'). The rustic lyricism of this design can also be seen in the image of a shepherd reclining in a landscape, often coupled with a grim scene of rural decay derived from a Bewick illustration to Goldsmith's *Deserted Village*, 'Only one master grasps the whole domain'.

The delicate sensibility sometimes evinced in Spence's tokens can be balanced against a more satirical vocabulary, revealing a knowledge of contemporary caricature. The 'Gagging Acts' of December 1795 are expressed in an image of *A Free Born Englishman* (no. 206k), probably derived from Isaac Cruikshank, and a padlock with the caption 'mum' was again a staple of contemporary caricature. George III is attached to a head of an ass with the mysterious inscription 'Odd fellows A million hogg a guinea pig', presumably a satire of current coinage, while the standard emblem of Britannia is subverted as 'rouse Britannia', as the liberty cap falls from her pike. A great many are openly self-advertising: the reverse sometimes bears only the simple inscription 'noted advocates for the rights of man/Thos. Spence/Sir Thos. More/Thos. Paine'; while others, both halfpenny and farthing sizes, show his own ideal profile with a reference to his seven months' imprisonment in 1794.

Tokens of the same size as normal currency, usually of halfpenny or farthing size, were produced in large numbers in the later eighteenth century, when the mint had produced too little small coinage, and for every radical token there are a great many more showing heads of royalty and naval heroes, or a company emblem. None the less, it is significant that the token should be the predominant vehicle for radical imagery from 1794 onwards. The printing of radical texts was always susceptible to laws against sedition; a token, on the other hand, could retain a certain immunity and could pass from hand to hand relatively inconspicuously. Furthermore, many of the radical supporters of the LCS were from London trades and could have had access to sympathetic die-sinkers.

The main attraction to radicals, however, was perhaps the fact that the token itself was a form of currency. With official currency the value and probity were effectively guaranteed by the king's image and therefore by his majesty. To subvert the currency implied in itself a denial of majesty, for it deconsecrated an emblem of kingship. Daniel Eaton's token celebrating his acquittal in March 1794 discussed above (no. 195b) was courting sedition not only in its address to the 'majesty of the people' but also in the way he replaced the head of the king with his own profile.

Despite the dangers of prosecution for sedition in the years 1794–6 inflammatory broadsides, sometimes illustrated, were published also by 'Citizen' Richard Lee of 'the British Tree of Liberty, 98 Berwick Street, Soho'. His broadsides have a strong visual impact which is enhanced by sensational titles, most notably *King Killing* of 1795 (no. 198), which was denounced in the House of Commons on 17 November 1795 and which helped to provide Pitt with an excuse to rush through the bills against treasonable practices and seditious meetings.[71] Lee was also the publisher of the notorious broadside *A Cure for National Grievances: Citizen Guillotine, A New Shaving Machine*, which includes a parody of 'God save the King' (no. 199). Other equally seditious broadsides are known to have existed, and they caused panic out of proportion to their numbers and indeed their content, which is invariably mischievous rather than sinister.

Publishers and pampleteers like Daniel Eaton and Richard Lee were used to spells in Newgate on account of their publications, but there can be no doubt that the Two Acts of November 1795 did eventually succeed in suppressing their more challenging efforts, and they both chose to emigrate to the United States by 1796.[72] Spence continued to propound his form of Utopian socialism into the nineteenth century, but for the few radicals left in England in the final years of the eighteenth century there was little left but the hope of a refuge where a new society could be built up from scratch, like Coleridge and Southey's projected settlement on the banks of the Susquehanna.[73]

War: external and internal

The execution of Robespierre on 28 July 1794 (10 Thermidor, l'an II) ended the period of the Terror and the most repressive phase of the Revolution. In France it was commemorated by violent assaults on imagery associated with the previous phase and the repudiation of the guillotine as a means of political control. Even so the new Thermidorean government remained committed to the Revolution, the Dauphin was still imprisoned, and, despite some peaceful overtures, France remained at war with Britain. From the British goverment's point of view the changes in France were of relatively little practical importance, and the fear of invasion remained constant through the last years of the eighteenth century and beyond, flaring up with justifiable intensity at the time of Bonaparte's Italian campaigns and the landing in Ireland of 1796–7.

In the years of the Thermidorean regime and the Directory, from late 1794 to 1799, British depictions of the Terror in France so far from being diminished actually seemed to increase in number and ferocity. Gory sans-culottes and guillotines became if anything more commonplace in caricature than they did during the Terror itself. Caricaturists, especially Gillray, frequently presented fantastic visions of Britain after a French invasion, in which the French come not to take power themselves but to put it in the hands of the Whig Opposition, who will institute their own British Terror.

199 Richard 'Citizen' Lee, publisher, *A Cure for National Grievances. Citizen Guillotine, A New Shaving Machine*, etching on printed broadside. British Library. See also p. 195.

CITIZEN GUILLOTINE,

A NEW SHAVING MACHINE.

Tune, "*Bob shave a King.*"

TO the just Guillotine,
Who shaves off Heads so clean,
I tune my String!
Thy power is so great,
That ev'ry Tool of State,
Dreadeth thy mighty weight,
Wonderful Thing!
Sweet Billy thee shall hail,
Johnny Reeves at his Tail,
Pride of our Days!
Placemen, Swan-like shall sing,
Guillotine, mighty King,
Echos from Crowds shall ring,
With thy juſt Praise.
No, Billy shall not swing,
An Hour upon a String,
To stop his Breath!
Right Honourable Friend,
The Swine shall ne'er suspend,
Thy Neck from Halters End,
In ling'ring Death.
No, no, the shining Blade,
Shall hail the *Felon's* Head,
Fraternal wise,
One blest, but happy stroke,
One soft tho' sudden shock,
Shall roll it from the Block,
'Midst joyful cries.
Long live great Guillotine,
Who shaves the Head so clean,
Of Queen or King;
Whose power is so great,
That ev'ry Tool of State,
Dreadeth his mighty weight,
Wonderful Thing!!!

A good example of the retrospective horror with which revolutionary events in Paris were viewed can be found in Johan Zoffany's scheme, possibly begun in July 1794, for a cycle of three paintings on the theme of the formation of the French Republic in August 1792.[74] One painting was exhibited at the Royal Academy in 1795, and two of the three paintings recorded in his sale catalogue have survived, both depicting the aftermath of the *journée* of 10 August 1792. The one to have been engraved in mezzotint (no. 46; the painting is in the Wadsworth Athenaeum, Hartford, Conn.) shows the invasion of the cellars of the Tuileries by the mob, while the other (Stadtmuseum, Regensburg) appears to depict the women of Paris dancing on the bodies of the Swiss guards killed in the assault, while Philippe Egalité seems to look on unconcernedly. The subject of the third painting is unfortunately unrecorded. The attack on the Tuileries which led to the establishment of the French Republic is revealed by Zoffany as the deed of a drunken, bloodthirsty rabble acting without civilised restraint. Yet on its exhibition in 1795 it must have been intended to act as a warning of the essential continuity of the French Revolution into the present and the potential for anarchy beneath the surface of French life.[75]

In Gillray's print *Patriotic Regeneration, – viz. – Parliament reform'd, a la Françoise* of 2 March 1795 (no. 189), which seems to have been distributed in unusually large numbers, the world is turned upside down after the Opposition has taken power

Fig. 4 Johan Zoffany, *The women of Paris dancing on the bodies of the Swiss Guards after the assault on the Tuileries, 10 August 1792*, oil, 1794–5. Stadtmuseum, Regensburg.

and the 'British Convention' has replaced the 'ci-devant Parliament', presumably with the aid of French arms. A white-gowned Pitt is arraigned in the dock while Lord Stanhope, the radicals' defender at the Treason Trials, reads out the charges. The judge, in the position of Fouquier-Tinville, is Charles James Fox, and his counsel, Sheridan and Erskine, recommend the guillotine. The grotesquely caricatured jury is made up of artisans and small tradesmen – butcher, tailor, hairdresser, chimney sweep, etc. – with the addition of a couple of starchy Puritans at the back, representing, therefore, all the groups associated with membership of the London Corresponding Society. With the addition of the direct participants in the trial one has the complete spectrum of the Opposition to the government.

Many other caricatures in the years 1794–9 also operate on the linked premises of continuing Jacobinism in France and the imminent danger of a radical takeover in Britain. In Gillray's *Promis'd Horrors of the French Invasion, – or – Forcible Reasons for negotiating a Regicide Peace* of 20 October 1796 (no. 190) the French Revolutionary Army marches down St James between White's and Brooks's clubs, while the Whig Opposition personally carry out atrocities associated with the Terror. A demonic Fox chastises Pitt tied to a Liberty tree, Erskine proclaims the triumph of the new law represented by the guillotine, and so on. The immediate political point of the caricature, however, is opposition to negotiations for peace with France, which would supposedly facilitate a French takeover.

Gillray's *The Consequences of a Successfull French Invasion* of March 1798 (no. 191) is unusual in showing the French in direct occupation, not entrusting power to British radicals but enslaving them. In the second plate of the series, entitled *Me teach de English Republicans to work*, misguided sympathisers with the Revolution, who include John Bull whose crime presumably is grumbling about the burdens of tax required to preserve liberty, are whipped into hoeing a field of garlic. Among those unfortunates are not only plebeian radicals but also a manufacturer, representing no doubt Midlands manufacturers like Thomas Walker, Wedgwood and Boulton, who are presumed not to have lost their earlier sympathies for the French Revolution. The prints in this series all bear the marks of indirect government support, and some of Gillray's correspondence concerning commissions from this period has survived. The *Consequences of a Successfull French Invasion* is one of four executed from a scheme to produce a series of twenty, proposed and closely supervised by an elderly Scottish gentleman, Sir John Dalrymple. Dalrymple's aim was explicitly propagandistic, to 'rouse all the People to an active Union against that Invasion; at a time when above five Millions of Vultures, with Beaks and Claws, hover over them; and when the Indolence and Divisions of the people themselves are more alarming than all foreign Enemies'.[76] Though the Dalrymple scheme was a private venture, he had hoped to get Treasury money for it.

Other ventures by Gillray brought him even closer to ministerial circles, and from late 1797 he was apparently in receipt of a pension.[77] In the years 1797–8 Gillray worked closely with George Canning, then a rising supporter of Pitt, and the circle around *The Anti-Jacobin* magazine. The consequence for Gillray was that he finally gave up attacks on Pitt and the royal family, and much of his work of the late 1790s depends upon suggestions and sometimes preliminary drawings emanating directly from ministerial circles, even, it has been claimed, occasionally from Pitt himself.[78] The most notable of these was the brilliant *Apotheosis of*

191 James Gillray, *Consequences of a Successfull French Invasion*, etching, coloured, published 1 March 1798. British Museum, Smith Collection. See also p. 189.

Hoche of 11 January 1798 (no. 175), of which the preliminary idea was suggested by John Frere and the revolutionary decalogue written by the Rev. John Sneyd. These interventions may account for the real knowledge shown of revolutionary symbolism everywhere in the print, though the underlying theme is still of the continuance into the present time in France of the Terror.

The work of Gillray in the years 1796–8 is evidence of the consolidation of attitudes towards France. Caricature has now a well-defined place in promoting national unity over what Dalrymple called the alarming 'Indolence and Divisions of the People themselves'.[79] No other image of France but one of perpetual Terror could be regarded as respectable, and this effectively destroyed the influence of those like Fox who refused to make such a categorical dismissal of the new French Republic. Yet a purely negative onslaught upon France and its influence was not regarded by Pitt and his supporters as enough in itself to rally public opinion, particularly in the face of the widespread discontent in the years 1794–6 caused by food shortages and the belief that war with France was draining the Treasury. An imagery of national contentment was gradually developed in the 1790s to reassure those susceptible to radical ideas that they lived, certainly in comparison to revolutionary France, in an island paradise. The poor were to be taught, in Burke's words of 1795: 'Patience, labour, sobriety, frugality and religion . . . all the rest is downright fraud.'[80] *The Contrast*, a print originally designed by Rowlandson and distributed by the Crown and Anchor Society in early 1793, employed a language of allegory: Britannia presided over Liberty and Prosperity, while France was represented by Disorder. Gradually pastoral conventions began to predominate in loyalist imagery: an ideal of rustic peace and harmony is set against the murderous head-chopping of France. In the medal *A Philosophical Cure for All Evils* of 1795 (no. 210) the contrast is made explicit: a headless figure appears to declaim, with a devil behind him, and is surrounded by a garland of decapitated heads. Britain, on the other hand, is represented by a young and loving family in a cottage, with all the signs of rural prosperity around them. The spade and the distaff represent constructive labour, while their table is laden with its rewards. The young husband, with two young children on his knee, raises a pint of porter to toast the king whose crown presides over the scene.

210 W. Whitley, medal, *A Philosophical Cure for All Evils*, 1795. British Museum. See also pp. 204–5.

Such images of rustic contentment derive, of course, from the traditional Georgic view of the countryside as yielding plenty to honest labour,[81] but the ultimate rewards of toil were now guaranteed by the king as father to his national family, despite the crippling shortages of the years 1794–6. Because the labouring classes evidently failed to understand that shortage of bread was due to crop failure, not to the corruption of society, simple parables or illustrations were produced in large numbers in the years 1795–6 in order to counteract Painite ideas. The connection between the Georgic vision of the countryside propagated by loyalists and the fear of revolution is brought out most clearly in Hannah More's scheme for Cheap Repository Tracts. This scheme had originally been inspired in 1791 by a plea by Beilby Porteus, the Bishop of London, for her to counteract the dangerous effects of the words 'liberty' and 'equality' upon the labouring classes by producing simple parables. *The Riot; or Half a Loaf is better than no Bread* of 1795 (no. 209) takes the form of a dialogue between two artisans who had previously appeared in Hannah More's *Village Politics* of 1792: Tom Hod, who had been influenced by reading Paine's *The Rights of Man*, and the loyalist Jack Anvil. The latter likens radicalism to destroying the mill because there is no bread, substituting strife and riot for constructive work:

> But tho' I can work, my brave boy, with the best,
> Let the King and the Parliament manage the rest;
> I lament both the War and the Taxes together,
> Tho' I verily think they don't alter the weather.
> The King, as I take it, with very good reason,
> May prevent a bad law, but can't help a bad season.

208 William Hamilton, engraved by Barney, *The Happy Cottagers*, from Macklin's Poets' Gallery, stipple engraving, published 1 January 1794. British Museum, Lucas Collection. See also p. 203.

Work and patience are seen as the answer to hunger, and there is also an emphasis in much popular patriotic imagery upon the joy and good fellowship of a stable society. There seems to have been in these years an immense production of mugs and domestic pottery with loyal toasts. Staffordshire mugs and bowls (for example, no. 215) were often inscribed with a toast to the king, with the hope that he would be protected from 'democratic wolves'. Behind such imagery there is an implied contrast with the miseries of France, which are to be read as following inexorably from popular involvement in politics. Contentment could be achieved by rejoicing in the simple life and not envying the wealthy.

Though the idea of rustic contentment is not new, there does seem to be a great increase in the mid-1790s of decorative prints in which it is celebrated. William Hamilton, for example, in the years 1794–6 when he was working on his large painting of *Marie Antoinette leaving the Conciergerie* (no. 136), was also involved in a large series of pastoral illustrations to Thompson's *Seasons*, which are notable for the sweetness of their vision of the countryside. His *The Happy Cottagers* of 1 January 1794 (no. 208) makes no explicit reference to political events and derives from a poem written in the first half of the century; yet the image and caption are full of discreet pointers to the virtues of the quiet acceptance of things as they are. The labourer returns to his cottage to be greeted by his loving young family, and the welcoming portal is gently played off against the village church behind. No taint of radicalism or dissenting religion lies upon this ideal way of life.

Military and naval victories could also be employed to bolster the government's claims to defend the stability of the realm. The Duke of York's taking of Valenciennes, on 28 July 1793, though short-lived, became the occasion for an immense painting commissioned by Valentine and Rupert Green to be engraved in a luxury edition (no. 179). At the same time a great many transfer-printed pots were produced which celebrate the Duke of York's victory, either by a print of the surrender itself or a toast (nos 179–80). In the absence of land victories patriotic attention became focused upon the navy, particularly after Howe's victory on 1 June 1794, which led to a veritable flood of commemoration: Loutherbourg immediately embarked upon a large painting of the battle to be paired with the one of Valenciennes (no. 181). A popular print published by Laurie and Whittle on 1 August 1794, *Jack's return after Lord Howe's Glorious Victory* (no. 182), expresses the notion of a *popular* victory, one which can be shared from the top to the bottom of society, as a triumph of British valour, yet there is also a hint in the caption of the navy's potential for mutiny in those years:

> Our fleet has engag'd and the French as expected,
> And wish'd by all ranks, save a few disaffected,
> Have not only been *tuck'd up* but also *dissected.*

The immense popularity of Nelson after the Battle of the Nile on 1 August 1798 tended to enhance the popularity of the king, yet it also made clear the limitations of George III's image of benevolence. Though George III himself had always been torn between reticence and display, it is notable that he played a more public ceremonial role after 1795 and became in person the focus of commemoration. As Linda Colley has pointed out,[82] an air of splendour was thought by Pitt to be a desirable attribute of royalty, and even the Prince of Wales was partially rehabilitated to take his place along with his more military brothers. In Beechey's spectacular painting and mezzotint of *George III with the Prince of Wales reviewing troops* of 1799 (no. 213) the king and prince appear in the unlikely role of military commanders themselves, along with the Duke of York; and in Loutherbourg's frontispiece to 'Nelson's Victories' of 1800 (no. 214) the king is represented as a bust on a plinth, upon which the sun shines, while an adoring Britannia offers him the domination of the sea. By the end of the century the slightly absurd figure of George III, satirised endlessly by Gillray and others as nervously observing the fate of his fellow monarch across the Channel, had been transformed into a symbol of political stability and military valour.

Revolution as myth: public art and private dissent

The works considered so far have all in one way or another been concerned to promote political ideas in the public sphere, and their political viewpoint can easily be discerned with hindsight. The artists considered in this section, William Blake, Henry Fuseli, George Romney and James Barry, present different problems: they were all admirers of the French Revolution in its early years, and their work of the revolutionary period appears to express a private as well as a public response to revolution and its place in human history. Yet few of their works make an *overt* reference to the French Revolution itself, and the intentions behind them may be difficult, and in some cases impossible, to recover, except by a process of inference from incomplete evidence. After 1794 to show even an awareness of the complexity of the revolutionary process might court the accusation of Jacobinism.[83]

In 1799 Farington recorded that in spring 1794 George III 'had imbibed a prejudice against the Academy' and refused to come to the opening of the annual exhibition because it 'was under the Stigma of having many Democrats in it'.[84] In a sense the king was right, for many of the higher officials of the Academy had been sympathetic initially to the French Revolution. James Barry, the Professor of Painting, was certainly a man of democratic temperament; Henry Fuseli, who was to succeed him, had close connections with radical intellectuals like Mary Wollstonecraft and William Godwin; and Robert Smirke worried the king with his 'democratic principles', though this did not prevent his occupying the Presidential chair in Benjamin West's absence.[85]

By 1794 these artists had evidently repented of their previous enthusiasm for the French Revolution and had joined in the business of presenting loyal addresses which seemed to take up so much of the Council's time. Even so there are hints in Farington's Diary that they were always under an aura of suspicion. Though a reputation as a democrat was enough to bar a candidate from the Professorship of History at the Academy,[86] some members retained radical sympathies beyond 1794, most notably Thomas Banks the sculptor, described by Farington as 'a violent Democrat', who was a member of the Society for Constitutional Information, and was actually brought before the Privy Council on suspicion of high treason in 1794.[87]

The 'contagion' also spread to some of the younger members: J. F. Rigaud's son described how in late 1792 'the peaceable students in the Antique Academy [were] continually interrupted in their studies by others of an opposite character, who used to stand up and spout forth torrents of indecent abuse against the King, and all that was sacred'.[88] From 1794 onwards one of the means for men to exhibit democratic sympathies in sophisticated circles was to wear their hair short and unpowdered. Farington describes a public meeting in November 1795, in Westminster Palace Yard, held in protest against the Sedition Bills. He noted that both Fox and the Duke of Bedford had cropped hair and 'In going out of the Hall, I met Banks & Smirke & his Son, who I joined, telling them as they were Crops and Democrats, I should be safe under their protection'.[89]

In fact hair cropping seems to have become a more general fashion in the last years of the century, but it still carried some connotations of radicalism. Thomas Girtin, for instance, was noted in 1798 as possessing a 'Brutus head/And curls not bigger than a bead'.[90] In addition two important artists who were not actually members of the Royal Academy, William Blake and George Romney, were certainly by the standards of George III 'violent Democrats'. Blake had in fact exhibited frequently at the Academy and was a friend and admirer of Fuseli, while Romney, though a portrait painter, had consorted with prominent French revolutionaries, including Jacques-Louis David in Paris in 1790.[91] Of all the artists mentioned so far only Banks is known to have actually joined a radical organisation, but William Sharp, thought to be the finest engraver of his age, was, like Blake, a link between Royal Academy circles and London radical artisans.[92] Also like Blake, Sharp's radicalism was strongly apocalyptic and after 1794 he moved increasingly towards the Messianic figures of Richard Brothers and Joanna Southcott, who predicted the imminence of the Second Coming.

Reynolds, who had been a close friend and supporter of Burke at the time of the publication of the *Reflections on the Revolution in France* in 1790, had already before his death in 1792 become disturbed by the rising tide of democratic sympathies within the Academy. Just before he died he wrote 'An Ironical Discourse' in which he satirised artists who believed in the unfettered expression of genius.[93] Such artists were ironically given the voice of political revolutionaries, especially of the French kind: 'Destroy every trace that remains of ancient taste. Let us pull the whole fabric down at once, root it up even to its foundation. Let us begin the art again upon this solid ground of nature and of reason. The world will then see what naked art is, in its uneducated, unprejudiced, unadulterated state.' Underlying Reynolds's nervousness was the realisation that the radicals like Barry and Fuseli were the very artists who had actually heeded his own call for an art which transcended the banalities and confusions of everyday experience.

Such artists, despite their sympathy for the French Revolution, generally avoided painting scenes from contemporary life because they wished to present moral situations of universal significance. At the same time they clearly thought the Revolution to be an event of such magnitude that it could be expressed only in epic terms. As Fuseli put it before the end of 1789, the age was 'pregnant with the most gigantic efforts of character, shaken with the convulsions of old, and the emergence of new empires: while an unexpected vigour seemed to vibrate from pole to pole'.[94] Blake also saw the French Revolution in an apocalyptic light from the beginning, and his work of the 1790s, particularly in the Prophetic books of 1793–5, is deeply bound up with events in France and especially their consequences for England. Romney has also left evidence in letters of his passionate and anxious response to the news from France, and he was perhaps the British artist most directly influenced by French revolutionary ideas. Yet the relationship between the Revolution and the work actually produced by these artists in the period remains problematic. It seems unavoidable that Fuseli's *Milton Gallery* cycle of paintings, conceived in 1790 and finished in 1801, must reflect in some way the artist's changing responses to the unfolding tragedy of the Revolution, though in what way is not immediately clear.

The same may also be said about Romney's abortive scheme for a series on *The Seven Ages of Man*, and James Barry's engravings from *Paradise Lost*, but perhaps the best starting-point for an enquiry into these projects is William Blake, for despite the complexities of his thought he at least has left a substantial body of material referring directly and indirectly to the French Revolution. Blake, through his London artisan background, was heir both to a 'levelling' tradition and to a Protestant fundamentalism which instinctively saw political and historical events within a framework of apocalypse.[95] This led to an uneasy

162 William Blake, *America a Prophecy*, relief etching, 1793. British Museum. See also p. 172.

relationship between his sympathy for the social radicalism of Paine and his detestation of the English rational tradition of Locke and Newton, of which Paine was the heir.

In Blake's poetic fragment *The French Revolution* of 1791 the events around the fall of the Bastille represent the end of despotism in France not as a stage on the way to 'the age of reason' but as the opening of an apocalyptic cycle which will free man from the moral tyranny that has confined him since the expulsion from the Garden of Eden.[96] Release from the Bastille is a metaphor of awakening from the dark night of despotism; it is also a metaphor of the awakening from life on earth into eternity through the liberation of death. In *America*, plate 6, the liberated soul is compared to a prisoner released from the Bastille:

> Let the inchained soul shut up in darkness and in sighing,
> Whose face has never seen a smile in thirty weary years,
> Rise and look out, his chains are loose, his dungeon doors are open.[97]

Imagery associated with Bastille-like confinement is to be found everywhere in Blake's work of the 1790s: in *Europe*, plate 13, the manacled prisoner responds in horror as the gaoler leaves his cell carrying an immense key.[98] In the sequence of images in *Europe* the Bastille represents another of the ghastly consequences of the tyranny of the old order. The identification of the liberation of the body with the liberation of the soul clings also to Romney's many energetic drawings made in 1791 of *Howard in the Lazaretto* (no. 160), where the great prison reformer appears as a Christ-like figure before the agonised prisoners in their foreign lazaretto. In a plaster model by Thomas Banks for a monument of 1791, now in the Soane Museum, angels release a captive from a dungeon, an emblem of the liberating power of death.[99]

Blake's poem *The French Revolution* consists of only one of the seven books proposed and it goes no further than the events of June–July 1789. The vision of revolution which emerges from the speech given to 'Sieyès' is an essentially pastoral one, in which the Old Order is sloughed off and all instantly enjoy equality and joyous labour. *America* (no. 162) and *Europe* (no. 163), written and published in the years 1793 and 1794, inevitably represent a later stage of revolutionary experience. In these two works the French Revolution is now presented as not the first but the second revolution of modern times, after the American Revolution: it is also the prelude to others, beginning with Britain and then ultimately engulfing Africa and Asia. In the continental structure which underlies the Prophetic books of the 1790s the French Revolution is Europe's revolution, the downfall of the system of spiritual and political despotism under the tyrannical aegis of the Roman Church, a view that would have been sympathetic to Tom Paine.[100] A perception of the destruction that can attend revolution is conveyed in the imagery of both books. On the Prophecy page of *America* the liberated Orc, flying free in his broken chains, is set against a family fleeing from a burning city beneath, while flames appear to burn up the page itself.[101] Revolution is a raging fire: no longer a universal celebration but 'a strife of blood'.

In these Prophecies of 1793–4 the figure of Orc integrates the American and French Revolutions into the larger current of universal history. Revolution becomes Energy, breaking the chains of the Old Order which has enslaved mankind since the Fall of Man. He is youthful and fiery, and in *America* he challenges the presiding deity of the Old Order, the Jehovah-like tyrant Urizen. In *The Marriage of Heaven and Hell*, probably finished by 1793, Energy's destructive and redemptive potential is contrasted with the passivity of conventional Christians or 'Angels' who seek to restrain the human desires of the 'Devils'.[102] The perception of energy as diabolic derives partly from an ironical reading of the role of Satan in Milton's *Paradise Lost*:'The reason Milton wrote in fetters when he wrote of Angels & God, and at liberty when of Devil & Hell, is because he was a true poet and of the Devil's party without knowing it.'[103] Satan and therefore

164 William Blake, *The Pope and Lucifer in Hell* (Isaiah 14: 4–12), engraving, *c.* 1793–4. British Museum. See also p. 173.

Orc's energy is contrasted with the passivity of Milton's Christ and God the Father: 'in Milton, the Father is Destiny, the Son a Ratio of the Five Senses, & the Holy-ghost Vacuum!'. Yet one cannot draw from this the conclusion that Blake identified completely with Satan's revolt, for as he makes clear Satan's history can be appropriated by both parties, and Satan can return to his role as the embodiment of evil outside the dialectical context of *The Marriage of Heaven and Hell*.

For Blake the bloodshed attendant on the Revolution in France would have appeared not as a sign of the failure of the Revolution but as the fulfilment of biblical prophecy: the Book of Revelation and the prophecies of the Old Testament are filled with images of the blood that must flow before judgement shall come, and of the downfall of the mighty of the earth. The powerful etching of this period of *The Pope and Lucifer in Hell* (no. 164) illustrates a passage from Isaiah on the King of Babylon, which gives an apocalyptic judgement on all monarchs, whose fate is eternal damnation. More than one recent critic has seen in the figure with a papal tiara a resemblance to George III,[104] but his jowly visage could just as easily be that of Louis XVI. The print was certainly made in 1793–4 and it must surely be a comment on the execution of Louis XVI, for the fate of kings – and this could apply equally to George III – was to join their tyrannical predecessors in hell. Blake's design may be compared with a French Jacobin image of the *Réception de Louis Capet aux Enfers*, designed and published by Villeneuve probably in early 1794 (no. 118), which shows the French king greeted by Charles I and other tyrants from the past. The Villeneuve print may itself be an answer to an English print, designed by the amateur John Warren and published in September 1793, *Louis XVI attended by Religion, & Charity, enters the Elysian Fields* (no. 117), in which he is presented with the Palm of Martyrdom by Charles I. It is possible that Blake meant his own print also to be an answer to Warren's, but it is instructively different from that by Villeneuve. Both assume the inherent corruption of monarchy and see Louis's fate in the very presumptions of kingship, but Blake's perspective is not that of an upholder of the new Age of Reason but of an Old Testament prophet reborn into an age of terminal moral decay.

Blake's writings, though difficult, allow us to see how a passionate involvement with the issues of revolution could be expressed in forms that are remote from the historical or descriptive. The maintaining of a distance from the events allows for the expression of the transcendental significance of revolution: it enables potentially dangerous thoughts to be disguised, and it also allows a flexibility of response as events unfold – indeed, the very project can redefine itself in the face of the unexpected. Most of these conditions would seem at first to apply to Fuseli's *Milton Gallery*. Though consisting of a gallery of large paintings rather than a series of illuminated books, it has in common with Blake's enterprise an implicit sense of a theological interpretation of the Revolution.

The *Milton Gallery* was conceived initially in 1791 as a series of paintings to be

157 Henry Fuseli, engraved by M. Haughton, *The Vision of the Lazar House* after Picture XXIV of the *Milton Gallery*, stipple engraving, published 10 October 1813. Victoria and Albert Museum. See also p. 168.

engraved, and Blake himself and William Sharp were asked to make some of the engravings.[105] The project is well enough documented for one to see its evolution over the years from 1791 to 1800, but it is curiously difficult to draw from it a clear sense of Fuseli's attitudes towards the Revolution. One of the first paintings, begun in October 1791 and finished in May 1792, was of the subject of *Satan, Sin and Death*, but this had been since Hogarth a popular Miltonic subject.[106] From the small version which has survived Satan appears in an Apollonian guise, but the choice of subject in itself demonstrates little. More telling, perhaps, is the fact that on 16 February 1793 he delivered the ghastly *Vision of the Lazar House* (no. 157), a dreadful scene in a madhouse presided over by Death. The choice of subject irresistibly suggests the horrific, disjointed and fratricidal image presented in England of the early months of the French Republic, and it also seems to parallel the words of Fuseli's own renunciation of the Revolution in an article in the *Analytical Review* of November 1793. He argues that after the collapse of despotism 'the anarchies that ensue will be little more than the temporary contests for rule of factions equally criminal . . . the bulk will subside again under the tyrant of the ruling party, and in degenerate silence subscribe to the law of force'.[107]

Fuseli's retreat from revolutionary hope reveals that despite his demonic posing, he was, unlike Blake, a man of the Enlightenment. For him the breakdown of order in France was conclusive evidence of the Revolution's failure. Paintings in progress in 1792, *Adam and Eve observed by Satan* and *Satan fleeing from Chaos*, might also subtly invite counter-revolutionary interpretations; the former shows Satan's envy of the more fortunate Adam and Eve, while the latter might be read as associating the Revolution with chaos. On the other hand, four paintings described also as finished on 16 February 1793 give less scope for a revolutionary interpretation: *The Creation of Eve*, two comic subjects from *L'Allegro* and *Milton dictating to his daughters*.[108]

It seems certain from such evidence, then, that Fuseli was not trying systematically to relate the subjects of the *Milton Gallery* to the events of the Revolution. It would be in character for Fuseli not to want to be seen as too 'Jacobinical', though at the same time he did not wish to break with his radical friends. He remained on close terms with Joseph Johnson until the end of the 1790s and was a constant companion of such radical thinkers as William Godwin (no. 167).[109] The first *Milton Gallery* paintings were conceived around the time of his affair with Mary Wollstonecraft, but, as Schiff points out, he was at the same time being supported by a group of liberal gentlemen like Roscoe, Coutts the banker and the Lockes of Norbury, who might have welcomed the humanitarian promise of the Revolution in its early days but not a Jacobin republic.[110] Fuseli not only succeeded in retaining the respect and loyalty of other members of the Royal Academy, who put on a grand banquet to boost visitors to the reopened Milton Gallery in 1800, but he was also able to persuade Blake that its commercial failure was due to the fear of the British establishment that the *Milton Gallery* had exposed its iniquities: 'O Society for Encouragement of Art! O King & Nobility of England! Where have you hid Fuseli's Milton? Is Satan troubled at his exposure?'[111]

Fuseli's predecessor as Professor of Painting of the Royal Academy, James Barry, also embarked on a series of engravings to *Paradise Lost* in the revolutionary years. In contrast to Fuseli he suffered greatly for his radicalism, or more precisely for his combative personality which always smacked of Jacobinism to his long-suffering colleagues in the Academy. His response to the French Revolution was complicated by his Roman Catholicism and his growing concern with Ireland in the 1790s. His vision of equality was conceived in terms of the peaceful coexistence of the different Christian sects under a benign papacy.[112] He dissociated himself from the anti-clericalism of the French Republic, yet, like Blake, his rejection of British religious and political hierarchies seems to have been absolute. Barry began his *Paradise Lost* series in 1792 and was still at work on them in 1794.[113] As with Fuseli it is difficult to define Barry's point of view from the works themselves, but Satan's heroism in his defiance of the Almighty is strongly emphasised.

Blake, Fuseli and Barry were all in their different ways stirred by the epic qualities of the events in France; George Romney is a different case for he had spent three weeks in Paris in August 1790, the most hopeful phase of the Revolution, meeting many of its most sympathetic protagonists, most notably David, with whom he and William Hayley dined.[114] Like Wordsworth who had been caught up in the celebrations of Fédération in the previous month, Romney seems to have been captivated by early revolutionary France. He was entertained by Madame de Genlis, the governess to the family of the Duke of Orleans and possibly his mistress, and it is likely that he mixed briefly with the kind of liberal pro-revolutionary aristocrat in Paris that Wordsworth found so captivating in the person of Michel Beaupuy.[115] Indeed, there is a strong Girondin flavour about Romney's ardent temperament, and this is reflected in his friendship with Tom Paine, who found Romney one of the few people in London he could visit in the period of notoriety which followed the publication of *The Rights of Man* in 1791–2.[116]

The impact of Romney's French visit is to be seen most strongly perhaps in the drawings of the great prison reformer John Howard visiting a lazaretto, which were studies for a painting commissioned by Hayley in honour of Howard who had died earlier in 1790.[117] Romney worked on the drawings after he returned from Paris, and the finished ones to survive all show Howard as a compassionate observer of ghastly scenes of imprisonment. The emphasis is upon the sufferings of the imprisoned, who are seen as heaped together in their misery under the cruel gaze of a single keeper. In one case (Fitzwilliam Museum, Cambridge, see fig. 5) a brutish gaoler holds a massive key suggestive of the Bastille and is fended off by Howard, while in the drawing exhibited here (no. 160) the gaoler appears as a malevolent, monkish figure apparently with a black cowl. The fact that in each case the gaoler is a single figure dominating the multitude of humanity surely suggests the inherent cruelty of despotism, while Howard represents not only mercy and courage but the power of reason to liberate humanity from suffering.

Romney's hopes for the French Revolution survived detailed accounts of the massacre of the Swiss Guards in the Tuileries on 10 August 1792, and in October of that year he reaffirmed that 'the present moment is an epock in Liberty that has never happened before since the Creation – I confess the Sublimity of it taking it together has interested and agitated me much'. By September 1793, however, his disillusionment in revolution was expressed by a nervous fear of the common people of London: 'the approach to London affected me in various ways. I observed a sharpness of countenance in the people I met: with passions so strongly marked, I suppose none could mistake. Deep design, disappointed ambition, envy, hatred, melancholy, disease and poverty'.[118]

Fig. 5 George Romney, *Howard in the Lazaretto*, pen and wash, 1790–1. Fitzwilliam Museum, BV152.

If the theme of the Howard drawings is one of liberation, the growing pessimism of 1793–4 was expressed in dark visions of human history which were to be brought together in a series on 'The Seven Ages', presumably to show the development of mankind up to the present era.[119] It is impossible to piece the series together from the sketches which survive, but it is likely that the powerful drawings of the *Fall of the Rebel Angels*, from *Paradise Lost*, Book I (no. 158), had a part to play in it. They show Satan, in contrast to Barry's heroic picture of him, at the moment he was cast down to 'bottomless perdition' in the failure of his 'impious war'.

The combination of the horrors reported from France and repression at home in the years 1793–5 effectively prevented the growth of a new generation of 'respectable' radical artists. Just as artists in France under the Revolution sought to paint pictures acceptable to each political phase, so most British artists, particularly those attached to the Royal Academy, sought after 1795 to wipe away the stain of Jacobinism. Though we may doubt that they all recanted in their hearts, their ability to express radical thoughts in public even in veiled form was severely curtailed by internal and external pressures. One artist who did not recant, in private at least, was William Blake: in 1798 he annotated the fervently loyalist Bishop Watson's *An Apology for The Bible in a series of Letters to Thomas Paine*, 1797,[120] taking Paine's part at every point and ending with the devastating conclusion that 'Tom Paine is a better Christian than the Bishop'.[121]

Postscript: the view from the mid-nineteenth century

The French Revolution did not become in England in the nineteenth century what it became in France – a touchstone for all political attitudes and alignments. Even so it lived on in such influential works as Carlyle's *French Revolution* of 1837 and Dickens's *A Tale of Two Cities* of 1859, and countless histories and memoirs, mostly of a sensational kind. The most insistent visual reminder, especially of the period of the Terror, was to be found, and still is to be found, in Madame Tussaud's waxworks in Baker Street in London, and Madame Tussaud herself lived on until 1850, still reminiscing about the revolutionary leaders and victims she claimed to have known so well.[122]

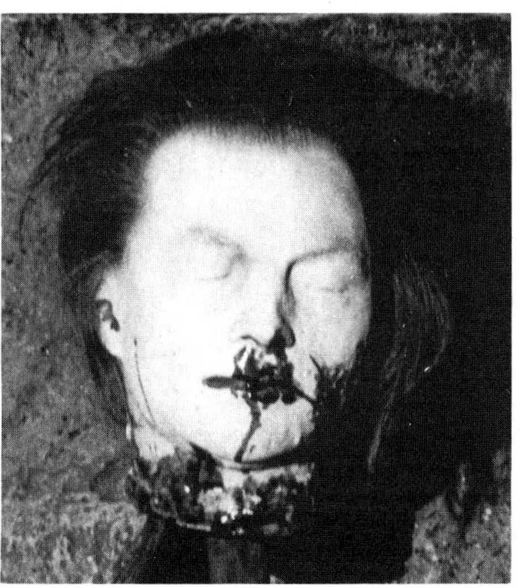

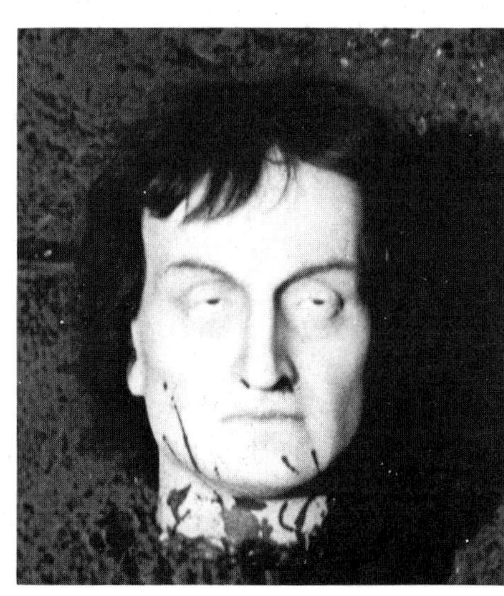

225 Madame Tussaud, two wax heads of Robespierre and Fouquier-Tinville. Madame Tussaud's, London. See also p. 212.

Madame Tussaud had brought with her from Paris in 1802 the moulds for the wax heads of Robespierre and others prominent in the Terror, and a great many relics of varying degrees of authenticity were added throughout the nineteenth century. Her uncle Curtius, the founder of the waxworks in Paris, had premises first in the Palais Royal and then in the Boulevard du Temple in the early days of the Revolution, and he claimed to have taken part in the attack on the Bastille, writing a pamphlet entitled *Les Services du Sieur Curtius, Vainqueur de la Bastille*.[123] He became a captain in the National Guard and was a loyal and active supporter of the Convention. He died on 26 September 1794, before his activities under the Terror might have come under scrutiny.

Madame Tussaud's *Memoirs and Reminiscences*, published in 1838, reveal that in old age, in so far as she wrote the *Memoirs* herself, she was torn by an understandable desire to demonstrate her close involvement with the Revolution and at the same time to dissociate herself from its excesses.[124] She claimed, of course, to have secretly been horrified by events, and though wax models of the decapitated victims of the guillotine were among the chief attractions of her waxworks, little credence should be given to her account of their creation. Her version, reinforced until a few years ago by a life-size tableau showing her in prison being forced to cast severed heads by a brutish sans-culotte, was that she served the Revolution under extreme duress and in imminent fear of her life.

The first catalogue of Madame Tussaud's to survive, of a display in Edinburgh of 1803,[125] consists simply of biographical accounts of various revolutionary leaders and victims, among other famous persons of history: her own intervention is not recorded. In the 1822 Manchester catalogue,[126] however, following the practice in the Paris display, the guillotined heads with a few other oddities were 'in consequence of the peculiarity of their appearance . . . placed in an adjoining room' for which an extra sixpence was charged. The catalogue now claims that Madame Tussaud had been forced to make a model of the head of the Princess de Lamballe after her murder, but in the case of the heads of Robespierre, Carrier, Fouquier-Tinville and Hébert, all of which still survive, the catalogue simply states that each one was 'Taken immediately after his execution, by order of the National Assembly'.[127] This sounds plausible insofar as the four heads are of precisely those revolutionaries who were most execrated under the Thermidor regime and the Directory, and it is perfectly possible that the post-Robespierre Convention could have commissioned them, or Madame Tussaud might simply have added them to her display. No mention is made at this point of the heads having been cast from the actual victims, though this later became part of the legend. In fact it seems unnecessary for a skilled wax modeller to have made them in such a messy way, and the claim seems not to have been made before the 1838 *Memoirs*.

From the early 1850s subjects from the French Revolution occasionally made their appearance in the Royal Academy, while the growing international trade in prints meant that many of the most familiar images of the Revolution were actually French in origin, being published in London and elsewhere as well as in Paris. Perhaps more than in the 1790s the guillotine became the principal emblem of the French Revolution, and the execution of Marie Antoinette, rather than of Louis XVI, the central and defining event, followed in frequency by Charlotte Corday before her execution. These subjects represent more than just the popular triumph of Royalism: the fate of the French royal family presented subjects of such drama that Romantic historians like Lamartine were captivated by its pathos. Victorian historical painters consulted the latest works of history in search of authenticity, and to some degree the vogue for French Revolution subjects tended to follow the spate of books, usually of a hagiographic nature, on the royal and aristocratic victims of the Revolution, which appeared from the middle of the century, emphasising their superior dignity and composure in the face of death.

Several artists, like Alfred Elmore and Frederick Goodall, made one or two paintings connected with the Revolution, but the one real specialist was the painter of historical subjects E. M. Ward, who exhibited between 1851 and 1875 as many as ten paintings of the last days of the French royal family or of Charlotte Corday.[128] The most successful was *The Royal Family of France in the Prison of the Temple* (see no. 233, Harris Museum and Art Gallery, Preston), exhibited at the Royal Academy in 1851 and subsequently in Paris in 1855 to great acclaim. The subject is derived from Lamartine's *History of the Girondins*, first published in 1847,[129] and it draws out the pathos of the family's confinement in the Temple before Louis's execution. The pathos is located in the contrast between the family's high position and their present plight: the text for the painting derives from Lamartine's description of how 'The Queen was obliged to mend the King's coat while he was asleep, in order that he might not be obliged to wear a vest in holes'. The royal family's quiet dignity is also contrasted with the brutality of the gaolers, one of whom blows tobacco smoke into the room. The work caused some controversy in Paris in 1855 because of its lack of histrionics, and the suggestion

Fig. 6 E. M. Ward, *The Royal Family of France in the Prison of the Temple*, oil, 1851. Harris Museum and Art Gallery, Preston. See also p. 77.

was made that the king had been depicted as a 'bon bourgeois faisant la sieste après diner', but it was also admired for its profound sadness and the dignity of the royal family.[130] According to a pamphlet produced by the publisher Gambart when it was to be engraved,

> When in 1855, this picture was at Paris, . . . it was surrounded by a crowd, among which might often be seen eyes wet with tears. Those who wept before it were, perhaps, as often the sons of parents who had bawled execrations against 'Monsieur Veto' or shouted 'A bas l'Autrichienne', as of those who had crowded the upper windows round the Temple to offer its prisoners their tribute of unavailing loyalty, or had treasured relics of Louis XVI and Marie Antoinette, as of saints and martyrs.[131]

Lamartine was also the source for paintings by Ward of the last days of Charlotte Corday, who emerges as 'among the great heroines of the world', a figure of mythical courage and self-sacrifice and also of compelling beauty. As such she incites the particular hatred and derision of those of base feelings, and for a painting of 1852 Ward borrowed from Lamartine the apocryphal story of Robespierre, Desmoulins and Danton watching her on her way to the guillotine (fig. 7).[132] As with the royal family Charlotte Corday is given all the true humanity, while her captors and enemies are seen as incapable of respect for finer feelings.

Ward's later paintings of Revolution subjects tend to focus upon the royal family in the Temple, emphasising, often relatively coarsely, the differences in bearing between Marie Antoinette and her tormentors. In *Marie Antoinette listening to the Act of Accusation* (McCormick family collection), as Susan Casteras has pointed out,[133] the Queen's dignity and composure are contrasted through Ward's pictorial language with the pretentious and insolent bearing of her elaborately dressed accuser Fouquier-Tinville, just as in Alfred Elmore's *The Tuileries, June 20, 1792* (no. 231) it is the queenly bearing of Marie Antoinette which prevails over the coarseness of the invading mob. In Ward's paintings, in particular, the representation of the sans-culottes, deriving from caricatures of the 1790s, enables the royal family to assert their blood royal through their bearing and not through their clothes, even in the dismal setting of a dank prison. This emphasis on regal bearing may also reflect the influence of Royalist prints from France, such as those published by Goupil simultaneously in Paris and London. In Paul Delaroche's *Marie Antoinette*, published by Goupil in 1857,[134] the Queen appears at her trial as a figure of heroic dignity, towering morally and physically over the common humanity of her accusers.

The result of all these images, popular and more elevated, was to establish in British consciousness, in place of the myriad complexities of the real French Revolution, a series of simple pictures and stereotypes which have proved virtually indestructible. If we still think of the French Revolution in terms of the guillotine, innocent aristocrats and brutish sans-culottes, then this represents the triumph of visual images which have a virtually unbroken history from the propaganda campaigns of the 1790s through the Victorian period to the present day.

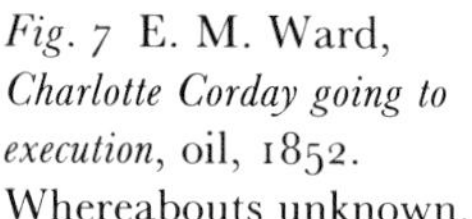

Fig. 7 E. M. Ward, *Charlotte Corday going to execution*, oil, 1852. Whereabouts unknown.

Catalogue

Notes to the catalogue

All works are in the British Museum unless otherwise stated, and are given their Museum number only. Most caricatures and certain other prints have the reference 'BMC': this refers to the *Catalogue of Personal and Political Satires preserved in the Department of Prints and Drawings in the British Museum*, the relevant volumes of which, v, vi and vii, were compiled by Mrs M. Dorothy George in 1935, 1938 and 1942 respectively. A certain number of prints in the exhibition which have been acquired since the publication of the George volumes have no catalogue number. 'de V' refers to the catalogue of the de Vinck Collection in the Bibliothèque Nationale, Paris. References to other publications have been kept to a minimum, and generally refer to recent works. A full list of abbreviated references will be found on p. 222. The provenance of objects has been included only if it is of particular relevance.

Measurements given are of the plate mark in the case of prints or image size if they are cut within it. All measurements are in millimetres, height preceding width.

Catalogue entries by Aileen Dawson and Mark Jones are indicated by their initials. All other entries are by David Bindman.

1 Before the Revolution

British responses to the French Revolution were conditioned by wars and trade rivalry between Britain and France in the previous century. At the same time French art and style had immense prestige in sophisticated circles in London, and many English gentlemen spent long periods in Paris. By 1789 a group of stereotypes of the French, many dating back to William Hogarth and beyond, had become well established in satirical art and literature. These stereotypes were often as much the product of middle-class suspicion of aristocratic Francophilia as of the French themselves.

Britain had its own social problems in the eighteenth century and popular disturbances were a feature of urban life. The experience of such eruptions as the Gordon Riots of 1780 undoubtedly affected later attitudes to revolutionary France, and the picture of Parisian sans-culottes in later caricature owed something to conceptions of the British 'mob'. The eighteenth century also saw widely based radical campaigns engaged in a struggle for the repeal of the Test and Corporation Acts, which kept Dissenters out of public life, and for a more equitable parliamentary system. The aristocratic oligarchy which effectively ran Britain in the second half of the eighteenth century was challenged by the American colonists and their many supporters in Britain, and by the growing power of manufacturers, who were often themselves Dissenters and took an interest in enlightened causes like the repeal of slavery. French philosophers like Voltaire and Rousseau had a great deal of prestige in England, and their rational objections to the domination of rank and the despotism of the *ancien régime* were influential in creating a climate in England initially sympathetic to the French Revolution. Merchants like Josiah Wedgwood were able to combine an admiration for the French Enlightenment with a strong sense of the commercial possibilities of the French market.

1

French stereotypes

H. W. BUNBURY

1 *The Kitchen of a French Post House*

etching, 415 × 442 mm, pub. 1 Feb. 1771 by M. Darly
J 6-2; Banks Collection
LITERATURE BMC 4764; Godfrey 1984, no. 68

The most famous of Bunbury's caricatures of French life, which remained influential to the end of the eighteenth century. Such caricatures purport to represent normal French life as seen by an English traveller, but in fact they both draw upon and reaffirm traditional stereotypes. The inn is sparsely furnished, suggesting poverty, and the religious broadsides on the wall and the print of the king suggest a people weighed down by superstition and authority, in implicit contrast to British liberty. The Frenchmen are characterised by their slender physique and absurd footware.

JAMES GILLRAY *(illus. p. 43)*

2 *Politeness*

etching, coloured, 200 × 275 mm, pub. 1779 by H. Humphrey
1868-8-8-5809
INSCRIBED 'With Porter Roast Beef & Plumb Pudding well cram'd
Jack English declares that Mons.[r] may be D-d
The Soup Meagre Frenchman such Language dont suit
So he Grins Indignation & calls him a Brute.'
LITERATURE BMC 5612

The classic confrontation between national archetypes. England is John Bull, four-square and direct like his mastiff, while the Frenchman is foppish and affected, accompanied by a greyhound. At the heart of the difference is food, symbolised by the joint of beef behind John Bull and the frogs behind the snuff-taking Frenchman. The contrast of national stereotypes is a stock-in-trade of eighteenth-century caricature and it occurs in different forms throughout the revolutionary period. This impression appears to have later colouring, so it may well have been issued towards the end of the century, when Gillray had achieved fame.

F. C. BYRON *(illus. in colour)*

3 *Breakfast at Breteuil*

pen and watercolour, 380 × 587 mm, 1790
1988-3-5-20
EXHIBITED Society of Artists, 1791, no. 38 (with *Inn Yard at Calais*, no. 37)
ENGRAVED F. C. Lewis, pub. 1 Nov. 1801 by W. Holland

One of a group of watercolours illustrating a journey through France in 1790, which were reproduced in etching and aquatint by F. C. Lewis in 1791 and 1801–2 (see nos 29 and 30 for prints from the set). Byron, who

3

4

was the poet Lord Byron's uncle, was an amateur who travelled in France at the time of the first Fédération ceremony of 14 July 1790 and made a large watercolour of the scene (Versailles Museum). The series employs traditional stereotypes derived from Bunbury even after the outbreak of the Revolution, including the postilion with enormous boots who now sports a cockade. A print of the fall of the Bastille can be seen hanging above the fireplace.

The English mob: the Gordon Riots

J. HEATH AFTER FRANCIS WHEATLEY

4 *The Riot in Broad Street, 7 June 1780*

engraving, 476 × 633 mm, proof before letters (published state inscribed: 'To the Gentlemen of the London Light Horse Volunteers and Military Foot Association, This Memorial of their Patriotic Conduct, is inscribed by their obliged Servants, John and Josiah Boydell, pub. Sep. 29 1790')
1866-2-10-468
LITERATURE M. Webster, *Francis Wheatley*, London, 1970, pp. 53–5; Bindman in *Kunst um 1800*, pp. 87–94

The scene is of 7 June when the London mob, which had rioted unchecked by the law for several days, was now confronted with the forces of the City of London militia under Sir Bernard Turner, who with discipline and humanity brought the disorder under control. The print was made from a painting commissioned by the great print publisher Alderman Boydell shortly after the event, probably to show the public spirit of City merchants and the inadequate response of the government to the Gordon Riots. The painting was destroyed in a fire apparently before the engraving was completed, and it was only published in 1790.

ATTRIBUTED TO JAMES GILLRAY

5 *No Popery or Newgate Reformer*

etching, 275 × 210 mm, pub. 9 June 1780 by I. Catch
1851-9-1-34; Smith Collection
LITERATURE BMC 5679; Bindman in *Kunst um 1800*, p. 89

If the publication date can be relied upon, this print appeared within days of the end of the Gordon Riots. Here the rioters are dissociated from the campaigns of the Protestant Association, whose anti-Catholic gathering had sparked off the riots, and are dismissed as street ruffians whose 'practice is only to burn and to thieve'. Compare with the behaviour of Parisian sans-culottes in Zoffany's mezzotint (no. 46) and see Introduction, p. 45.

5

British radicalism

JAMES BARRY

6 *The Phoenix or the Resurrection of Freedom*

etching and aquatint, 460 × 640 mm, pub. Dec. 1776 by J. Almon
1848-11-25-563
LITERATURE Pressly 1981, p. 268, no. 8, II; Pressly, *Barry* cat., 1983, no. 21

This print is a fierce and radical attack on the king and court at the time of the American Revolution, and at the same time an affirmation of Barry's adherence to the British republican tradition going back to the Commonwealth and the writers Algernon Sydney, John Milton and Andrew Marvell. They, and also Locke and Barry himself, are gathered round the bier of Britannia whose traditional liberties, inherited from Athens, Florence and republican Rome, have now, in the face of government attack, migrated to America. It is inscribed beneath: 'O Liberty though Parent of whatever is truly amiable & Illustrious, associated with virtue, thou hatest the Luxurious & Intemperate & hast successively abandon'd thy lov'd residence of Greece, Italy & thy more favor'd England when they grew Currupt & Worthless, thou hast given them over to chains & despondency & taken thy flight to a new people of manners simple & untainted.'

6

Barry was an associate of Edmund Burke who, though he was later to be the first and most influential scourge of the French Revolution, was at the time of the American Revolution a fierce opponent of government policy towards the colony. Barry seems, with reservations, to have been in sympathy with the French Revolution, and it may be significant that he reissued the print about 1790. According to Goodwin (1979, p. 33), 'In the 1790s radical publicists and even popular demagogues never tired of invoking the hallowed names and political doctrines of Milton, Algernon Sydney, Harrington and Locke in support of their protests and remonstrances against clerical intolerance, Loyalist reaction and ministerial repression'.

THOMAS STOTHARD, ENGRAVED BY WILLIAM SHARP

7 *Declaration of Rights*

engraving, 615 × 440 mm, no pub. line, 1782
1853-12-10-197
LITERATURE Bindman 1977, pp. 26–7; Bennett 1988, p. 4

This little-known print was dedicated to the Society for Constitutional Information by the painter Thomas Stothard, later well known as a Royal Academician, and the engraver, William Sharp, who were both associated with the young William Blake. The former seems not to have maintained his interest in politics while the latter became a notable radical in the 1790s before becoming a follower of the prophets Richard Brothers and Joanna Southcott. The Society for Constitutional Information, which was founded in 1780 by Major Cartwright who appears in profile at the bottom of the print, was an important link between the middle-class radicalism of the period of the American Revolution and that of the French Revolution. It was revived as an active organisation in 1790, and some of its most prominent members, like Horne Tooke (no. 166), were involved in it from its beginnings until its collapse in 1795. The basis of the Society, as its name suggests, was the conversion of public opinion to parliamentary reform by presenting the case as widely as possible throughout the country, and this print, judging by its rarity, was an abortive attempt to present it in decorative form.

8 *Wedgwood plaque, Am I not a Man and a Brother?*

caneware and black basalt, inscription impressed and filled in black, H. 97 mm
1909, 12-1, 260; presented by Mr and Mrs Isaac Falcke
LITERATURE Dawson 1984, p. 45 and pl. 13

An example of Josiah Wedgwood's humanitarian interest in the campaign for the end of slavery, which parallels the concern of some, if not all, French revolutionaries. Though Brissot had formed 'La Société des amis des noirs' in 1788, it was not until 4 February 1794 (16 Pluviose, l'an II) that slavery was abolished by the Convention. The medallion, modelled by Josiah Wedgwood's chief modeller, William Hackwood (employed 1769, d.1839), is based on the seal of the Society for the Abolition of the Slave Trade established in 1787, and was issued in quantity in a smaller size for jewellery and for the lids of snuffboxes. The same image was used in early 1789 by the Sèvres factory, but at the command of the French colonial administration the medallions were withdrawn lest they provoke unrest among the Negroes. AD

J. SAYERS

9 *The Repeal of the Test Act: a Vision*

etching, 495 × 355 mm, pub. 16 Feb. 1790 by T. Conell
Sayers Album, 298.d.2(Y10-125)
LITERATURE BMC 7628

This print was published after the outbreak of the French Revolution and makes an attack upon the Rev. Richard Price, the central figure in the pulpit, famous for his rapturous welcome to the French Revolution. In fact the print was originally conceived in 1788 as a comprehensive attack on the Dissenting radicals, most notably Joseph Priestley and Price himself, and their passionate advocacy of motions in Parliament for the repeal of the Test and Corporation Acts which imposed disabilities upon Dissenters. Here the Dissenting clergymen who supported the motions are satirised as atheists and republicans who seek the return of a Cromwellian Commonwealth. After the French Revolution Price's notoriety was much increased by his sermon of 4 November 1789 which was followed by an address of congratulation to the French National Assembly. It provoked Edmund Burke to a ferocious reply in his *Reflections on the Revolution in France* of 1790, for which see no. 48.

The French trade

10 *Wedgwood figure of Voltaire after J. C. Rosset*

caneware, impressed Wedgwood & Bentley, H. 313 mm
1909, 12-1, 440; presented by Mr and Mrs Isaac Falcke
LITERATURE Dawson 1984, p. 86, pl. 13

An example of contacts between England and France, and the great prestige of the French *philosophes* like Voltaire and Rousseau in England in the years before the Revolution, especially among the increasingly assertive circles of Midlands manufacturers and scientific amateurs.

The figure, perhaps modelled by William Keeling (fl.

11

1763–90) working from drawings to which Thomas Bentley put the finishing touches, is based on a small-scale marble of 1773, measuring 350 mm in height, by the Swiss sculptor Jean-Claude Rosset called Du Pont (1703 or 1706–86). It was issued by Wedgwood in 1778 in both basalt and caneware. A letter of 16 October 1779 from Josiah Wedgwood to his partner Thomas Bentley discusses problems experienced in firing caneware, mentioning the companion figure of Jean-Jacques Rousseau. AD

11 *Wedgwood plaque, Mercury uniting the hands of Britain and France*

solid blue jasper ware, white jasper relief, H. 250 mm
Lent by Castle Museum, Nottingham, 92-404
LITERATURE *Flaxman, R. A.*, no. 52; 'Wedgwood at Woburn', exh. cat., Woburn Abbey, 1973, no. w4; A. Dawson, 'The Eden Service, Another Diplomatic Gift', *Apollo*, CXI, no. 218, pp. 295–6, fig. 12

The subject celebrates the signing of the Treaty of Navigation and Commerce on 26 September 1786 which was strongly advocated by Josiah Wedgwood. The plaque was commissioned from the sculptor John Flaxman jun. (1755–1826), whose pen and wash drawing survives in a private collection. The wax from which the mould was created was ready by 26 March 1787 at a cost of 13 guineas. It belongs to the Wedgwood Museum, Barlaston, Staffordshire. On 16 June 1787 Wedgwood wrote to William Eden (1744–1814), Minister Plenipotentiary to France, who had played a leading part in the negotiations for the Treaty, that he had sent him the first pair of bas-reliefs representing the commercial treaty with France by the diligence through Monsieur Dominique Daguerre, a leading dealer. The other plaque represents 'Peace Preventing Mars Opening the Gates of Janus'. AD

2 The first year of liberty: Bastille to Fédération

The events that led to the fall of the Bastille have often been described, and are only briefly restated here. On 17 June 1789 the Third Estate declared its autonomy from the king and constituted itself as a National Assembly, and on 20 June the deputies swore the famous Tennis Court oath to sit until a new constitution had been established. In the state of uncertainty which followed troops were ordered by the king to build up in and around Paris to keep order in the face of popular discontent, mainly caused by the rising price of bread. The dismissal of the finance minister Necker on 11 July raised popular fears of an 'aristocratic plot' to crush the people of Paris. Crowds of people in fear of attack began to gather arms, setting up on 13 July what was to become the National Guard. On the morning of 14 July crowds went to acquire arms from the Invalides while others went to the Bastille to take over a supply of gunpowder which was reputed to be kept there. Delaunay, the governor, had only a small garrison, but opened fire, treacherously it was believed by the invaders, on the crowd, killing many people. This caused a troop of National Guards to return with cannon, and in the late afternoon Delaunay surrendered and was beheaded by the vengeful crowd on the way to the Hôtel de Ville.

The storming and demolition of the Bastille

The predominant image of the fall of the Bastille was established very quickly, probably before the end of July 1789. Within a short period a companion image of the demolition of the Bastille was added, representing symbolically the dismantling of the institutions of despotism. Many British images derive directly from French prototypes, but there are numerous caricatures which celebrate uninhibitedly the discomfiture of the King and Queen of France and welcome what they presumed to be the establishment of a British-type constitutional monarchy.

12

13

ANON. FRENCH

12 *Prise de la Bastille par les bourgeois et les braves gardes françaises de la bonne ville de Paris, le 14 juillet 1789*

etching with aquatint, 345 × 450 mm, pub. by Bance
1868-8-8-7434; Slade Collection

A characteristic example of the many different prints of the fall of the Bastille produced in subsequent months, but which contain roughly the same scenes. In effect three phases of the action are depicted: the assault of the guards on the left, the forced entry into the inner courtyard in the rear, and in the middle distance the apprehension of Delaunay, the governor of the Bastille. Other elements can also be observed which inform almost all views of the scene: the humanity of the attackers contrasted with the facelessness of the defenders, and the impregnable solidity of the Bastille itself. At this early date the citizens and National Guard of Paris are given credit for the assault, not 'the people'.

J. WELLS AFTER CHARLES BENAZECH

13 *The Taking of the Bastile on the 14 of July 1789*

etching and aquatint, coloured, 380 × 505 mm, pub. 20 Nov. 1789 by B. van der Gucht and J. White
1951-6-6-1
LITERATURE de V 1598

The first of a series of coloured aquatints of the first events of the Revolution, of which only three were published. Though claiming to have been 'Drawn on the Spot by an eminent Artist', we can now, on the basis of a signed drawing in the Maidstone Museum (no. 26), firmly attribute the design to Charles Benazech, an artist of French parentage based in London (see no. 91). The fanciful nature of the scene and its obvious derivation from such prints as no. 12 make the claim that the artist was an eyewitness extremely unlikely. On the right there lie copies of books which had 'exposed' conditions in the Bastille, like the memoirs of Latude which suggest the artist's sympathy with the assault, but Governor Delaunay is made into an unusually dignified figure. The print suggests an interest in England in the fall of the Bastille, while the inclusion of a French title implies the hope of French sales as well.

ANON. FRENCH

14 *Monument du Despotisme*

etching and aquatint, 340 × 465 mm, pub. by Bance
1868-8-8-7435; Slade Collection

This print is paired with no. 12, and it reflects the symbolic importance given to the demolition as well as to the fall of the Bastille. If the attack on the Bastille expressed the power of the people, then the demolition expressed their determination that despotism should never return. The demolition, carried out by the unscrupulous figure of Palloy, gave rise to an enormous

14

number of relics. Each new *département* in France was presented with a model of the Bastille supposedly made from its stones, manacles were melted down to make medals, while the bones of 'victims of despotism' were buried in a memorial chapel.

15 *Jug printed in black with the storming of the Bastille*

creamware, probably Staffordshire, H. 240 mm
Private Collection

On one side is a scene inscribed 'The Destruction of the BASTILLE.' and on the other the *Death of Wolfe* after Benjamin West. Beneath the spout is inscribed 'Robert Stitt Marchant Comber 1791'. A particularly fine jug in the Schreiber Collection, Victoria and Albert Museum (Sch II 383), has scenes of the assault on both sides. These jugs testify to the popularity of the Revolution in England in the first two years after the fall of the Bastille. AD

16 *Wedgwood medallions*

a) *Le Triomphe de la Valeur Francoise, 1789*
b) *Le Despotisme Abattu, 1789*

white jasper ware dipped blue, applied white jasper reliefs, (a) DIAM. 61 mm, impressed WEDGWOOD; (b) 73 mm
(a) Manchester City Art Galleries, 1906. 85; (b) Castle Museum, Nottingham 92-426A
LITERATURE *Mr Wedgwood*, exh. cat., Castle Museum, Nottingham, 1975, (a) no. 355 (Nottingham example illus. p. 47), and (b) no. 356; J. K. des Fontaines, 'The Bastille Medallion', *Proc. Wedg. Soc.*, no. 3 (1959), pp. 149–51, and no. 6 (1966), p. 107

A ledger in the Wedgwood MSS. kept at Keele University (E50-29982) suggests that the Bastille medallions were produced at the same time as most of the portrait medallions of revolutionary leaders (nos 37a–g), i.e. *c.* 1789–90. Despite their extreme rarity Wedgwood was still prepared to make impressions according to a catalogue as late as 1912/13.

Wedgwood wrote to his friend Dr Erasmus Darwin (grandfather of Charles Darwin) in July 1789, 'I know you will join me in the glorious revolution which has taken place in France. The politicians tell me that as a manufacturer I shall be ruined if France has her liberty, but I am willing to take my chance in that respect, nor do I yet see that the happiness of one nation includes in it the misery of its next neighbour'. AD

16a

16b

W. DENT

17 *Revolution, or Johnny Bull in France*

etching, coloured, 182 × 246 mm, pub. 25 July 1789 by W. Dent
Lent by Andrew Edmunds

The bull, representing curiously both John Bull and Revolution, tosses Marie Antoinette, often thought to be the real power of the French court, in the air while Louis XVI observes in supplication. The bull has 'Tiers Etat' on his horns and 'Orleans' on his collar, suggesting that revolution has been initiated by the Anglophile Duke of Orleans, later to be a regicide (see no. 109), while the soldiers look forward to their reward in 'de Roast Beef of Old England'. Despite its crudity Dent's print expresses the common, but in retrospect absurdly complacent, belief that the French Revolution was nothing more than a rejection of despotism in favour of British common sense.

17

JAMES GILLRAY

18 *France. Freedom. Britain. Slavery*

etching, coloured, 275 × 460 mm, pub. 28 July 1789 by J. Aitken
1851-9-1-468; Smith Collection
LITERATURE BMC 7546

Gillray's first response to the fall of the Bastille, showing Necker, the French finance minister, returning in triumph after the fall of the Bastille and his dismissal by Louis XVI on 11 July which had provoked much public anger. The balancing of cap of liberty and crown by Necker expresses more subtly than Dent (no. 17) the hope that the fall of the Bastille might inaugurate in France a British-type constitution. He is carried aloft by, among others, the Duke of Orleans (the bearer front left), and cheered by a grateful populace, while in the contrasting image of Britain Pitt arrogantly tramples on the Crown and enslaves both king and people by his transfer of tobacco tax from customs to excise. Like no. 71 it is a 'Contrast' print, but highly unusual in contrasting Britain unfavourably with France, and full of ironies in view of future attitudes towards the Revolution and the execration the Duke of Orleans was to attract. This print was extensively copied in France, usually as a pair of separate prints.

18

ANON.

19 *La Chute du Despotisme/The Downfall of Despotism*

etching, coloured, 462 × 536 mm, pub. 14 August 1789 by William Holland
1925-7-1-11
LITERATURE BMC 7550

A characteristically radical print published and perhaps designed by William Holland, who was imprisoned for publishing seditious works in 1793 (see Introduction,

19

p. 33), with an eye to the French as well as the British market, and containing advertisements for other prints as well as 'Hollands Exhibition Rooms [where] may be seen the largest Collection in Europe of Humourous Prints Admittance One Shilling'. The hero is the Duke of Orleans (see no. 17) who introduces the two emaciated prisoners to freedom with the words 'Regardez Mes amis les effet louables d'aristocracie! [*sic*]', while Louis XVI supplicates the distraught figures of the Comte d'Artois, Louis's younger brother who fled on 16/17 July, and Marie Antoinette, both framed by a setting sun surrounded by instruments of torture. Liberty arises above the Bastille accompanied by Necker and probably Lafayette. The print is unusual in its affirmation of the role of Enlightenment philosophers Montesquieu, Raynal, Voltaire and Rousseau in the triumph of liberty, rather than seeing the new Revolution as merely the acceptance of the superiority of the British constitution.

SAMUEL COLLINS, ETCHED BY BARLOW

20 *An Amphitheatrical Attack of the Bastile*

engraving, 148 × 241 mm, pub. 1 Nov. 1789 by Bentley and Co.
1868-8-8-5891
LITERATURE BMC 7561

A satire on the 'Bastillemania' which struck fashionable London in the months after the fall of the Bastille. The subject is the rivalry between two stage reconstructions of the attack, at Astley's amphitheatre and Hughes's Royal Circus. The strange perspective and scale express the flimsiness and absurdity of the stage scenery (the drawbridge is inscribed 'this is a drawbridge') and the actors, despite the claims on a piece of paper in the foreground: 'Mr Centaur can assure the publick since his return from Paris [Dublin is struck through] that this here Bastile is the most exactest of any of the Bastiles existin'. Mrs George mentions also an opera produced at the time entitled *Island of St Marguerite* by the Hon. John St John in which a Temple of Liberty arises from the ruins of the Bastille.

HENRY SINGLETON, ENGRAVED BY W. NUTTER

21 *The Destruction of the Bastile*

engraving, 497 × 636 mm, (proof impression, dated Jan. 1792), pub. 1 March 1792 by B. B. Evans
1877-8-11-944

Henry Singleton was typical of the kind of painter produced by the Royal Academy in the late eighteenth century, who could turn his hand with equal facility to a wide range of subject-matter from heroic subjects to rustic genre. In this case it is the genre of contemporary history painting made popular by Benjamin West and John Singleton Copley, though the large painting from which the engraving was presumably taken is now lost. A painting in the Musée Carnavalet, Paris, in an oval format on metal (570 × 740 mm) may be an original small version of the final work.

20

21

Singleton's print is the only British work to have come to light which offers an heroic view of the attack on the Bastille from the years 1789–92, when such a subject would have been acceptable. For a comparable rendering of the actual entry into the Bastille see no. 24. Singleton's design, which emphasises the rich humanity of the common people and National Guard united in their struggle, is clearly based upon the famous Andrieu medal (Mark Jones, *Medals of the French Revolution*, London, 1977, p. 1, illus. 2), which it follows in general composition and telling details. The attackers in the foreground are drawn from the vocabulary of sentimental genre: ardent young men, women of tender feelings and gallant elderly gentlemen, while the defenders are given no human face.

The prisoners of the Bastille

There were only seven prisoners in the Bastille when it was liberated on 14 July 1789, and the conditions in which they were kept in no way corresponded to the legend of the prison's horrors in earlier times. Yet this legendary history was important not only to the revolutionaries but as part of the imaginative appeal of the event both in France and abroad, and led to the invention of an exemplary prisoner, the Comte de Lorges, who makes an appearance in both French and the few English pictures of the liberation of the Bastille.

JOSEPH WRIGHT OF DERBY, ENGRAVED BY T. RYDER

(illus. p. 38)

22 *The Captive* (from Sterne)

stipple engraving, 450 × 525 mm, pub. 1 Oct. 1786 by Josiah Boydell

1917-12-8-3425; Lucas Collection

LITERATURE Nicolson 1968, no. 216

Engraved from a lost painting (Nicolson 1968, no. 216) painted by Wright in 1774. *The Captive* (from Sterne) was a favourite subject of Wright's, and intriguingly he seems to have returned to prison scenes in the late 1780s or early 90s (Nicolson 1968, nos 218, 219). For the popularity of this subject from Sterne's *Sentimental Journey* see p. 37.

L. CARPANTIER

23 *L'Heure Premiere de la Liberté*

engraving, 273 × 341 mm

1861-3-9-1574

LITERATURE de V 1628

This print by a little-known French artist appears to have been made shortly after the fall of the Bastille, and it shows the just-released prisoners being escorted from the Bastille, along the Rue Saint-Antoine to the Hôtel de Ville. The leader of the group of prisoners is an elderly

23

white-bearded figure who could be the French-Irish lunatic Whyte who believed himself to be Julius Caesar, Saint Louis or God (Godechot 1970, p. 92), or the fictitious figure of the Comte de Lorges who had been held in the Bastille supposedly for thirty-two years and who died shortly after his release.

JAMES NORTHCOTE, ENGRAVED BY JAMES GILLRAY *(illus. p. 15)*

24 *Le triomphe de la Liberté en l'élargissement de la Bastille, dédié à la Nation Francoise*

engraving, 490 × 610 mm (cropped), pub. 12 July 1790 by R. Wilkinson
1851-9-1-1353; Smith Collection
LITERATURE Hill, *Gillray*, 1965, p. 42

Northcote's original painting is now lost and this engraving was paired with one designed by Gillray, showing the prison reformer John Howard visiting prisoners, entitled *The Triumph of Benevolence*, dated 20 April 1788 (Hill, *Gillray*, 1965, p. 34). Given the date of the print the original design must have been made in the first enthusiasm in England for the new age of liberty begun by the fall of the Bastille. Here the emphasis is on the horrors of despotism as reflected in the ghastliness of the Bastille, which is depicted as a place of torture and utter inhumanity. In Northcote's fictional conception the young heroes of the siege are horrified at the cruelty they discover, and in the central group an elderly manacled figure, perhaps intended to be the Comte de Lorges (see Introduction, pp. 38–41, and no. 25 below), is tenderly escorted out of the building while the governor and executioner are politely gestured towards the lower depths. This appears to have been the only heroic rendering in British painting of a scene inside the Bastille, though prison scenes had been made fashionable by the career of John Howard who died in 1790 (see no. 160).

MADAME TUSSAUD *(illus. p. 41)*

25 *Wax model of head of Comte de Lorges and photograph of Comte de Lorges in cell*

Lent by Madame Tussaud's, London

The 'discovery' of the Comte de Lorges in a cell in the Bastille and the continuity of the legend of this mythical prisoner are discussed in the Introduction, pp. 38–41. Madame Tussaud was not the only one, apart from his creator Jean-Louis Carra, to have claimed to have met him after his release on 14 July 1789; a soldier and *vainqueur* of the Bastille, Aubin Bonnemère, claimed to have released the Comte from his gloomy cell ('cachot ténébreux') and also to have kept the stone which sealed it up for the rest of his long life, leaving it to the city of Saumur (A. Begin, 'Les Prisonniers de la Bastille', *L'Intermédiaire des Chercheurs et Curieux*, no. 502, 10 April 1889). The wax head, or a cast from the same mould, appears to have been brought over by Madame Tussaud from France in 1802: certainly it is recorded as early as the 1803 Madame Tussaud catalogue, and it seems to have been on continuous display in the nineteenth century as part of the French Revolution group (see no. 225), remaining on view until as late as 1968. The photograph shows the Comte in one of his incarnations in the late nineteenth century, closely corresponding to Dickens's description in *All the Year Round*, 7 January 1860, p. 252: 'To enter the Chamber of Horrors rather late in the afternoon, before the gas is lighted, requires courage. To penetrate through a dark passage under the guillotine scaffold, to the mouth of a dimly-lit cell, through whose bars a figure in a black serge dress is faintly visible, requires courage. Your eye-witness entered, on the principle which causes judicious persons to jump headlong into the sea from a bathing-machine instead of gradually and timidly emersing themselves from the ankle upwards. Let the visitor enter this very terrible apartment at a swift pace and without pausing for an instant, let him turn sharply to the right, and scamper under the scaffold, taking care that this structure – which is very low – does not act after the manner of the guillotine it sustains, and take his head off. Let him thoroughly master all the circumstances of the Count de Lorge's imprisonment, the serge dress, the rats, the brown loaf – let him then hasten up the steps of the guillotine and saturate his mind with the blood upon the decapitated heads of the sufferers in the French Revolution – this done, the worst is over.'

Madame Tussaud claimed to have met the Comte de Lorges on his release from the Bastille and to have cast the head from him the same day. In the 1803 Tussaud catalogue he is confused with the 'Chevalier' Latude who staged a sensational escape from the Bastille and who is the subject of the famous painting by Vestier in the Musée Carnavalet, Paris.

The new regime: the first year

For the first year after the fall of the Bastille everything ostensibly went well: the king appeared to have accepted the Revolution, a moderate constitutional government was in power, and pressures from below were still contained. With the great ceremony of Fédération held on the Champ de Mars on 14 July 1790 a kind of apogee was reached: Wordsworth, who passed through France at the time, remembered how 'Unhoused beneath the evening star we saw/Dances of liberty', and F. C. Byron also recorded his impressions of France at the time though in a more sardonic way. The increasing disorder in France which began to grow in 1791 attracted intermittent attention from satirists, who were mainly concerned to extract as much humour as possible from events that at first had little resonance in Britain. Attitudes expressed in caricature, at least until the summer of 1792, were equally cynical towards the royal family and the revolutionaries.

Bringing back the King from Versailles, 5 and 6 October 1789

CHARLES BENAZECH

26 *The Paris Militia setting out for Versailles, on the 5th of October 1789*

pen and wash drawing, 245 × 581 mm, signed and dated 1789
Lent by Maidstone Museums and Art Gallery

The original drawing for an aquatint published 24 November 1789 by C. van der Gucht in the same series as no. 13. The print claims to have been 'Drawn on the Spot by an eminent Artist', but this drawing proves the anonymous artist to have been Charles Benazech (see no. 91). The scene is of the women of Paris setting out for Versailles to bring the king and queen back to Paris. They were joined by the National Guard under Lafayette who is presumably represented on horseback in the foreground.

W. DENT

27 *Female Furies or Extraordinary Revolution*

etching, coloured, 255 × 422 mm, 18 Oct. 1789
1948-2-14-464

A caricatural version of the events depicted by Benazech above but showing the actual assault on Versailles. Here the women of Paris are seen as fierce *poissardes* routing the king's bodyguard and chopping off some of their heads, in a comic reversal of the natural order of things. Though not particularly sympathetic to the French royal family, it is unusual at this early date for dwelling on the violence of the assault, which lead to the heads of some of the bodyguard being returned to Paris in triumph on the top of pikes.

The Fête de la Fédération, 14 July 1790

LE ROY, ENGRAVED BY J. B. CHAPUY

28 *Vue perspective du Champ de Mars*

aquatint, colour printed, 355 × 538 mm
1924-11-18-1; presented by F. B. Maule
LITERATURE de V 3762

The Fête de la Fédération was an enormous public celebration of the first anniversary of the fall of the Bastille which took place at the Champ de Mars, now the site of

27

the Eiffel Tower, and in many provincial centres. The idea was for the National Guard from the new departments to take an oath of loyalty to 'la Nation, la Loi et le Roi'. This oath was sworn at an altar by Lafayette, presided over by Talleyrand, then Bishop of Autun. Contemporaries, including Helen Maria Williams (*Letters written in France, in the summer 1790*, letter II), testify to the joyful atmosphere of the ceremony: for Madame de Staël it 'was the climax of a great surge of national fervour' (Furet and Richet 1970, p. 109). In retrospect it was the last time that a real political balance seemed to have been achieved after the Revolution.

Fédération was also a great opportunity for visual artists of all kinds and there was a great production of banners, fans and commemorative prints like the present one, which gives a panorama of the Champ de Mars at the moment of the oath, with the *fédérés* lined up, and immense crowds watching the ceremony.

30

29

F. G. BYRON

29 *A Trip to the Federation: A Scene near Amiens*

etching, coloured, 361 × 501 mm, pub. 12 Feb. 1791 by William Holland
Lent by Robert Douwma

F. G. BYRON, ENGRAVED BY F. C. LEWIS

30 *Returning from a Review at the Champs de Mars in Paris*

etching, coloured, 475 × 660 mm, pub. 1 Nov. 1802 by W. Holland
1881-6-11-27
LITERATURE BMC 8275

Nos 29 and 30 were both etched from the same series of watercolours by Byron as no. 3. Byron seems to have travelled to France mainly for the Fédération ceremony in July 1790, and he made a large watercolour of the ceremony itself, now in the Versailles Museum. Byron's attitude is wholly that of a gentleman amateur, seeking comic scenes in the manner of Bunbury (see no. 1). Except for the cockades they could have been done at any time before the Revolution, though there may be a contemporary point in no. 30 in the elderly *fédéré*'s anger at the way the fat monk and nun have joined the procession. The publishing history of these prints is obscure. The existence of no. 29 is the only evidence, unknown to Mrs George, that an attempt was made to publish the series in 1791, before the publication in 1802. The first publication may have been a victim of the increasingly ill-natured attitude towards French foibles in 1791–2, while their re-publication in 1801–2 may have been an attempt to exploit the negotiations for the Peace of Amiens which enabled British travellers to go once more to France.

The new French market: exports to France, 1789–91

The Anglo-French trade treaty of 1786, in the promotion of which Wedgwood played a key part, helped to open up the French market for luxury pottery, and for him and other manufacturers the Revolution of 1789 must have seemed an opportunity to sell appropriate wares not only to France but to revolutionary sympathisers in England. The new revolutionary government had reduced some of the customs barriers, and were likely to welcome the sympathetic attention of such manufacturers as Wedgwood and Boulton who had supported the cause of reform in England. For exporters, then, the Revolution was another opportunity to take advantage of the increasing ability of Midlands manufacturers to come up rapidly with new designs, though the attempt foundered as the symbolism associated with the constitutional phase of the Revolution became rapidly obsolete.

31 *Plate printed in red-brown with a vine leaf scroll around 'Vive Les Tiers Etats' [sic]*

creamware, impressed T. & J. Hollins, DIAM. 240 mm
Lent by Royal Pavilion, Brighton Art Gallery and Museums, Willett no. 366
LITERATURE Willett cat. 1899, no. 366

The incorrect reference to 'Le Tiers Etat' (or Third Estate, which was represented at the Estates-General on 5 May 1789 and on 17 June declared itself the National Assembly) strongly suggests that the printing was done in England and dates the plate fairly conclusively to May–June 1789.

T. and J. Hollins of Shelton, Hanley, Staffordshire, are believed to have been making earthenwares and Wedgwood-type wares between about 1795 and 1820. AD

32 *Metalwork pattern book, with engraved designs for commode handles*

Birmingham, *c.* 1790–1800
Lent by Victoria and Albert Museum, M. 61g

A pattern book of commode handles many of which were clearly designed for export. Several of them contain revolutionary designs, including one very close to no. 36d, of a liberty cap on a *fasces* with emblems of prosperity, and others are inscribed 'Vive la République'. There is also one of a willow enfolding a tomb of Louis XVI, dating from 1793 or later. No doubt many such objects are to be found on French furniture, and they reflect the commercial acumen of Birmingham manufacturers in the 1790s.

33 *Copper-plate printed cotton valance, the fall of the Bastille and other events*

76 × 25 mm, 1789–90
Lent by Victoria and Albert Museum, T.63-1936
INSCRIBED 'Gordon sculp.' and 'H. M. & Co.'
LITERATURE *English Chintz*, Victoria and Albert Museum, 1960, no. 180

This piece of textile was undoubtedly intended for export to France, and the reference to events of July and August 1789 suggest that it was printed soon after. There is another piece of the same material in the Cooper Hewitt Museum, New York, measuring approximately 152 × 50 mm (Inv. no. 1945-7-1).

34 *Plate printed in black with inscriptions referring to the Fête de la Fédération, 1790*

creamware, probably Leeds, DIAM. 250 mm
Lent by Leeds City Art Galleries (Temple Newsam House), 49.1/82

Shaped rim with six lobes, the border with six printed flower sprays. In the centre below a ribbon inscribed 'VIVRE LIBRE OU MOURIR' are scantily clad winged figures of Liberty each holding a pole surmounted by a bonnet and supporting the French royal arms with the motto below it 'LA CONSTITUTION OU LA MORT'. Underneath on a ribbon is inscribed 'LA NATION LA LOI ET LE ROI'. The plate was clearly intended for export, and examples are known in French private collections; it is possible that the printed design was added in France on imported blank plates.

There is a very similar plate in the Musée Joseph Dechelette, Roanne (Loire), no. 988.10.16. AD

33

35a

35b

AUGUSTIN DUPRÉ

35a *Medal, Le Pacte fédératif*

gilt copper, 35 × 28.5 mm, 1790
1947-6-7-565
LITERATURE Charles Saunier, *Augustin Dupré*, Paris, 1894

The obverse shows the *fédérés*, carrying a banner bearing the cap of liberty, taking their oath before France, who holds up to them tablets on which are engraved the Rights of Man. The reverse inscription reads 'NOUS JURONS DE MAINTENIR DE TOUT NOTRE POUVOIR LA CONSTITUTION DU ROIAUME'.

Dupré executed the medal on his own initiative and sold 3,000, many of which were worn on red, white and blue ribbons on which there was a profile of the king with the inscription 'His virtues have put him there'. A plan to strike 100,000 for distribution to the army came to nothing, but the Monneron brothers used his die for their money medals. MJ

MATTHEW BOULTON AND THE MONNERON BROTHERS

35b *Money medals*

copper, 39.5 mm, 1792
S. S. Banks, p. 195–49, 1947-6-7-590, S. S. Banks, p. 195–51 and p. 196–68
LITERATURE Richard Margolis, 'Matthew Boulton's French ventures of 1791 and 1792: Tokens for the Monneron Brothers of Paris', *British Numismatic Journal*, 1988, vol. 58

By the beginning of the Revolution Boulton had expended a great deal of money and effort on applying steam power to coin production. Aware of the radical overhaul of the French monetary system undertaken by the National Assembly, in January 1791 he put forward a proposal to strike an entire new French coinage at the Soho Mint, from the confiscated French church bells, which he would melt down and refine. His initial approach, through John Motteux, put him in touch with the Monneron brothers and, although the government did not take up his proposals, the Monnerons were eager to launch a token coinage on their own account.

The design for the obverse of the five *sol* pieces was taken from the Dupré medal for the Pacte fédératif (see no. 35a) which the Monneron brothers purchased. The oval of Dupré's medal is set within a circle containing the legend 'VIVRE LIBRES OU MOURIR'. The reverse, which was engraved by Noel-Alexandre Ponthon, a young French engraver working in Soho, reads 'REVOLUTION FRANÇAISE 1792' and, across the centre, 'MEDAILLE QUI SE VEND A PARIS CHEZ MONNERON/PATENTÉ/CINQ-SOLS'. Around the rim is engraved 'LA CONFIANCE AUGMENTE LA VALEUR'.

The Monneron brothers' tokens were initially very popular. They distributed over 11,000 *livres* worth, to a crowd so large that they had to call upon the cavalry to maintain order. The Monnerons' plans, which also included the issuing of a series of patriotic medals three of which, the 'Serment du roi', 'Rousseau' and 'Lafayette', were struck at the Soho Mint, were disrupted by their bankruptcy in March 1792. Augustin Monneron, however, continued in business. Over forty tons of tokens were shipped to France in July and a new design, Hercules failing to break a bundle of sticks, was adopted for the five *sols* medals. This too was taken from an earlier design by Augustin Dupré, for a *jeton* for the merchants of Paris.

In September 1792 the National Assembly forbade the import or issue of private tokens and, although Boulton continued work on a new Republican token, showing Hercules breaking the symbols of monarchy on one side, with the inscription 'LA SAGESSE GUIDE SA FORCE/LA FIN DU DESPOTISME', and on the other side a pyramid labelled 'RESPUBLICA GALLIA ANNO I/AERE PERENNIUS/1792' (S. S. Banks, p. 196–68), until January 1793, no further shipments were made. MJ

Wedgwood's exports to revolutionary France: 'French cameos'

This section includes examples of all the known medallions and other objects produced by Wedgwood, sometimes from earlier designs, celebrating the French Revolution. They were produced at the earliest in July 1789 (the portrait of Necker was already in production

36

that month) and at the latest early 1792. Though export was undoubtedly predominantly on Josiah Wedgwood's mind, it is known that some were on sale in England, and one stockist is recorded in Manchester. Wedgwood's sympathy, along with other manufacturers like Boulton, for the Revolution is recorded below.

36 *Medallions celebrating the fall of the Bastille, 1789*

a) *Medallion, France and Liberty holding hands by an altar*

white jasper ware, dipped dark blue, applied white reliefs, edge polished, DIAM. 51 mm, dated 1789, impressed WEDGWOOD; metal mount with suspension ring
Pot. Cat. I. 676; Franks Collection
LITERATURE *Pot. Cat.* I. 676

At the left France in a helmet rests her left hand on top of an oval shield decorated with fleurs-de-lis in relief and shakes hands with Liberty who holds a pole surmounted by a cap of liberty in her left hand. Between them is an altar ornamented in relief with a caduceus between two cornucopiae. On the altar stands a figure holding a sheaf of corn in one hand and a basket of fruit in the other. At her left is a lamb. The border is decorated with a stylised floral design between dots. Josiah Wedgwood jun. wrote to his father on 29 July 1789: 'Inclosed is the sketch of the medallion I mentioned to you last night. The figure on the altar with the Caduceus in one hand & the Cornucopia in the other is Public Credit or Faith & instead of the caduceus on the Altar there ought, I think, to be the words Fid. Pub. for fides publica, the goddess of liberty with the cap of liberty in her left hand takes hold of France in her right.' AD

b) *Medallion, France and Liberty holding hands by an altar inscribed FIDEI PUBL.*

white jasper ware, dipped dark blue, applied white reliefs, edge polished, DIAM. 61 mm, impressed WEDGWOOD
1853, 11-4, 12 H
LITERATURE *Pot. Cat.* I. 675

At the left Liberty holding a pole, on which is a cap of liberty, in her left hand shakes hands with France who wears a helmet and holds an oval shield decorated with fleurs-de-lis in relief in her left hand. Between them is an altar impressed FIDEI PUBL. on which stands a figure of Public Faith holding a sheaf of corn in one hand and a cornucopia in the other (for Wedgwood jun.'s comments see no. 36a). Another example of this medallion in the Wedgwood Museum, Barlaston (M-0151-1), is set into an ivory-mounted snuffbox. AD

c) *Medallion, Liberty with a cornucopia, inscribed EN QUAM SAEPE OPTASTIS LIBERTAS*

white jasper ware, dipped dark blue, applied white reliefs, edge polished, DIAM. 60 mm, impressed WEDGWOOD; metal mount with suspension ring
Pot. Cat. I. 674; Franks collection
LITERATURE *Pot. cat.* I. 674

Beneath a pillared arch, at the lower left side of which rests an oval shield ornamented with three fleurs-de-lis in relief, stands a figure of Liberty turned to the left. In her right hand she holds a pole surmounted by a bonnet of liberty and in her left a cornucopia. Within a white line in relief is a raised Latin inscription in blue, which can be translated, 'Behold! The liberty which you have often wished'. AD

d) *Button, cornucopia, cap of liberty on pole and laurel branch*

white jasper ware, dipped dark blue, applied white reliefs, edge polished, DIAM. 26 mm, impressed WEDGWOOD and I; metal mount with suspension ring
Pot. Cat. I. 673
LITERATURE *Pot. Cat.* I. 673: Dawson 1984, pl. 12

In the cornucopia are a pineapple and other fruits, flowers and corn. The fleur-de-lis motif around the border suggests a date of 1792 at the latest. The cornucopia indicates the prosperity and honour attendant upon liberty. AD

(illus. in colour)

37 *Medallions of revolutionary leaders, 1789–92*

a) *Jacques Necker (1732–1804)*

white jasper ware, dipped dark blue, applied white jasper reliefs, edge polished, DIAM. 60 mm, impressed WEDGWOOD and J
1853, 11-4, 11
LITERATURE *Pot. Cat.* I. 101: Dawson 1984, p. 84 and pl. 12

In 1776 Necker, a banker, became Director of the Treasury. Following his appointment as Director-General of Finance in 1777 he attempted taxation reform, making many enemies. He resigned in 1781. Recalled in 1788, he recommended the summoning of the Estates-General and granted double the number of deputies to the Tiers Etat. His sudden departure for Brussels in July 1789, after being ordered to leave France by the King, precipitated the storming of the Bastille by the mob. He was recalled in July 1789 but, his views proving too conservative, he resigned office in September 1790. In a letter to his father in July 1789 Josiah Wedgwood jun. wrote 'We are making Mr. Necker's head of a size proper for snuff box tops', showing that they were already in production. The portrait is based on an anonymous medal. AD

b) *Honoré Gabriel de Riqueti, comte de Mirabeau (1749–91)*

white jasper ware, dipped dark blue, applied white jasper reliefs, edge polished, DIAM. 60 mm, impressed WEDGWOOD and I
1853, 11-4, 9
LITERATURE *Pot. Cat.* I. 102

Author of *Essai sur le Despotisme* and other political works, Mirabeau became a member of the National Assembly where he advocated a new constitution on the English model. He joined the Jacobin Club in 1790 and was appointed President of the National Assembly in 1791 but died in April that year. AD

c) *Jean-Sylvain Bailly (1736–93)*

white jasper ware, dipped dark blue, applied white jasper reliefs, edge polished, DIAM. 60 mm, impressed WEDGWOOD
1853, 11-4, 10
LITERATURE *Pot. Cat.* I. 103

Bailly, author of *Histoire de l'Astronomie*, 1775–87, shared with Fontenelle the honour of belonging to the Académie des Sciences, the Académie Française and the Académie des Inscriptions. He was Mayor of Paris and President of the National Assembly during the Revolution but after allowing the National Guard to fire on the mob left Paris. He was arrested and guillotined in Paris in November 1793. The portrait is after a medal by Duvivier of 1789 (*Trésor de Numismatique Française: Médailles de la Révolution Française*, Paris, 1836, pl. IX, 2). Like the Duvivier medal of Necker, it was offered to the National Assembly in August and October 1789. The Wedgwood version was on sale by 23 December 1791 at twelve shillings. AD

d) *Louis-Philippe-Joseph, Duke of Orleans, called Philippe Egalité (1747–93)*

white jasper ware, dipped dark blue, applied white jasper reliefs, edge polished, DIAM. 55 mm, impressed WEDGWOOD; metal mount with suspension ring
Pot. Cat. I. 48; Franks Collection
LITERATURE *Pot. Cat.* I. 48

The sitter succeeded to the Orleans title in 1785 but adopted the name of Philippe Egalité in 1792. As a member of the convention he voted for the death of Louis XVI but was himself arrested and guillotined in 1793. From being a figure of admiration in England he became, as a result of his vote for Louis's death, perhaps the most execrated of all the French revolutionaries (see no. 109). AD

e) *Louis XVI (1754–93)*

white jasper ware, dipped dark blue, applied white jasper reliefs, edge polished and laminated, DIAM. 60 mm, impressed WEDGWOOD and I
1853, 11-4, 8
LITERATURE *Pot. Cat.* I. 18; Dawson 1984, p. 84 and pl. 12

The portrait, the latest of the three Wedgwood versions of this sitter, is based on a medallic portrait by Benjamin

37, 38

Duvivier (*Trésor de Numismatique Française: Médailles de la Révolution Française*, Paris, 1837, pl. LV, 6) and shows the king wearing the star and sash of the Order of St Louis. The border is ornamented with ovals alternating with fleurs-de-lis. The growing reaction in France against Louis XVI's exercise of power from early 1791 onwards suggests an earlier date for the production of this medallion. AD

f) *Marie Joseph Paul Roch Yves Gilbert Motier, marquis de Lafayette (1757–1834)*

white jasper ware, dipped dark blue, applied white jasper reliefs, edge polished, DIAM. 60 mm, impressed WEDGWOOD
1909, 12-1, 263; presented by Mr and Mrs Isaac Falcke

Lafayette joined the army of the American colonies in 1777 and returned to France a hero of that campaign. In 1787 he sat in the Assembly of Notables and in the States General and National Assembly of 1789. Although he favoured the abolition of titles and other measures, he remained supportive of the king and queen, especially as their isolation increased, and took the Oath of Fédération on behalf of the French nation in 1790. He became a figure of deep suspicion to radicals in 1792, finally fleeing France and surrendering to the Austrians before he became an almost certain candidate for the guillotine. He was liberated by Napoleon in 1797. The portrait is based on a medallic portrait by Benjamin Duvivier (*Trésor de Numismatique Française: Médailles de la Révolution Française*, Paris, 1836, pl. IX, 3), completed early in 1790. The Wedgwood version was in production by December 1791. AD

g) *Charles Maurice de Talleyrand-Perigord (1754–1838)*

recent impression cast from mould still belonging to Wedgwood factory, 60 mm
LITERATURE Reilly and Savage 1973, p. 319.

The extreme rarity of this medallion, of which only one finished example is recorded in an American private collection by Reilly and Savage (1973), suggests that it was not normally offered with the rest of the set. Talleyrand remained in the forefront of politics from 1789 when he was the leading clergyman, as Bishop of Autun, to support the Civil Constitution of the Clergy. After a period of exile from 1792 to 1796 he returned to France to become Foreign Minister to the Directory, achieving immense influence under Napoleon, whom he eventually betrayed to the Allies. He was celebrated more than anything else for his extraordinary ability to negotiate the dramatic shifts of power of his period, while always remaining on top.

38 Perfume bottles and buttons, 1790–2

a) *Perfume bottle, portraits of Bailly and Lafayette*

pale blue jasper ware, applied white jasper reliefs, white jasper, collar, stopper missing, H. 60 mm
Pot. Cat. I. 745; Franks Collection
LITERATURE *Pot. Cat.* I. 745; Reilly and Savage 1973, p. 208 AD

b) *Perfume bottle, portraits of Mirabeau and Philippe Egalité*

pale blue jasper ware, applied white reliefs, blue jasper collar, stopper missing, H. 55 mm
Lent by Castle Museum, Nottingham, no. '92-288 AD

c) *Two Wedgwood buttons of Philippe Egalité*

white jasper ware, dipped dark blue, applied white jasper ware reliefs, edges polished, left-hand button pierced and ornamented with rosettes, DIAM. (of both) 24 mm, left impressed WEDGWOOD and H
Pot. Cat. I. 49 and I. 50; Franks Collection
LITERATURE *Pot. Cat.* I. 49 and I. 50

These buttons probably date from about 1790–2. According to a private ledger (1786–1890) belonging to Wedgwood, Josiah supplied buttons to M. Darnandery, button-makers to the French king, as early as 1786. AD

39 Other medallions

a) *Sydney Cove Medallion*

dark brown unglazed earthenware, moulded, DIAM. 57 mm, 1789, impressed on reverse MADE BY JOSIAH WEDGWOOD OF CLAY FROM SYDNEY COVE
1985, 5-6, 1
LITERATURE L. R. Smith, *Josiah Wedgwood's 'Slave Medallion'*, Sydney, 1986; A. Dawson, 'No Common Clay', *British Museum Society Bulletin*, no. 51, March 1986, p. 36; recent acquisitions of post-medieval ceramics and glass in the British Museum's Department of Medieval and Later Antiquities (1982–8); *Burlington Magazine*, CXXX, May 1988, p. 402

39a

Designed with a scene of Hope encouraging Art and Labour under the influence of Peace by Henry Webber (1754–1826) and modelled by William Hackwood, the medallion is made of clay dug in January 1788 on the orders of Captain Arthur Phillip who reached 'the first harbour in the world' on 21 January. The clay was sent to Sir Joseph Banks, President of the Royal Society, and forwarded by him to Wedgwood. Finished medallions were sent to Banks in November 1789 and reached Botany Bay in May 1790. AD

b) *Framed medallion, Hope Addressing Peace, Labour and Plenty*

white jasper ware, dipped dark blue, applied white jasper reliefs, DIAM. 66 mm, impressed WEDGWOOD
Lent by Castle Museum, Nottingham, no. 92-403
LITERATURE *Mr Wedgwood*, Castle Museum, Nottingham, 1975, no. 362; *Flaxman, R. A.*, 1979, no. 55c

The Sydney Cove medallion was adapted for this one, apparently at the suggestion of Josiah Wedgwood II, who wrote to his father on 29 July 1789: 'inclosed is a sketch of

39b

the medallion I mentioned to you last night . . . the goddess of liberty with the cap of liberty in her left hand takes hold of France in her right. The figure of Hope in the Botany Bay medal would come in exceedingly well for the figure of liberty'. AD

c) *Plaque, Liberty*

white jasper ware, dipped blue, applied white jasper reliefs, H. 118 mm, impressed 'ENOCH WOOD,/SCULPSIT'
Lent by National Museums and Galleries on Merseyside, Liverpool Museum, M. 1367

A French Revolution motif with the figure of Liberty holding a key to the Bastille in her left hand and a bonnet of liberty on a pole in her right hand.

Enoch Wood (1759–1840) was apprenticed to H. Palmer of Hanley and set up in partnership with his cousin Ralph Wood at Fountain Place, Burslem, Staffordshire, in 1783. Wood, a talented modeller, apparently created a creamware plaque moulded with the Wood arms when in his twelfth year (British Museum, Franks Collection, *Pot. Cat.* H. 45), and signed a large jasper plaque of the Descent from the Cross in 1777 (examples in Victoria and Albert Museum and Hanley Museum, Stoke-on-Trent). In 1790 he went into partnership with James Caldwell until 1818 when the firm became Enoch Wood and Sons. It closed down around 1846. Little is known of Enoch Wood's own political sympathies and it must be assumed that he took the lead from Josiah Wedgwood who had identified a market for medallions and plaques with revolutionary subjects. AD

3 The collapse of the French monarchy

The contrast in France between the sense of national unity observed at the Fête de la Fédération of 14 July 1790 and the murderous conflict which prevailed little more than two years later can hardly be exaggerated. The unity of the constitutional phase of the Revolution was gradually fragmented, as splits developed between revolutionaries and counter-revolutionaries, and ever more deeply among the revolutionaries themselves. Financial measures hit different sections of the community, and the Civil Constitution of the Clergy, which demanded an oath of loyalty from the Clergy to the State, broke the unity of the Revolution and the Catholic Church. The classes who still retained most of their privileges after the Revolution were challenged from below by a disillusioned intelligentsia increasingly joined by artisans who had expected a dramatic improvement of their lot from the new order.

From the British point of view there were two conspicuous manifestations of the changing situation: the increasingly beleaguered position of the king, whose attempted flight on 20 June 1791 ending at Varennes effectively destroyed his position as a constitutional monarch, and the growing political presence of plebeians demanding economic reform. The two came together dramatically in the popular invasion of the Tuileries on 20 June 1792 when the king was humiliated by a crowd which had smashed its way into his palace. The growing internal conflict was exacerbated by war with Austria and the threatening presence of Prussia, creating an intolerable and often justified suspicion among ordinary people of betrayal by the country's leaders and generals. As the military situation and public order deteriorated in the summer of 1792, a great many men in arms predominantly radical in sentiment poured into Paris to defend it against internal as well as external enemies. By July the king was virtually powerless, with many of his supporters like Lafayette completely discredited, and on 10 August 1792 he was deposed by a military attack on the Tuileries.

Growing disorder, 1791–10 August 1792

The flight to Varennes and the arrest of Louis XVI, 20–2 June 1791

Louis XVI and his family left the Tuileries, where they had been detained, in a carriage on the night of 20 June 1791, it was assumed with the intention of reaching *émigré* forces on the German border. He was recognised by the postmaster of Sainte-Menehould, who had the king arrested a little further along at Varennes, and he was brought back to Paris to face hostile crowds. Though the Assembly agreed to the obvious fiction that the royal family had been kidnapped, the flight effectively destroyed the king's claim to have accepted the Revolution and ultimately undermined also the credibility of those who sought to maintain a constitutional monarchy.

JOHN NIXON, ETCHED BY J.C. *(illus. p. 44)*

40 *Le Gourmand, Heavy Birds Fly Slow, Delay Breeds Danger. A Scene at Varennes June 21, 1791*

etching, coloured, 327 × 481 mm (no address, date 1791)
1948-2-14-491
LITERATURE Jouve 1983, p. 55

This print, though extremely rare, was copied early in France. It continues the tradition of mockery of French life with the familiar stereotypes of the obsequious and affected public official and the brutalised soldiery behind. Louis is also invested with his standard image of gluttony: it is his greed for his supper which leads to his capture. He is saying 'Je me f___ de tout cela Laisse moi manger tranqillement', while Marie Antoinette replies unconcernedly 'Come my dear Louis havn't you finish'd your two Turkeys & drank your six bottles, you know we shall dine at Mont medy'.

JAMES GILLRAY

41 *The National Assembly Petrified. The National Assembly Revivified*

etching, coloured, 408 × 298 mm, pub. 28 June 1791 by S. W. Fores
1851-9-1-534; Smith Collection
LITERATURE BMC 7883

This caricature of the National Assembly's response to Louis's flight and then to his recapture is notable for the characterisation of the Assembly as absurd plebeians and tradesmen, foreshadowing Gillray's later figures of sans-culottes (see p. 122). His enthusiasm for the Revolution had apparently cooled after the publication of Burke's *Reflections* in late 1790 (see no. 49).

The Civil Constitution of the Clergy and the assault on the Church

Among the most important and contentious issues in France in 1790–2, comparable with the English Reformation of the sixteenth century, were the demand that the clergy should take an oath of allegiance to the state and the state's confiscation of church property, neither of which were fully resolved before 1800. Because such issues of Church and State had been resolved in England in the sixteenth and seventeenth centuries, the French struggles had little popular resonance in England and were only rarely reflected in caricature, though they deeply disturbed Burke. For English caricaturists it was an occasional excuse to revitalise traditional stereotypes of French monks and nuns, without involving themselves in the more intricate issues.

JAMES GILLRAY

42 *A Representation of the horrid Barbarities practised upon the Nuns by the Fish-women, on breaking into the Nunneries in France*

etching, coloured, 270 × 398 mm, pub. 21 June 1792 by J. Aitken
Lent by Andrew Edmunds

INSCRIBED 'N:B: This Print is dedicated to the FAIR SEX of GREAT-BRITAIN & intended to point out the very dangerous effects which may arise to Themselves, if they do not exert their influence to hinder the "Majesty of the People" from getting possession of the Executive Power'
LITERATURE BMC 8109 (an altered and damaged impression)

This outrageously cynical print appears, as Mrs George suggests, to refer back to an incident in Paris in Easter week 1791, when some nuns were whipped by market women in Paris, because their priest had refused to accept the Civil Constitution of the Clergy. This incident was picked up by Burke in a parliamentary speech on 6 May 1791, and the print may owe something to a French caricature entitled *La Discipline Patriotique* (Hennin, no. 10,952). However, the presence of fisherwomen, or *poissardes*, well known to travellers in northern France – indeed, they carried visitors ashore from their ships at Calais – suggests a more general assault upon nunneries. The picture of the destruction of civilisation at the hands of the 'swinish multitude' and the ironic reference to the 'Majesty of the People' in the inscription suggest the strong influence of Burke. The prurient display of the nuns' pink bottoms is, however, entirely Gillray's own invention.

The invasion of the Tuileries, 20 June 1792

The anniversary of the king's flight to Varennes the previous year became the occasion for a *journée* in the form of a popular assault on the Tuileries. The demonstrators, from the Faubourgs Saint-Marceau and Saint-Antoine, entered the Assembly and offered petitions, then marched

42

on the Tuileries with the aim of persuading the king to renounce his powers of Veto over the Assembly. This he refused to do, but he did agree to drink a toast to the nation and wear the *bonnet rouge*. In retrospect the *journée* of 20 June was a rehearsal for the more serious military assault on the Tuileries of 10 August. It revealed the powerlessness of Louis's position and the futility of compromise. By this stage civil war seemed imminent and the threat from Prussia was very great.

43

ANON., FRENCH, AFTER J. BOZE

43 *Louis Seize with bonnet rouge*

engraving, coloured (cut impression), 265 × 212 mm
Lent by Musée de la Révolution Française, Vizille
INSCRIBED 'Bonnet de la liberté, Presente au Roi par le peuple Francais, le 20 Juin, 1792'
LITERATURE de V 397 (the print before alteration is de V 396)

This astonishing print commemorates the humiliation of Louis XVI on 20 June 1792 when he was forced to wear the *bonnet rouge* by the invading crowd. It is not from a new plate but an altered version of a much earlier print of the king, after a painting by J. Boze. The *bonnet rouge*, hand coloured, is the principal addition, but Louis's title has been altered in the plate from Roi de France to Roi des Franceais in reference to the title conferred upon him on 19 October 1789.

44

W. DENT

44 *A Limited Monarchy*

etching, coloured 249 × 174 mm, pub. 23 July 1792 by J. Aitken
1948-2-14-467
INSCRIBED 'A Limited Monarchy, or, the NEGATIVE power of France surrounded by the patriotic Furies of the 20 Ult.'
LITERATURE BMC under no. 8114

This is half of a print; the other half, which is not in the British Museum's collection, is entitled *An Unlimited Democracy*, and it shows the scene in the Assembly on 7 July 1792, when in the face of the declaration of war by Prussia men from all parties embraced fervently on the motion of Lamourette. Dent's hostility to the sans-culottes and the Assembly is self-evident, though they are not completely equated with each other.

The Assault on the Tuileries, 10 August 1792

The *journée* of 10 August 1792 was one of the decisive events of the Revolution, and in Jacobin mythology comparable to the fall of the Bastille itself. It led directly to the suspension of the monarchy and the end of all constitutional compromise. Louis became a prisoner and the Republic was proclaimed on 21 September. The assault itself was the work of the combined forces of *fédérés* from the provinces (see no. 45) and local sections, and it led to much bloodshed, especially among the Swiss guards whose massacre was the subject of a horrifying picture by Zoffany (see Introduction, p. 46), and much later the famous monument in Lucerne by Thorwaldsen known as the Lion of Lucerne.

46

PUBLISHED BY VILLENEUVE

45 *Journée du 10 Aoust 1792*

etching and aquatint, 334 × 399 mm
1925-6-15-131
LITERATURE de V 4898

This print, dedicated 'Aux Braves sans Culottes', is a characteristic example of propaganda associating the suspension of the monarchy and the creation of the Republic with the will of the common people. Villeneuve was the chief publisher of such prints throughout the period of Robespierre's ascendancy, mid-1793–July 1794 (see also no. 118). The victory is given not to a 'mob' but to a disciplined military force led by *fédérés* from Brittany and Marseilles who overcame fierce opposition.

45

JOHAN ZOFFANY, ENGRAVED BY R. EARLOM

46 *Invasion of the Cellars of the Louvre, 10 August 1792* (not 1793 as on title of finished engraving)

mezzotint (scratched letter proof), 567 × 640 mm, pub. 1 Jan. 1795
1856-10-11-106
LITERATURE Webster, *Johan Zoffany*, 1976, no. 108; Bindman in *Kunst um 1800*, pp. 92–4

This mezzotint after Zoffany's painting (Wadsworth Athenaeum, Hartford, Conn.) begun in 1794 is a precise antithesis of Villeneuve's print above, depicting the invaders as a bloodthirsty mob seeking gratification of their animal desires. Though such a view was undoubtedly taken of the attackers of the Tuileries in England, the ferocity of the characterisation owes much to the more nervous climate of late 1794–5 when invasion was threatened (see Introduction, p. 58).

47

RICHARD NEWTON

47 *Louis dethron'd; or Hell broke loose in Paris!!!*

etching, coloured, 248 × 365 mm, pub. 16 Aug. 1792 by W. Holland
Lent by Andrew Edmunds

One of a number of caricatures produced in response to the events of 10 August in Paris which focus not on the events themselves but on the supposed reactions of George III. He is shown here in a panic for his own life as well as Louis's, while the queen hides bags of money in the privy.

The first disquiet in Britain: Burke and Paine

Edmund Burke's *Reflections on the Revolution in France*, published in November 1790, was the first coherent British attack on the French Revolution, and its passion and eloquence made it the central text for all loyalists as the Revolution progressed. The intention behind the work was not just to condemn the Revolution but to distinguish what was happening in France from the British experience of constitutional monarchy. Burke wholly rejected the common assumption that France had essentially adopted a British-style constitutional model, and he strove to drive a sharp wedge between those who were sympathetic to the French Revolution and those he defined as true upholders of the British constitution.

There were a great many replies to Burke, including one by Mary Wollstonecraft: in a strict sense the first part of Tom Paine's *The Rights of Man*, published in March 1791, was not a reply to Burke, though the title-page declares it to be. Paine's treatise explicitly rejects the claims of the past, basing its vision of society not upon precedent but upon the natural rights of man, which were legitimised by reason, and by the success of the American and French Revolutions. The power of Paine's book, part II of which was published in February 1792, lay not in its originality but in its eloquence which rivalled Burke but employed a plain language to appeal to the unlearned. It was the potential of Paine's message to spread to the unenfranchised that worried conservatives: the nightmare of the dormant mass of the lower orders being roused into political action by a flood of copies of *The Rights of Man* lay behind the huge campaign against 'seditious' writings that gathered momentum throughout 1792. It culminated in the setting up of the Crown and Anchor Society (see

p. 117) in November of that year with the specific object of denouncing sedition and providing cheap loyalist tracts and prints to counteract and overwhelm it.

In the caricature and popular imagery of this period Burke is at first a target of ridicule as he had been for many years, along with Charles James Fox, but increasingly the light is turned on Paine, particularly after the publication of the more inflammatory *The Rights of Man*, part II, in February 1792. Paine became a symbolic demon for a great amount of popular propaganda in a wide range of media. The visual material shown here should be seen in the context of a vast number of anti-Paine pamphlets and also a great deal of popular street theatre in which Paine was burned in effigy or symbolically trampled under foot. A broadside of as late as 1820 tells of 'A Dying Infidel' on his deathbed who cries out: PAINE'S AGE OF REASON HAS RUINED MY SOUL! (Louis James, *Print and the People*, Harmondsworth, 1976, p. 30).

ANON. *(illus. p. 17)*

48 *The Knight of the Woful Countenance*

etching, coloured, 365 × 255 mm, pub. 15 Nov. 1790 by W. Holland
1868-8-8-5972
LITERATURE BMC 7678

One of a remarkable number of caricatures which appeared shortly after the publication of Burke's *Reflections on the Revolution in France* in November 1790. Burke was second only to Charles James Fox as a target for caricaturists, and the *Reflections* appeared as a reversal of his previous sympathy with the American colonists. In this print the gaunt figure of Burke is seen quixotically taking on all the trappings of a supporter of the *ancien régime* with its implications of despotism and Catholic bigotry. The identification of Burke with Don Quixote was not uncommon and was provoked by the famous passage in the *Reflections* in defence of Marie Antoinette, whose image is contained in a locket around Burke's neck, and whom Burke claimed to have revered from seeing her at Versailles sixteen or seventeen years before: 'little did I dream that I should have lived to see such disasters fallen upon her in a nation of gallant men, in a nation of men of honour, and of cavaliers. I thought ten thousand swords must have leaped from their scabbards to avenge even a look that threatened her with insult. But the age of chivalry is gone. That of sophisters, economists, and calculators, has succeeded; and the glory of Europe is extinguished for ever'.

JAMES GILLRAY

49 *Smelling out a Rat*

etching, 248 × 351 mm, pub. 3 Dec. 1790 by H. Humphrey
1851-9-1-501; Smith Collection
LITERATURE BMC 7686

Gillray had been actively involved in projects sympathetic to the Revolution (see no. 24), but the evidence of this print suggests that he was almost instantly converted to hostility by Burke's fierce rhetoric. This print is unusual at the time in taking Burke's part, though still satirised as a Jesuitical inquisitor carrying crown and cross. Dr Price was the author of the famous sermon preached before the Revolution Society on 4 November 1789, which according to Burke provoked the publication of the *Reflections*. The

49

51

association with the execution of Charles I made by the picture on Price's wall is also derived from Burke: 'That sermon is in a strain which I believe has not been heard in this kingdom, in any of the pulpits which are tolerated or encouraged in it, since the year 1648.'

W. SHARP AFTER GEORGE ROMNEY

50 *Thomas Paine*

engraving, 305 × 228 mm, pub. 20 April 1793 by W. Sharp
1853-12-10-328
LITERATURE Jaffé 1977, p. 66

Engraved by William Sharp, the most highly regarded engraver of his day and active member of the Society for Constitutional Information, after the lost portrait of Paine by Romney. Both engraver and painter were among the few friends that Paine could trust after he became notorious with the publication of *The Rights of Man*. A contemporary newspaper (Jaffé 1977) seems to have picked up the fact that Romney was deeply involved in designs for Milton at the time of painting Paine's portrait: 'Romney is said to be painting Tom Paine; but whether for an individual likeness or the hero of *Paradise Lost*, is not yet known. Those, however, who have seen the sketch of it, say it is devilish like.'

ANON.

51 *Contrasted Opinions of Paine's Pamphlet*

etching, coloured, 247 × 560 mm, pub. 26 May 1791 by W. Holland
Lent by The Lewis Walpole Library, Farmington, Conn.

This fascinating print shows the varied reactions of famous readers to *The Rights of Man*, at the same time quoting some of the most eloquent passages in the book. Holland's sympathy with Paine could hardly be in doubt from the print and this may account for its extreme rarity, though it was copied in a cheap version at the time. The readers, from left to right, are Burke, Fox, George III, Baron Hawkesbury, Queen Charlotte, Hannah More, Pitt and Sheridan.

JAMES GILLRAY

52 *Tom Paine's Nightly Pest*

etching and aquatint, 246 × 343 mm, pub. 16 Nov. 1792 by H. Humphrey
1851-9-1-624; Smith Collection
LITERATURE BMC 8132

The aquatint version of a design which was published later in a more elaborate form (BMC 8137). The rarity of this version suggests it was never published properly, perhaps because of problems with the aquatint. The picture of Paine is wholly unsympathetic and suggests a ruffianly Grub Street hack in a garret, producing absurd levelling fantasies, including 'The Rights of Farthing Candles proving their Equality with the Sun & Moon'. He is motivated according to the charges beneath the judicial wigs, by 'Ignorance, Poverty [and] Envy' while guilty of 'Libels, Scurrilities, Lies etc.'. His guardian angels are Priestley and Fox. Paine appeared in court on 8 June 1792 as a consequence of the publication, in February 1792, of *The Rights of Man*, part II, a work which was regarded as more inflammatory than part I. Because of the threat of prosecution Paine fled to France, never to return to England, and was given French citizenship on 17 August 1792, becoming a member of the Convention the following month. The growing concern about the distribution of his works led to a campaign to counteract their effect, and Gillray's print expresses the supposedly demonic aspect of his doctrines.

52

53

53 *Jug printed in black with a portrait of Tom Paine on one side and caricature of Burke addressing pigs on the other*

creamware, probably Staffordshire, H. 180 mm
Lent by Royal Pavilion, Art Gallery and Museums, Brighton, Willett no. 518
LITERATURE Willett cat. 1899, no. 518

A figure of Edmund Burke mouthing a verse, 'Ye pigs who never went to college,/You must not pass for pigs of knowledge', holds in his hand a paper inscribed 'Loaves & Fishes' and has another attached to his arm with the legend 'Thoughts on Frch Revolution'. The vicar proclaims 'Church & State' and 'Tythes'. One boar represents 'BUDGET' and 'A SINKING FUND', another quotes 'I eat the straw who gets the pease'. On the other side is a portrait captioned 'Mr Thomas Paine'.

A satire on Burke's famous reference to 'the swinish multitude' in the *Reflections on the Revolution in France*, 1790, which is carried by Burke. The pigs represent here 'the people', and they are here treated with condescension by Burke who rides a pig himself, followed by a Church of England clergyman. The source of the caricature has yet to be discovered but is probably to be found in a radical periodical of the kind published by Daniel Eaton (no. 195g) or Thomas Spence (no. 206) in the years 1794–6. AD

54a *Token, The End of Pain*

copper, 29.5 mm
S. S. Banks, p. 193–156, 1947-6-7-157 and 1947-6-7-161
LITERATURE Spence 1795, no. 257; Bell, *Political Tokens*, pp. 263, 264

Tom Paine hangs, while a flag flies from the church in the background. The reverses found with this token read 'MAY THE KNAVE OF JACOBIN CLUBS NEVER GET A TRICK' and 'THE WRONGS OF MAN, January 21 1793'. MJ

54b *Medallet, A tree is known by its fruit*

tin, 31.5 mm
M5000

The reverse of this medallet reads 'MAY THE TREE OF LIBERTY EXIST TO BEAR TOMMY'S LAST FRIEND'. On the obverse Paine is seen hanging from the tree, beneath the inscription 'TOMMY'S RIGHTS OF MAN', saying 'I DIED FOR THIS DAMN'D BOOK'. Around the edge is a legend reading 'A TREE IS KNOWN BY ITS FRUIT'. MJ

54c *Token with scratched design, End of Pain*

halfpenny, copper, 26 mm
Lent by A. H. Baldwin and Sons

This anti-Paine token may have been cut at the time of the widespread anti-Paine demonstrations in 1792–3 (see nos 55–6 below). Its function is not known, but it perhaps gives an idea of the shoe nails mentioned by Conway (*Paine*, 1909, p. 167): 'These nails, with heads so lettered [T.P.], were in great request among the gentry, who had only to hold up their boot-soles to show how they were trampling on Tom Paine and his principles.'

ANON. *(illus. p. 21)*

55 *The last Dying Speech, Confession, Behaviour, Birth, Parentage and Education of Thomas Paine*

broadside, 325 × 220 mm, late 1792
Lent by Guildhall Library, Broadsides 8.145

Paine, of course, was not executed at Taunton on 18 December 1792 but lived on until 1809, dying peacefully at the age of seventy-two in the United States. However, popular feeling against him in late 1792 was very strong in some provincial towns, and the broadside probably refers to a hanging in effigy of the kind that took place in many West Country towns to commemorate Paine's trial which was due to take place on 18 December 1792.

56 *Glass window pane with hole probably made during anti-Paine riot in Taunton 1792*

glass panel in oak frame, glass 300 × 420 mm
Private Collection
INSCRIBED 'In the Year 1790, Dr Toulmin, and others met at Taunton to Celebrate the French Revolution: this render'd him obnoxious to the High Tory Party then in the Town, he was much persecuted, and at a meeting to burn Tom Paine in Effigy, Stones and Fire-works were thrown at the Doctor's Windows. The HOLE in this Pane was made by a Roman Candle. Joshua Toulmin DD. Born in London, 11th May. 1740. Died at Birmingham, 23rd July. 1815.'

This extraordinary object seems to have been conceived as a memorial window to Dr Toulmin who was a Unitarian Baptist clergyman, follower of Joseph Priestley and friend of Coleridge. The latter occasionally preached in his chapel in Taunton, walking over from Nether Stowey

54a

54c

54b

(B. Laurence, *Coleridge and Wordsworth in Somerset*, Newton Abbott, 1970, pp. 40–1). According to a memorial sermon written shortly after Dr Toulmin's death (Israel Worsley, *Observations on the state and changes in the Presbyterian Societies*, 1815, p. 22), 'At one time Paine was burnt in effigy before his door, and but for the interference and remonstrance of particular friends, he would have undergone a similar fate . . . One evening a large stone was aimed at his head through his study window, where he was sitting, with an evident intention to strike a mortal blow'. It is known that Dr Toulmin was one of a group who celebrated the anniversary of the Revolution in 1790 (R. Bush, *A Taunton Diary*, Taunton, 1988), but it was late 1792 when Paine was burned in effigy in several towns in the West Country (see no. 55 above). There is a strong possibility, therefore, that this window refers to the same events as the broadside above. There are traces of emblems, now painted over in the four corners of the frame, which can be read as follows: a *bonnet rouge* with cockade, a broken crown, a man on a gibbet (Tom Paine?) and an open book (the Bible?). (I am grateful to Miss Louise Simson for her help with this entry.)

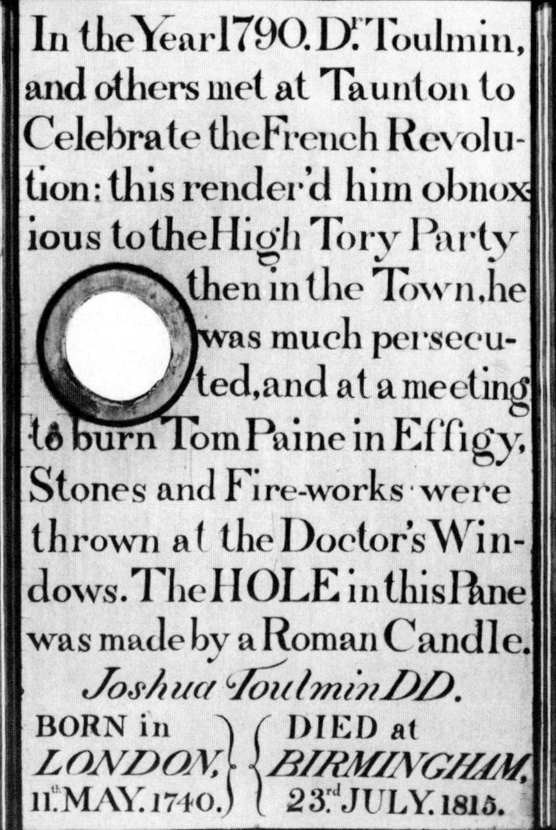

In the Year 1790. Dr. Toulmin, and others met at Taunton to Celebrate the French Revolution: this render'd him obnoxious to the High Tory Party then in the Town, he was much persecuted, and at a meeting to burn Tom Paine in Effigy, Stones and Fire-works were thrown at the Doctor's Windows. The HOLE in this Pane was made by a Roman Candle.

Joshua Toulmin DD.

BORN in *LONDON*, 11th MAY. 1740. DIED at *BIRMINGHAM*, 23rd JULY. 1815.

56

57a *Mug printed in red with a medallion portrait of Tom Paine and verses*

creamware, probably Staffordshire, grooved loop handle, H. 95 mm

Lent by Royal Pavilion, Art Gallery and Museums, Brighton, Willett no. 521

LITERATURE Willet cat. 1899, no. 521; May 1972, pp. 127–8

The verses read: 'Prithee, Tom Paine, why wilt thou meddling be/In others Business which concerns not thee;/ For while thereon thou dost extend thy Career/Thou dost at home neglect thy own Affairs', and 'Observe the wicked and malitious Man,/Projecting all Mischief that he can;'. Within the frame enclosing the portrait and first verse is inscribed 'GOD save the KING'.

The mug probably dates from 1792 to 1793 when anti-Paine sentiment was at its height, but it could be slightly later.

AD

57a

57b *Mug printed in brown with verses*

creamware, probably Staffordshire, grooved loop handle, H. 122 mm

Lent by Royal Pavilion, Art Gallery and Museums, Brighton, Willett no. 520

LITERATURE Willett cat. 1899, no. 520; May 1972, pp. 127–8

The verse is the same as on no. 57a; the portrait and lower verse are omitted and scrolls fill the upper part of the oval reserve which has a more elaborate border including a ribbon bow.

AD

58 *Jug printed in brown with 'Courtship and Matrimony' and patriotic verses*

creamware, probably Staffordshire, H. 170 mm
Lent by Royal Pavilion, Art Gallery and Museums, Brighton, Willett no. 519
LITERATURE Willet cat. 1899, no. 519
INSCRIBED 'God save the King/And all his subjects Too,/Likewise his forces/And Comanders true./May HE their Rights/Forever hence Maintain/Against all strife/Occasion'd by Tom payne.'

The jug was probably made *c.*1792–3. AD

59 *Kerchief printed on linen, Paine surrounded by royal family and monarchs*

580 × 550 mm
Lent by Sussex Archaeological Society, Lewes

This object is clearly anti-Paine for it implicitly attributes to him the execution of Louis XVI which is shown below adapted from a popular broadside published by Lane (see no. 102), with the implied threat that the other monarchs and royal personages may suffer the same fate. The fact that Catherine the Great is present suggests that the kerchief dates from before her death in November 1796, though this should not be relied upon. The purpose of the object is unclear: it could simply be a wall-hanging or a kerchief, but the idea might also have been for one to blow one's nose on an image of Tom Paine (see no. 54c).

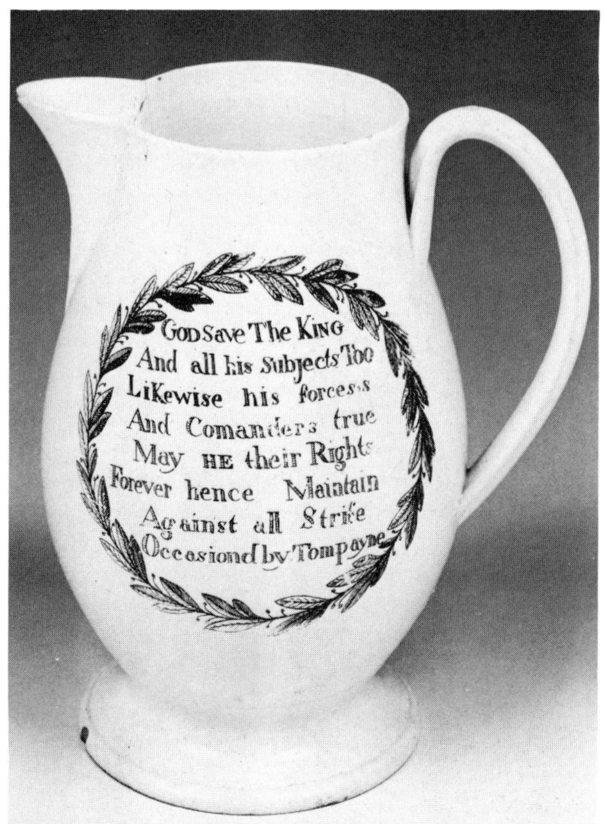

58

59

60

WILLIAM KENT, ENGRAVED BY LOVEGROVE

60 *The Monkey who had seen the World*

illus. to Gay's *Fables*, 1793, Fable XIV, p. 63, 80 × 93 mm (image)
1856-5-10-707; Pressmark 1* b.3

An adaptation of an illustration for Gay's *Fables*, first published in 1727 and repeatedly copied. The 1793 edition is notable for containing ten engravings freely adapted from the earlier engravings by William Blake. This illustration by the lesser-known Lovegrove shows the Monkey who had seen the World as a Frenchified fop carrying Paine's *The Rights of Man*. The facial resemblance is close enough (see no. 50) to raise the possibility that it is intended to be of Paine himself, who was by 1793 a French citizen, but perhaps more likely it was meant to associate the reading of Paine with French affectation as the 'radical chic' of the 1790s.

61

ATTRIBUTED TO SAMUEL COLLINGS

61 *A Gentleman of Moderate Income. Making himself decent to dine out*

etching, 249 × 185 mm, pub. 28 Nov. 1796 by Laurie and Whittle
Lent by The Lewis Walpole Library, Farmington, Conn.

The penurious gentleman living in a garret is revealed by the peeling print on the wall behind to be a supporter of Tom Paine.

'Church and King': campaigns against 'sedition', 1791–2

By November 1792, with the formation of John Reeves's Crown and Anchor Society devoted to 'Church and King', the framework of a nationwide system of anti-radical propaganda had been established, with the tacit encouragement of the government. This was the culmination of a process which can be effectively dated back to the events surrounding the famous dinner held in Birmingham on 14 July 1791 to commemorate the second anniversary of the fall of the Bastille. The sequence of events can be traced clearly through the objects displayed below. The chief guest at the dinner was to be the radical scientist Joseph Priestley, though in fact he did not turn up, having been warned that there might be trouble. As a consequence of the uproar initiated by an anti-radical mob, with possibly some encouragement from local magistrates, Priestley's house and laboratory were burned down, as were the houses of his most noted radical supporters. Gillray's caricature of the dinner marks the beginning of the identification, rapidly to become a 'given' of loyalist satire for the rest of the decade and longer, between English radicalism of all shades and the most extreme 'levelling' tendencies within the French Revolution. In May 1792 the first proclamation against sedition was brought in by the king, and by the end of the year popular prints with simple anti-French messages were beginning to be distributed widely through the Crown and Anchor Society (see p. 117).

62 *Wedgwood plaque, Dr Joseph Priestley (1733–1804)*

pale blue jasper ware with dark blue dip, applied white jasper relief, H. 274 mm, impressed WEDGWOOD & BENTLEY; metal frame

Pot. Cat. I. 66; Franks Collection

LITERATURE *Pot. Cat.* I. 66; H. Tait, 'The Wedgwood Collection in the British Museum, part II', *Proc. Wedg. Soc.*, no. 5 (1963), p. 35

The portrait is based on an original plaster by Giuseppe Cerrachi (1751–1802), still kept at the Wedgwood Museum (T. Clifford, 'Wedgwood at the National Portrait Gallery', *Burlington Magazine*, CXV, 1973, pp. 832–5), and was modelled in 1779 as part of a series of large portraits, including Franklin, Solander, Banks, Sir William Hamilton and Sir Isaac Newton. Wedgwood wrote to his partner Thomas Bentley on 24 March 1779, 'Dr Priestley is arriv'd & we are with great reverence taking off his presbyterian parsons wig & preparing a Sr I. Newton as a companion to him'. Wedgwood corresponded with Priestley for many years and was a fellow member with him of the Lunar Society of Birmingham, sharing his scientific interests. After the mob had burnt Priestley's house at Birmingham, Wedgwood wrote him several sympathetic letters in September and October 1791 and counselled him on the phrasing of his 'Appeal to the Public on the subject of Riots in Birmingham, 1791'. Priestley emigrated to America in 1794. AD

62

63a,b *Two tickets to Birmingham French Revolution Dinner, 14 July 1791*

Lent by Birmingham Public Library

63c *Medal worn by Charles Jennens at the French Revolution Dinner*

tin, 33 mm

Lent by Birmingham Museums and Art Gallery

This was one of a large number of medals struck to celebrate the centenary of the Glorious Revolution in 1788. The obverse legend reads 'WILLIAM III OF BLESSED MEMORY'; the reverse 'REVOLUTION JUBILEE NOVR IV 1788/BRITONS NEVER WILL BE SLAVES'. MJ

JAMES GILLRAY

64 *A Birmingham Toast, as given on the 14th of July, by the Revolution Society*

etching, coloured, 271 × 500 mm, pub. 29 July 1791 by S. W. Fores

1851-9-1-538; Smith Collection

LITERATURE BMC 7894

A highly fictionalised account of the celebrated Birmingham dinner of 14 July 1791. Not one of those depicted was actually at the dinner. Even Priestley, seen holding a Communion dish and brimming chalice calling out 'The [King's] Head, here!', though he was the chief victim of the riots which followed the dinner (see no. 65), was not present. The others, from the left Sheridan, Sir Cecil Wray, Fox, Horne Tooke, Dr Lindsay and the grotesquely caricatured Dissenters, belong to Gillray's standard repertory of radical types. Gillray's general intention in the print was to characterise the dinner as belonging to the tradition of covert celebrations of the execution of Charles I, and the notion of the radicals as 'king-choppers' was already expressed in his print *The Hopes of the Party*, published on 19 July 1791. The Bastille dinner is seen by Gillray not so much in terms of French influence but more in terms of the continuity of seventeenth-century 'Levelling' ideas.

64

AFTER JOHANN ECKSTEIN, PRINTED BY J. HULLMANDEL

65 *Dr Priestley's House and Laboratory after their destruction in the Birmingham Riots, 1791*

lithograph, 396 × 499 mm, early 19th century
Lent by Birmingham Public Library, BRL LV.1
INSCRIBED 'From a Picture sketched on the Spot in the possession of Joseph Parkes'
LITERATURE *Priestley in Birmingham*, 1980, no. 44

The print is taken from a painting by Eckstein of 1791, now in a private collection in Portugal. It shows the 'Church and King' mob destroying Priestley's house. The painter was closely involved in Birmingham radical circles.

P. H. WITTON, ENGRAVED BY W. ELLIS

66 *Views of the ruins of the Principal Houses destroyed during the Riots at Birmingham, 1791*

8 aquatints (volume open at ruins of Priestley's house), 128 × 197 mm
Lent by Birmingham Museums and Art Gallery, 800'40
LITERATURE *Priestley in Birmingham*, 1980, no. 43

The views show the ruins of the houses of Priestley and his supporters following the attacks of the rioters. The accompanying text is in both English and French.

66

67a

67a *Medal, Nourished to Torment, July 14 1791*

copper, 34.5 mm
S. S. Banks, p. 5-1
tin, 34.5 mm
1906-11-3-413
LITERATURE Bell, *Political tokens*, p. 77

The obverse shows a monstrous harpy with the features of Joseph Priestley, representing revolution (see also no. 67b), carrying a banner on which a crown is deluged by drops of blood. Several offspring suckle at her breasts. One is carrying a scroll labelled FACTION; another has set off carrying a dagger and a burning brand. The legend above explains: 'OUR FOOD IS SEDITION'. On the reverse a snake in the grass appears beneath the legend 'NOURISHED TO TORMENT', with the date of the Birmingham Revolution dinner to which it clearly refers. MJ

67b

67b *Token, Pandora's breeches, 1792*

copper, 28.5 mm
T 6518
LITERATURE Bell, *Political Tokens*, pp. 82, 261

In May 1792 it was discovered that an attempt had been made to set fire to the House of Commons by hanging an old pair of worsted breeches, filled with combustible matter, in the ceiling of a room below it. The human head, severed by a dagger from a snake's body, is that of Joseph Priestley. This design was often paired with 'The End of Pain' – see no. 54a. In the *Public Advertiser* of 11 May 1792 there was a skit in which Thomas Paine is claimed to have said that 'he could not attend the enquiry about the fire, because his breeches had gone to be new seated'. MJ

ANON.

68 (a) *Miniature of Thomas Pougher Russell, 1775–1851*, and (b) *hat which belonged to him with cockade*

(a) pen and watercolour, 126 × 104 mm; (b) beaver felt, trimmed with silk, H. 244 mm, L. 500 mm
Lent by Birmingham Museums and Art Gallery, 39'42 and 24'49
LITERATURE *Priestley in Birmingham*, 1980, no. 56 (miniature only)

Russell was a supporter of Priestley who also had his house destroyed in the 1791 riots. He visited Priestley in Northumberland, Pennsylvania, where the latter had settled after leaving for America in April 1794. Russell eventually settled in France, becoming a French citizen in 1809, and according to family tradition he wore the hat with its cockade, and a court suit which still survives, at Napoleon's wedding to Marie-Louise of Austria on 2 April 1810.

RICHARD NEWTON

69 *A Bugaboo!!!*

etching, coloured, 341 × 448 mm, pub. 2 June 1792 by W. Holland
1868-8-8-6209
LITERATURE BMC 8102

A satire on the proclamation against 'tumultous meetings and seditious writings' of 21 May 1792, which was the first governmental attempt to counteract the influence of Paine's writings and was the forerunner of many more legal measures against radicalism. Here it is seen as a panic measure by George III, driven on by Pitt to impose despotic rule by building Bastilles in all the centres of dissent, like Bristol, Birmingham and Manchester. Holland as a publisher of radical tracts, who was jailed for seditious publications, would have been particularly sensitive to attempts to strengthen the law against sedition.

69

4 The first year of equality, September 1792–June 1793

This section covers the period from the formal abolition of the monarchy on 21 September 1792 and the declaration of the Republic the following day, inaugurating 'l'an I de la République française', to the *journée* of 2 June 1793 when the Convention was forced to vote for the arrest of twenty-nine Girondin deputies, thus inaugurating the rule of the 'Mountain'. The monarchy fell to a popular uprising, possibly partly organised by Danton, on the *journée* of 10 August 1792, and on 13 August the king and his family were imprisoned in the Temple. One consequence was the declaration by the Duke of Brunswick that he intended to raze Paris if the Assembly did not surrender the king immediately. In the ensuing panic the September Massacres took place in Paris, in which many imprisoned aristocrats and clergy were killed, and calm was restored only as a result of the astonishing French victory of Valmy on 20 September, which effectively secured the survival of the Republic. This was followed by the equally decisive victory of Jemappes on 6 October, which led to the offer by the Convention of aid to any uprising in another country.

By the end of 1792 the king's position weakened dramatically, as a result of the discovery of an iron chest containing incriminating papers, and on 20 December his trial began. On 17 January 1793 he was condemned to death by a vote of the Convention which replaced the Assembly after the fall of the Tuileries, and on the 21st he was publicly guillotined in the Place de la Révolution in Paris. War with Britain now became inevitable and it was declared on 1 February. In Paris the political situation became ever more confused, with the government under the ostensible power of the Girondins, or moderate revolutionaries, but they were under constant challenge from the radicals of the 'Mountain', or Montagnards, who finally expelled them in June, inaugurating a period of a year when the guillotine was used with increasing frequency until the fall of Robespierre in July 1794.

The Association for Preserving Liberty and Property against Republicans and Levellers, November–December 1792

On 20 November 1792 at a meeting at the Crown and Anchor tavern in the Strand, John Reeves set up the Association for Preserving Liberty and Property against Republicans and Levellers. Its aim was explicitly to counteract the effects of the circulation of radical literature throughout the kingdom and 'the circulating of mischievous opinions, founded upon plausible but false reasoning . . . [which is] carried on by the industry of Clubs and Societies of various denominations in many parts of the Kingdom'. A letter to Reeves in the British Library (Add. MS. 16,919) of 2 November 1792 is even more explicit in revealing the purposes of the society: 'a gentleman willing to communicate any information to the loyal & spirited Society now established at the Crown & Anchor Tavern will relate such observations, as he thinks may prove useful to their designs, & open the eyes of the people, who will then see, how they have been misled by the Rights of Man, & the Soldiers Friend & the low price these books are sold for, make them common in the poorest houses; it is therefore necessary to open the eyes of the people, before it is too late, in order to counteract the mischief the above books have done'. The intention was to set up a nationwide network on the lines of the radical Society for Constitutional Information to produce propaganda to counteract such writings and encourage their suppression. Reeves, therefore, invited his supporters to send to him any seditious material they could find, and nos 70a–c are taken from a collection of such material which still survives with accompanying letters in the British Library (Add. MSS. 16,919–16,928).

70

(a) *Flier for The Star of Liberty: or The Constitutional Cockade by R. Hawes*

(b) *Letter to Reeves enclosing it, signed Detector*

(a) 250 × 180 mm; (b) 255 × 115 mm
Lent by British Library, Dept of Manuscripts, Add. MS. 16,922, f1, 2

(c) *Seditious tobacco paper*

160 × 160 mm
Lent by British Library, Dept of Manuscripts, Add. MS. 16,922, f13

The flier (no. 70a) for *The Star of Liberty* by R. Hawes was sent in anonymously by an informer, calling himself 'Detector' on 11 December 1792, who wrote 'A Friend of

Juſt publiſhed, Price 3d. Plain, or 6d. Gilt.

The STAR of LIBERTY:
OR
The *Conſtitutional* COCKADE!
CONTAINING

I.

FORTY-FIVE Patriotic and Sentimental TOASTS, Doubled—ſo arranged that any Perſon's moſt private Choice of any of them may be told in an Inſtant. They will alſo afford an agreeable Winter Evening *Diverſion*, called Robin's Game.

II.

An Advertiſement, with the Preamble to an American Act of Congreſs, by THOMAS PAINE, never before publiſhed in Europe; and which may be juſtly eſteemed as *one of* the moſt choice Productions of PAINE's incomparable Pen.

III.

The Emblems of Philanthropy and Juſtice, (with the *Bandage* removed from the Eyes of the latter) ſupporting the above Fragment and other Compoſitions; in particular, an Acroſtical *Addreſs* to the London Correſponding Society.—

IV.

A ſmall Bundle of ACROSTICS, on SIR THOMAS GRESHAM—THOMAS PAINE,—MAJOR PETER LABELLIERE—DEI GRATIA, &c. alſo on COMMUTATION—MENE MENE TEKEL—King George the Third—William Pitt—&c. &c. *N. B.* The two latter *Acroſtics* are poſited in a curious Hieroglyphic, Emblematic of a *Ladder* with ONE STEP, or BAR:—which alſo nearly reſembles the Type of the new Planet called the *Georgium Sidus.*

V.

The RIGHTS OF MAN, an Acroſtical Song.

VI.

The PROCLAMATION OF LIBERTY, an Acroſtical Song, with a few ſhort Notes, of material *importance* to the Public in General at this juncture.

As divers Schemes from various Cauſes ſpring,
Fair FREEDOM's *STAR*, we here preſume to bring:
A PROCLAMATION for the Times, deſign'd—[Ezek. XLV. 9!]
At once t'amuſe and *liberate* Mankind.
All Ranks all Orders may this Emblem wear:
Let Kings diſpute your Title—if they dare!
Zone, Garter, Favor, may from each be made;
A Curious Shoe-Knot, or a neat Cockade—
A Prieſt's *Phylactery*; a Judge's *Band*;
A *Flag* of PEACE:—GOOD WILL TO EVERY LAND!——
An *Ornament*, by G—RACE, for each degree:
A LEGAL *badge* of JUST EQUALITY!
With one let Faſhion but adorn her Head,
The flame will ſoon thro' all aſemblies ſpread.
I'll lay them at your feet, ye Friends of Art,
If Stars are Honors——Bind them on your heart!

LONDON:
Invented, Printed, and Sold, by R. HAWES, at the CONSTITUTIONAL LIBERTY PRESS, 107, White-Chapel Road: Sold alſo by Meſſrs. RIDGEWAY, York-Street, St James's Square; DAWSON, Covent-Garden Market; PARSONS, Paternoſter-Row; WOOD, at the Royal Exchange; and by the Bookſellers and Newſmen in Town and Country.

70a

the Constitution, whose opinion perfectly coincides with that of your excellent institution sends you the enclosed inflammatory Paper, in order to point out to you the Arts & intentions of our Enemies'. No. 70c is a tobacco paper which the informant claimed to have picked up in a tavern in Kennington. Its seditious message reads 'I am puzzled how to live while kingcraft may abuse my rights and tax the joys of day'.

70c

LORD GEORGE MURRAY, ENGRAVED BY THOMAS ROWLANDSON

71 *The Contrast, 1792*

etching, coloured, 305 × 470 mm, pub. Dec. 1792
J 4-50; Banks Collection
LITERATURE BMC 8149; George 1959, II, p. 1

Probably the most widely disseminated design of the whole anti-radical campaign, for it was used on a variety of objects. A note on the back in the hand of Miss Sarah Sophia Banks, who gave the print to the British Museum, tells us that it was 'Designed by Lord George Murray. Sent by Him to the Crown & Anchor from whence they have been distributed. & likewise sold by Mrs Humphrey [Gillray's publisher] in Bond Street Dec. 1792'. In fact this seems to apply to the copy (no. 72) dated 1793 which was clearly intended for wide and subsidised distribution.

Towards the end of 1792 with news of the September Massacres, the deposition of Louis XVI and the proclamation of the French Republic, the propaganda offensive against radicalism tended to emphasise the consequence of 'levelling' in France as a lesson to England, rather than seeking to answer Paine's arguments directly.

AFTER THOMAS ROWLANDSON

72 *The Contrast, 1793*

etching, coloured, 249 × 350 mm, pub. 1 Jan. 1793 by S. W. Fores
1861-10-12-47; H. W. Martin Collection
LITERATURE BMC 8284

Copied from the previous print by Rowlandson, it was clearly intended for distribution, for it could be bought by the hundred at one guinea plain and two guineas coloured. According to Mrs George it was advertised by the Crown and Anchor Society on 26 December 1792 as showing 'The happy and flourishing State and Wealth of Great Britain, contrasted with the Horrors, Massacres, and Poverty of France'.

THE CONTRAST
1792
BRITISH LIBERTY
FRENCH LIBERTY
MAGNA CHARTA
RELIGION. MORALITY.
LOYALTY OBEDIENCE TO THE LAWS
INDEPENDANCE PERSONAL SECURITY
JUSTICE INHERITANCE PROTECTION
PROPERTY. INDUSTRY. NATIONAL PROSPERITY
HAPPINESS
ATHEISM PERJURY
REBELLION. TREASON. ANARCHY MURDER
EQUALITY. MADNESS. CRUELTY. INJUSTICE
TREACHERY INGRATITUDE IDLENESS
FAMINE NATIONAL & PRIVATE RUIN.
MISERY
WHICH IS BEST

71

THE CONTRAST
1793
BRITISH LIBERTY
FRENCH LIBERTY
MAGNA CHARTA
RELIGION, MORALITY,
LOYALTY, OBEDIENCE to the LAWS,
INDEPENDANCE, PERSONAL SECURITY
JUSTICE, INHERITANCE, PROTECTION of
PROPERTY, INDUSTRY, NATIONAL PROSPERITY
HAPPINESS.
ATHEISM, PERJURY
REBELION, TREASON, ANARCHY, MURDER
EQUALITY, MADNESS, CRUELTY, INJUSTICE,
TREACHERY, INGRATITUDE, IDLENESS,
FAMINE, NATIONAL & PRIVATE RUIN,
MISERY.
WHICH IS BEST?

72

73 left

73 right

73 *Mug printed in dark blue with 'The Contrast' after Rowlandson*

pearlware, probably Staffordshire, H. 150 mm
1982, 11-1, 1

The printed design is certainly copied from Rowlandson's design above, probably about 1793, but it could have remained in production for some years.

To the left of the title 'THE CONTRAST/1793/WHICH IS BEST' is FRENCH LIBERTY: within a medallion is a man hanging from a lamp post to the right of Discord running over a prostrate body, a sword in her left hand and in her right a pole surmounted by two hearts between which is a severed head. Inscribed below: 'ATHEISM. PERJURY. REBELLION. TREASON. ANARCHY. MURDER. EQUALITY. MADNESS. CRUELTY. INJUSTICE. TREACHERY. INGRATITUDE. IDLENESS. FAMINE. NATIONAL & PRIVATE. RUIN. MISERY.' To the right is BRITISH LIBERTY: within a medallion is Britannia seated under a tree at the left by a shield bearing the Union Jack, her right hand resting on 'MAGNA CHARTA' and holding a pole surmounted by a cap of liberty. In her left hand she holds scales. In front of her is a lion and a sailing ship. Inscribed below: 'RELIGION. MORALITY. [L]OYALTY. OBEDIENCE TO THE LAWS. [I]NDEPENDENCE. PERSONAL. SECURITY. JUSTICE. INHERITANCE PROTECTION. PROPERTY. INDUSTRY. NATIONAL. PROSPERITY. HAPPINESS. There is a printed design of vine leaves and grapes round the inner and outer rim and on the handle. AD

AFTER THOMAS ROWLANDSON

74 *The Contrast, with song The New Hearts of Oak*

broadside, 385 × 107 mm
Lent by British Library 648, c. 26, no. 28

This design, probably from the same block, appears in a broadside with *God save the King!* and also on the title-page of *The Antigallican Songster*, no. II, pub. J. Downes, 1793.

75 *Jug printed in black with hand-painted additions and coloured, with design from Gillray's 'French Liberty. British Slavery'*

creamware, probably Staffordshire, H. 168 mm
Lent by Royal Pavilion, Art Gallery and Museums, Brighton, Willett no. 375
LITERATURE Willett cat. 1899, no. 375

The printed design is clearly copied from Gillray's very popular print (no. 84), probably about 1793, though it could be a little later. AD

THE CONTRAST.

1792.

Religion, Morality, Loyalty, Obedience to the Laws, Independence, Personal Security, Justice, Inheritance, Protection, Property, Industry, National Prosperity, Happiness.

Atheism, Perjury, Rebellion, Treason, Anarchy, Murder, Equality, Madness, Cruelty, Injustice, Treachery, Ingratitude, Idleness, Famine, National and private Ruin, Misery.

WHICH IS BEST?

The New Hearts of Oak.

I.

COME rouſe up my lads,
And defend the great Cauſe
Of our Country and King,
Our Religion and Laws;
Theſe, in ſpite of the maxims
Of Prieſtly and Paine,
Each true hearted Briton
Would die to maintain.

CHORUS.

Hearts of oak are our ſhips,
Hearts of oak are our men,
We always are ready,
Steady, boys, ſteady,
Be firm in the cauſe
Of our Country and King.

II.

Shall a nation, for wiſdom
And valour long fam'd,
Hear their Laws and their Council
Seditiouſly blamed;
But let Levellers talk,
And let rioters ſwear,
We have thoſe at the Helm
Who know well how to ſteer.
Hearts of oak, &c.

III.

The French had long bowed
To Oppreſſion's ſtern rod,
And mad to be freed,
Drenched their footſteps in blood;
But we, who are bleſſed
In ſo gentle a reign,
Have no cauſe to rebel,
And no right to complain.
Hearts of oak, &c.

IV.

The Frenchmen we long
Have conſider'd as foes,
And did ever with courage
And vigour oppoſe;
Tho' we ſhelter their poor,
For protection who fled,
Yet by Frenchmen's example
We ſcorn to be led.
Hearts of oak, &c.

V.

May Commerce long flouriſh,
And faction ſoon ceaſe,
And George long reign o'er us,
In glory and peace;
Whilſt Soldiers and Sailors
And Citizens ſing
Of the bleſſings of Britons,
And long live the King.

CHORUS.

Hearts of oak are our ſhips,
Hearts of oak are our men,
We always are ready,
Steady, boys, ſteady,
Be firm in the cauſe
Of our Country and King.

74

75a

75b

76

B. JACOBS AFTER JAMES GILLRAY

76 *Medal, French Liberty. English Slavery*

copper, 29.5 mm
S. S. Banks, p. 188-14, and T6504

On one side a free Frenchman is seen seated on the floor, gnawing bones; on the other a well-fed English slave is seen, seated at table, tucking into roast beef with a large pudding to follow. The picture behind him shows an equally corpulent figure drinking in an ale house.

Tokens and medals, being two sided, were particularly well suited to this kind of comparison. MJ

THOMAS ROWLANDSON AFTER G.L.S

77 *Philosophy Run Mad or a Stupendous Monument of Human Wisdom*

etching, coloured, 247 × 353 mm, (no address) Dec. 1792?
1851-9-1-626; Smith Collection
LITERATURE BMC 8150

This print seems also to have been directly inspired by the activities of the Crown and Anchor Society. It was designed by an amateur and etched by Rowlandson, and must date from late 1792 as a response to the aggressive foreign policy of the Girondin government in France. The imagery is more complex than most produced at the time, and it may reflect a desire to challenge intellectual radicals, for it argues that the misunderstanding of the true nature of Liberty and Equality must lead inevitably to their opposites. A woodcut version of part of the design appeared on the title-page of *The Anti-Levelling Songster*, no. 1, pub. J. Downes, 1793 (information from Richard Spencer).

JOHN NIXON, ENGRAVED BY THOMAS ROWLANDSON

78 *French Liberty*

etching, working proof tinted with wash and with extensive MS. inscriptions by Nixon and dedicated to Mrs Nicols, 471 × 581 mm, late 1792?
1868-8-8-6265
LITERATURE BMC 8334; Duffy 1986, no. 96

Dated by Mrs George to possibly as late as 1793, though in fact it certainly belongs to late 1792. The references are to the invasion of the Tuileries on 10 August and the September Massacres, and the print precedes the almost universal adoption of the stereotype of the sans-culotte in 1793 satires. It also has the didactic character of prints associated with the Crown and Anchor Society: Paine is depicted as a mountebank. According to the published state of the print, 'this represents his work to be froth & Airy Vapour: tending to delude & mislead a Nation who it is hoped, are by this time so well convinced of the Blessing they enjoy, as to have no wish to change it for any other'. On the left the arts and trades are forced into exile, presumably in the direction of England, for the scene, though schematic, suggests northern France, particularly the church which is of a northern French type.

THOMAS ROWLANDSON

79 *Reform Advised. Reform Begun. Reform Compleat*

etching, coloured, 440 × 275 mm, pub. 8 Jan. 1793 by J. Brown
1932-2-26-17
LITERATURE BMC 8289

Probably the print advertised by the Crown and Anchor Society as 'Reform. Several degrees of Modern Reform, and its fatal consequences, contrasted with the settled, constitutionally protected, affluent, happy Briton'. Though the print shows John Bull wheedled and then assaulted by a group of sinister Frenchmen, the aim of the print is to attack the idea of constitutional reform which lay at the heart of all radical dissent in England. Reform is characterised as inherently Jacobin and destructive of British contentment. The Frenchmen are classic stereotypes who begin with ingratiating courtesy and end with brutality.

The sans-culottes

The revolutionary sans-culottes were in reality a complex phenomenon, brutally travestied in British caricature. In French terms they represent the ideals of the artisan class who took part, though rarely on their own initiative, in the popular uprisings, or *journées*, which marked changes of power as the Revolution progressed. The sans-culotte ideal was adopted by the Montagnards, the more radical members of the Convention, though they themselves were rarely artisans, and by the revolutionary government which fell with Robespierre in July 1794. The ideal was essentially that of plain manners and conduct, opposed at all points to what were perceived as the 'aristocratic' ideal of rank, gentility and privilege based on ancient custom. Sans-culottes represented 'the people' who were universally invoked by French revolutionaries as the bedrock of the Revolution, though in practice their power was intermittent, and they were essentially eliminated as a political force under the Directory.

Le bon sans Culotte

80

In British loyalist mythology they were reduced to a bloodthirsty mob, whose excesses, in the September Massacres of 1792 and the Terror of 1793–4, were taken as representative of the French Revolution in action and the consequences which would follow from a French invasion of England. British Opposition Whigs and radicals were tarred in many caricatures with the sans-culotte brush, to the point that any sympathy with the Revolution or desire for a peace treaty with France was taken as approval of the brutal massacre of all upholders of the British constitution. Sans-culottes in British caricature served to travesty all the nuances and complexities of revolutionary sympathy in both France and England, and the over-simplification of their role was reinforced in popular literature throughout the nineteenth century.

ANON. FRENCH

80 *Le bon sans Culotte*

engraving, colour printed, 230 × 170 mm
Lent by Musée de la Révolution Française, Vizille
LITERATURE de V 6112

A sympathetic contemporary representation of the sans-culotte enjoying the simple life, eating soup and feeding his dog. There is a companion print of 'Madame sans Culotte' knitting while a cat plays with the wool.

81

JAMES GILLRAY

81 *Un petit Souper a la Parisienne – or – A Family of Sans-Culotts refreshing after the fatigues of the day*

etching, coloured, 252 × 353 mm, pub. 20 Sept. 1792 by H. Humphrey
1868-8-8-6230
LITERATURE BMC 8122

One of the most ferocious of Gillray's anti-French satires, it reflects an early British response to the news of the September Massacres in Paris. It is one of the first prints to note the existence of the sans-culottes, who are depicted as a mob without human feelings. The humour lies in the witty parallel to the familiar motif of John Bull eating roast beef (see no. 84), for the starving French revolutionaries are eating the only meat they can obtain. The publication of this print precedes by some months the Crown and Anchor Society campaign of late 1792 (see p. 117).

RICHARD NEWTON *(illus. p. 46)*

82a *A Party of the Sans Culotte Army marching to the Frontiers*

etching, coloured, 217 × 678 mm, pub. 1 Oct. 1792 by W. Holland
1925-7-1-34
LITERATURE BMC 8123

RICHARD NEWTON

82b *The Duke of Brunswick attacking the Rear of the Sans Culottes*

etching, coloured, 276 × 439 mm, pub. 2 Oct. 1792 by W. Holland
Lent by Robert Douwma

These two prints commemorate the defence of France, threatened by the invasion of the Prussians, whom she

82b

unexpectedly defeated at Valmy on 20 September 1792. Judging by the buoyant figure of the Duke of Brunswick in no. 82b the French victory had not been confirmed by the time the prints appeared. Brunswick, who had earlier issued a manifesto threatening the virtual destruction of Paris, seemed almost invincible and his defeat at Valmy saved the Revolution, but the threat he presented created a fear of treachery within France that contributed greatly to the September Massacres and ultimately to the execution of the king. Newton's characterisation of the sans-culottes plays on the idea that the word 'sans-culotte' meant without trousers rather than without aristocratic knee-breeches, and the scatological potential of this mistranslation has been taken to its comic limit. Though the Duke of Brunswick is seen as the victor in no. 82b, when his defeat became known in England he also became the butt of satire, especially as dysentery had played a part in weakening his armies (see BMC 8125).

83 *Two song sheets*

(a) RICHARD NEWTON, *Ça Ira*

etching, coloured, 162 × 224 mm, pub. 18 Nov. 1792 by W. Holland
Lent by Andrew Edmunds

(b) RICHARD NEWTON, *Marche des Marseillois*

etching, coloured, 384 × 241 mm, probably late 1792
1988-10-1-4

(c) ANON. FRENCH, *Figure playing violin* (from which (b) was copied)

etching, coloured, 223 × 176 mm, summer 1789
1988-5-14-9
INSCRIBED 'Chantons, Célébrons, la Réunion des trois Ordres.'
LITERATURE de V 2022

These song sheets record two of the most celebrated revolutionary songs, the *Ça ira* and the *Marseillaise* in a good-natured spirit which probably reflects the publisher William Holland's radical sympathies. No. 83b borrows

83a

83b

the design from a French print (no. 83c) which celebrates the excitement of the period just before the fall of the Bastille and must date from the summer of 1789. The *Ça ira* was later regarded as highly inflammatory and with *La Carmagnole* associated with the excesses of the sans-culottes (see *A Tale of Two Cities*, pp. 307–8); however, the version used here is the mild earlier one, composed *c.* 1790, referring to 'le prudent La Fayette', and lacking the notorious cry 'les aristocrates à la lanterne' (Constant Pierre, *Les Hymnes et Chansons de la Révolution*, Paris, 1904, p. 486).

JAMES GILLRAY

84 *French Liberty. British Slavery*

etching, coloured, 247 × 348 mm, pub. 21 Dec. 1792 by H. Humphrey

J 3-14; Banks Collection

LITERATURE BMC 8145; Jouve 1983, p. 51

Perhaps the most famous of Gillray's anti-Revolution caricatures, its enormous popularity led to the design being copied in several media, including pottery and medals. It was also known in France and copied in Germany, and the figure of John Bull was adapted as a symbol of England in the print of 1795 *Le Neuf Thermidor ou la Surprise Angloise* (no. 172). The print belongs with those encouraged by the Crown and Anchor Society, though it was probably initiated by Gillray himself. The imagery of

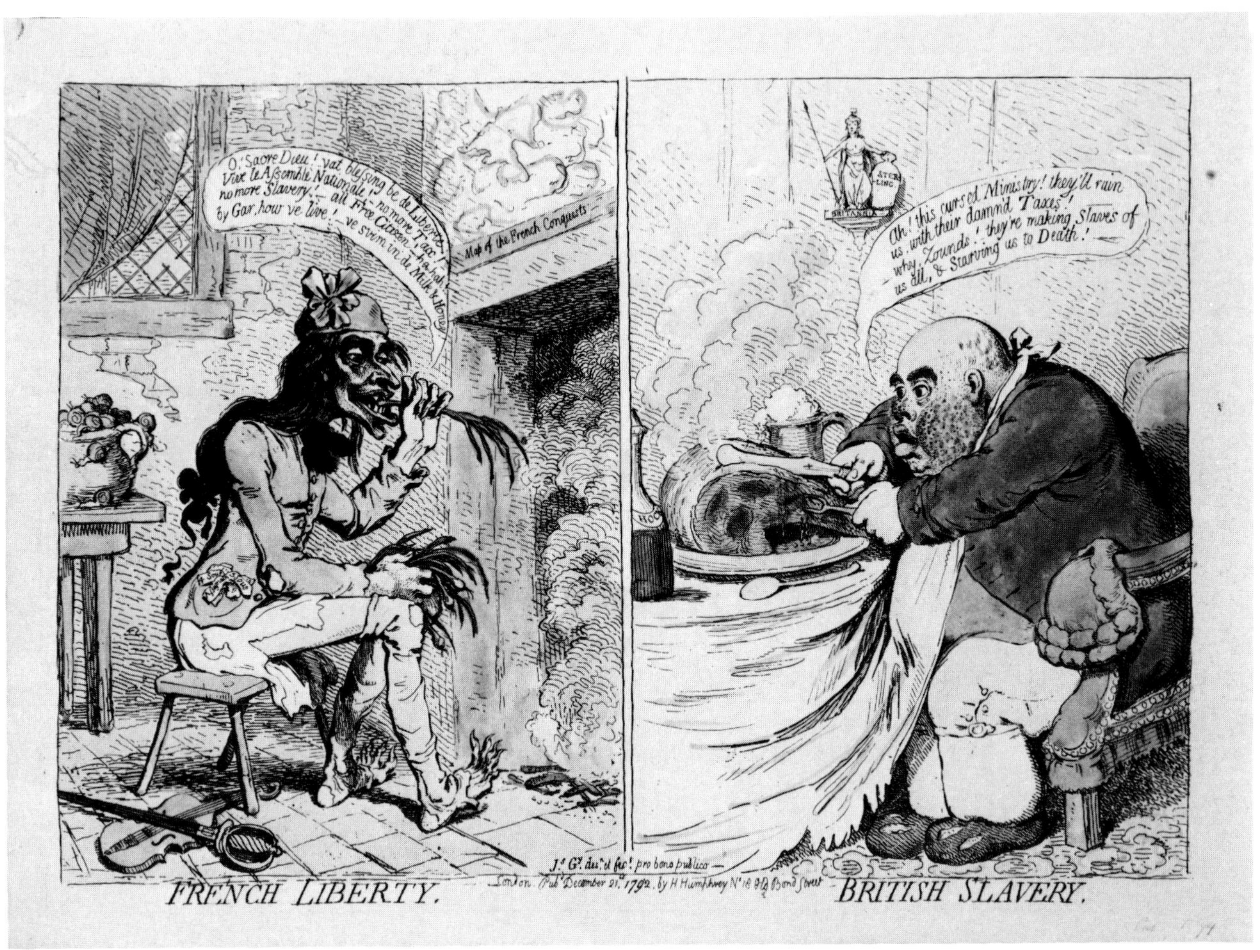

84

the contrast between France and England, defined in terms of food, is wholly traditional (see no. 2). John Bull is ridiculed for complaining of taxation while enjoying the benefits of prosperity, especially compared to starving Frenchmen.

The Opposition unmasked: Charles James Fox as sans-culotte

Charles James Fox's combination of elevated principles and a rakish private life made him an easy target for satirists: he was possibly the most caricatured politician of the eighteenth century. Before the French Revolution it was common to show him as a cunning fox, and to reveal crude self-interest behind his seemingly high-minded actions, but after 1789 he was invariably depicted as a covert sans-culotte. The plausible and gentlemanly façade of 'the Friend of the People' was often contrasted with his 'real' identity as a ruthless and calculating Jacobin. In fact Fox was neither a true radical nor unusually dissolute by the standards of the day, but a Whig gentleman who had espoused constitutional reform about 1780 and attracted a devoted aristocratic following. He argued eloquently in the Commons on behalf of the repeal of the Test and Corporation Acts and on behalf of basic human rights, though he was emphatically not a 'Leveller' as his opponents claimed. Radicals like Thelwall (no. 201) increasingly complained of his establishment sympathies, despite his appeals to public opinion over the head of Parliament.

J. NOLLEKENS

85 *Charles James Fox*

terracotta bust, H. 527 mm, *c.* 1791
Lent by National Portrait Gallery, no. 139

The distinguished sculptor Nollekens had a successful trade in busts of politicians, and there are many versions of his bust of Fox which acted as signs of allegiance in the country houses of his supporters. There are two types of bust: the first, to which the present example belongs, was conceived about 1791 and shows him with flowing locks. The version of about 1802 shows Fox as a 'crop' (see no. 170), with his hair cropped in the Roman manner. This version is probably a contemporary cast from a terracotta model.

JAMES GILLRAY

86 *A Democrat, – or – Reason & Philosophy*

etching, coloured, 342 × 241 mm, pub. 1 March 1793 by H. Humphrey
1851-9-1-647; Smith Collection
LITERATURE BMC 8310

Fox is reduced in Gillray's caricature to the most blood-thirsty of sans-culottes and *septembriseurs*, drunk on the blood of his victims. He is depicted as jowly and unshaven in implied contrast to his open assumption of the manners of a country gentleman, which led him on occasions to appear in the House of Commons 'booted and whip in hand from Newmarket' (Goodwin 1979, p. 93).

ANON. *(illus. on cover)*

87a *The Hopes of the Party! or the Darling Children of Democracy!*

aquatint, coloured 377 × 300 mm, pub. 28 Feb. 1798 by W. Holland
1871-11-11-535
LITERATURE BMC 9178

ANON.

87b *John Bull Consulting the Oracle!*

aquatint, coloured, 381 × 502 mm, pub. 20 March 1798 by W. Holland
1868-8-8-6713
LITERATURE BMC 9190

These remarkable prints by an unknown artist show the ferocity which Fox still attracted in 1798, and his continued identification with sans-culottism long after

86

87a

the latter's virtual demise under the Directory. In no. 87a the figure of Democracy in *bonnet rouge* and cockade is the hideous mother of Fox and Horne Tooke, while in no. 87b Fox is a ghastly nightmare terrorising an honest citizen. These two prints are evidence of the renunciation of radicalism by the publisher William Holland, whose prints of the years 1789–92 are notable for their sympathy with the French Revolution.

The imprisonment of the royal family and the trial of Louis

With the invasion of the Tuileries Louis XVI and his family became helpless prisoners and were confined to the Temple prison on 13 August 1792. The new Republic was proclaimed on 21 September 1792 following the transformation of the National Assembly into a Convention to draw up a new constitution. The discovery of an iron chest in the Tuileries containing hints of the king's counter-revolutionary activities made it inevitable that he should be tried, and on 5 December it was decided that it should be by the Convention itself. He was brought before the Convention on 11 December and after lengthy debate the voting began on 14 January 1793. The vote was nearly unanimous for his guilt, but the manner of his punishment was intensely debated. In the end, on 19 January, those

87b

who felt that only the king's death could ensure the irreversibility of the Revolution prevailed by a small majority. On the evening of the 20th Louis received the Abbé Edgeworth as his confessor and said farewell to his family. The next morning he was taken with his confessor to the Place de la Révolution, and before 20,000 armed men and a large crowd he was guillotined.

ANON. FRENCH

88 *Louis le dernier et sa famille conduits au Temple le 13 Aoust 1792*

etching, coloured, 331 × 475 mm
1861-10-12-240; H. W. Martin Collection
LITERATURE Vovelle 1986, III, pp. 154–5

Louis was confined to the Temple on 13 August 1792, and was kept there, except for his trial, until his execution. Though Louis is touching in his vulnerability, the print is Jacobin in spirit, emphasising his lack of the regal dignity which informs the sympathetic images that follow. It is captioned 'Louis le Dernier', and he is deprived of his ability to dominate his people, who are shown as on the same physical level and are able to force upon him the ultimate humiliation of wearing a *bonnet rouge* (see no. 43).

CHARLES BENAZECH, ENGRAVED BY L. SCHIAVONETTI

89 *The Separation of Lewis the Sixteenth from his Family in the Temple*

engraving, 518 × 650 mm, pub. 1 June 1793 by Colnaghi
1854-8-12-207

The scene probably shows the cruel and unnecessary separation of Louis XVI from his family in the Temple on the orders of the Mayor of Paris on 29 September 1792. However, the setting appears to be not the Temple but the Palace of the Tuileries, despite the title. The figure with the scroll on the right may well be Pétion, the Mayor of

89

Paris, who was particularly reviled in England, perhaps because of his visit to London in late 1791 when he met many prominent English radicals (Goodwin 1979, pp. 186–8).

W. MILLER, ENGRAVED BY L. SCHIAVONETTI

90 *The Memorable Address of Louis the Sixteenth at the Bar of the National Convention After his Counsel Mr. Deseze had closed his Defence on the 26 of December 1792*

engraving, 534 × 649 mm, pub. 20 Nov. 1796 by Testolini
1917-12-8-3954; Lucas Collection

Louis is seen at his trial before the Convention as a figure of regal dignity. The deputies are identified in a key provided with the print, and include the painter Jacques-Louis David, who voted for Louis's execution. He is the figure second from the end on the right of the third row. Robespierre is just below him. Despite the name of the publisher this seems to belong to the series after Benazech and others published by Colnaghi from 1794 onwards. The design itself probably dates from after Benazech's death in 1794.

Louis's last farewell to his family, 20 January 1793

Within days of the execution of Louis XVI on 21 January 1793 a version of the events had reached England which included a declaration of innocence on the scaffold and last words of forgiveness to the nation. The event provoked a flood of broadsides, including hastily produced views of the scene on the scaffold, copies of Louis XVI's will, dated 25 December 1792, and a great many prints by all the main caricaturists of the day. The tendency of all these productions was to emphasise the exemplary conduct of Louis and to reinforce his Christ-like innocence. In addition, accounts appeared shortly after the execution describing Louis's farewell to his family the night before his execution, and though they are not always compatible with the later account of the Duchess of Angoulême who was a witness to the scene, they rapidly became fixed in substance and a source for visual images.

A typical account of Louis's parting from his family in the Temple prison the night before his execution is contained in a contemporary broadside (John Johnson Collection, Bodleian Library, Oxford): 'The KING passed two hours with his family; it was for the first time since his imprisonment that he had been allowed to see them without witnesses. Dreadful indeed was the moment in which he tore himself from them, although they hoped to see him once more on the following morning. The QUEEN, delirious and convulsed, embraced the KING's knees with so much violence, that two men were obliged to use all their force to tear the KING from her arms. Madame ELIZABETH and the DAUPHIN extended on the ground at his feet uttering the most dreadful screams: Madame ROYALE senseless on her bed. Such was the situation of this Family when His MAJESTY took his last farewell of them!' The following items all present a version of this event.

CHARLES BENAZECH

91 *The Last Interview between Lewis the Sixteenth and his Disconsolate Family*

pencil, pen and wash drawing, 360 × 520 mm
1896-5-11-4

A sketch for the following print. Though apparently squared for transfer to the copper, it shows considerable differences from the print, most notably in the relative placing of the Bible and crucifix and the window. In the final version Louis looks towards both window and crucifix, which suggest the idea of death as the Christian's release from the material body.

CHARLES BENAZECH, ENGRAVED BY L. SCHIAVONETTI
(illus. p. 32)

92 *The Last Interview between Lewis the Sixteenth and his Disconsolate Family*

engraving, 514 × 644 mm, pub. 10 March 1794 by D. Colnaghi
1917-12-8-2929; Lucas Collection

Though dated 1794 on this impression, the design in its painted form was clearly in existence early in 1793, for Gillray's print (no. 96) surely refers to Benazech's version and is dated 20 March 1793. Benazech's design emphasises the king's Catholic faith and has a strong *pietà*-like composition. There is a small painted version, dated 1793, in the Musée de Versailles (reproduced in *Wordsworth*, 1987, fig. 17), paired with a scene of Louis's execution. Benazech died in May 1794 before he could illustrate the later history of the royal family.

93 *Historical Account of the last interview of Louis XVI. with his family, before his execution; to elucidate the second print of the series formed on that interesting event*

broadsheet accompanying no. 92
etching, 225 × 285 mm
1881-11-12-258

Keys like this were published by Colnaghi to accompany the set of prints designed by Benazech and others of the last days of the royal family.

M. BOVI AFTER D. PELLEGRINI *(illus. p. 50)*

94 *The King's Departure from his Disconsolate Family*

engraving, 454 × 578 mm, pub. 1 Jan. 1794 by M. Bovi
1917-12-8-997; Lucas Collection

This print was issued as part of a series published by the engraver Mariano Bovi. Artist and engraver continued to depict the fate of the rest of the family, after Louis's execution. Six of the engravings were gathered together in book form and given a text under the title *A Graphic History of Louis the Sixteenth, and the Royal Family of France*. The claim that the pictures were made on the spot need not be taken seriously. Pellegrini's version is altogether more Neoclassical than Benazech's above and may show the influence of Jacques-Louis David's paintings of the 1780s. Pellegrini was a painter from the Veneto who seems to have been part of the engraver Bartolozzi's circle.

MATHER BROWN, ENGRAVED BY P. W. TOMKINS *(illus. p. 23)*

95 *The final interview of Louis the Sixteenth*

engraving, 543 × 654 mm, pub. 1 Jan. 1795 by Jee and Eginton, Birmingham
1987-10-3-24
LITERATURE Dorinda Evans, *Mather Brown*, Middletown (Conn.), 1982, pp. 117–21, nos 271–3

The engraving is derived from an oil-painting by Mather Brown which is known in three versions, the first of which can be dated 1793. The painting was announced as begun on 1 February 1793 in the *Morning Chronicle*, and the large version of the painting (now Wadsworth Athenaeum, Hartford, Conn.) was sent on a tour of northern towns later in the year. Brown also worked on a painting of the *Massacre of the Princess Lamballe*, but no trace of it is known.

JAMES GILLRAY *(illus. p. 33 and in colour)*

96 *Louis XVI taking leave of his Wife & Family*

etching, coloured, 248 × 378 mm, pub. 20 March 1793 by J. Aitken
Lent by Andrew Edmunds
INSCRIBED 'NB: The above is an exact Copy of an infamous French Print, which has lately appeared in Paris, among numberless others, intended to bring the Conduct of their late Monarch in his last moments, into Contempt & Ridicule;– It is now Copied & publish'd, in order to hold up a Nation of unfeeling Assassins to that detestation which every true Englishman must feel for Wretches, who can sport with the sufferings of the unfortunate.'
LITERATURE Hill, *Gillray*, 1965, p. 44

Gillray's inscription should not be taken seriously. The print is, in fact, a satire on engravings by British not French artists, and it has all the hallmarks of Gillray's anti-Catholicism and urge to ridicule royalty. Louis is shown as a glutton and drunkard (see no. 40), while Marie Antoinette has become a hysteric. They bear, perhaps intentionally, a close resemblance to Gillray's depictions of George III and Queen Charlotte. The rarity of the print suggests that it had little circulation.

97

97 *Mug printed in black with 'Louis XVI taking leave of his Family'*

creamware, Staffordshire, H. 117 mm, print signed Fletcher & Co. Shelton
Victoria and Albert Museum, 3638-1901
LITERATURE C. Williams-Wood, *English Transfer-Printed Pottery and Porcelain*, London, 1981, pp. 160–2, fig. 91

The mug is inscribed below the print of the king in a windowed cell, with his wife and sister and two kneeling children: 'LOUIS XVI taking leave of his FAMILY the morning of his EXECUTION. Farewell Queen Children Sister Louis cries/Abate your grief & dry those streaming eyes/And O! my son if e'er the Crown you wear/think of my fate and steer your course with care'.

Thomas Fletcher (fl. 1786–1810) became a partner in a pottery run by John Baddeley I at Shelton in 1761 continuing under his son, Ralph Baddeley, until 1775. Nothing is known of him from then until 1786 when he was in business as a decorator and transfer-printer with Sampson Bagnall II. In 1796 Fletcher took new partners, Thomas Thompson and John Hewitt. The firm was dissolved in 1800, Fletcher continuing as a transfer-printer until about 1810. This print has been attributed to the engraver Thomas Radford (fl. 1778–1802) who had been employed by the Baddeleys. AD

98

98 *Mug printed in black with 'The last interview of Louis the Sixteenth with his Family'*

creamware, attributed to Liverpool, H. 149 mm
1986,10-17,1

The print shows the king in a gloomy cell, with a crucifix on the wall, embracing his wife and son, whilst his daughter lies at his feet. It is not known for certain where mugs like this one, often of indifferent quality, were made; this piece could equally well have been produced in Staffordshire. AD

CONRAD HEINRICH KÜCHLER

99 *Medal, The Last Interview*

gilt copper, 48 mm, 1793
M2589
LITERATURE Pollard 1970, pp. 259–318

C. H. Küchler fled to England from Amsterdam early in 1793. On 2 March, through Richard Chippindall, Matthew Boulton's agent in London, he suggested to Boulton that he should engrave 'a medal on the fate of the late King of France'. Boulton agreed to the production of a series of medals as a joint speculation with Küchler, the profits to be divided equally between them. The dies for this medal were completed by 6 July 1793.

The portraits are similar to those executed by Benjamin Duvivier in the 1780s, but the portrait of the king may be more directly derived from a medallic portrait commissioned by Boulton in 1792 from another artist, which he mentioned in a letter to Küchler dated 23 April 1793. MJ

99
100

100 *Medal, The Last Interview*

tin, 38 mm
1913-3-1-17

It is not clear whether the signature W.M.F. is that of William Mossop, who worked in Dublin, or William Mainwaring, who worked in Birmingham, but the poor quality of the engraving suggests the latter. MJ

The execution of the king, 21 January 1793

ANON. FRENCH

101 *Complainte sur le mort de Louis le dernier*

broadside with verses, 138 × 203 mm, pub. 1793 'chez le citoyen Auger'
1861-10-12-90; H. W. Martin Collection
LITERATURE mentioned under de V 5171

A contemporary French broadside of Jacobin sympathies celebrating, as if in Louis's own words, his execution on 21 January 1793 and the hoped-for end of the dynasty.

ANON. (*illus. p. 29*)

102 *Massacre of the French King!*

broadsheet, woodcut with text, 468 × 309 mm, n.d. but pub. early 1793 by William Lane
1856-7-12-1101

A highly opportunistic publication for the woodblock had originally been used for a broadside illustrating approvingly Dr Guillotin's new invention, before the execution of Louis XVI. Despite its doubtful source and unemotional presentation it was a very popular image in England of the execution, and it reappears in adapted form on a number of objects (see nos 113–14, 121).

CHARLES BENAZECH, ENGRAVED BY A. CARDON (*illus. p. 49*)

103 *Louis the 16th with his Confessor Edgeworth ascending the fatal Steps*

engraving, 384 × 466 mm, pub. 1 March 1797 by Colnaghi, Sala
Lent by Her Majesty the Queen

A re-engraving by Cardon of a print first published by Colnaghi on 1 February 1795 and engraved by L. Schiavonetti, after the death of the artist in May 1794.

COMPLAINTE SUR LA MORT DE LOUIS LE DERNIER.

LA NATION ET LA LOI. LIBERTÉ ÉGALITÉ

SUR L'AIR : de Chambort.

Peuple Français sans égal,
Me voilà au rang des morts ;
Mais priez dieu pour mon sort :
Il n'y a plus d'interval,
Voilà ce que j'ai mérité.
Chantez vive la liberté !

Peuple souverain de la terre,
Qui n'avez jamais été,
Par ma mort vous voilà lavé.
Hélas ! je finis ma carrière,
A la place de la Révolution, pour certain,
Voilà donc ma triste fin.

Du crime le plus atroce,
Ce fut dans le mois d'août,
Je voulais vous faire périr tous,
Croyant en faire une noce.
Hélas ! pour moi, quel malheur !
On me découvre à dix heures (1).

C'est dans l'assemblée nationale
Où je me sauve à l'instant,
Retiré comme un enfant
Qui venait de faire du mal ;
De-là on m'a fait emmener,
Au temple pour prisonnier.

Étant dans la Tour.
Quelle horrible résidence !
Je me vois environné ;
De moëlon ma chambre est pavée.
Mais me voilà tout en trance :
On vient pour me faire coucher :
Je ne puis y résister.

Hélas ! sept mois se passèrent
Dans cette horrible prison :
J'entends troupe et bataillon,
Qui se disent, nous sommes frères :
Il faut garder sans façon,
Ne point perdre le Cochon.

Hélas ! voilà l'alarme :
C'est quand on vient m'avertir,
On me dit qu'il faut partir,
Que le peuple est sous les armes,
Pour mon dernier jugement :
Allons, partons, il est tems.

A la convention je jure,
On me conduit à l'instant,
Pour entendre mon jugement,
Où l'on me connaît pour parjure :
De-là je fus aussitôt
Conduit dessus l'échaffaud.

Les adieux qu'il fait au peup
Adieu peuple de la terre :
Adieu donc Peuple François,
Je vais voir le roi des rois ;
Je vais fermer la paupière
Sous le glaive de la loi,
Comme étant ci-devant roi.

FIN.

L'exécution a eu lieu le lundi 21 janvier, à dix heures du matin.

Et se trouve à Paris, chez le citoyen AUGER, rue de Rohan, N°. 439.

(1) Qui fut le 10 août.

101

105

A version of the original painting is in the Versailles Museum and is dated 1793. Anthony Cardon was a Belgian engraver who settled in London in 1792. The design was enormously popular and was copied several times in Germany and in France after the Terror. This print is apparently the third in the series published by Colnaghi. Louis is shown in an attitude of calm resignation, at the point at which Abbé Edgeworth supposedly said to him, 'Offspring of St Lewis, ascend to Heaven'. For a discussion of the change in inscription between the two versions see Introduction, p. 48.

104 *Historical Account, explanatory of the third print, representing Louis XVI on parting from his confessor Edgeworth, the moment before a period was put to his existence, On the 21st of January 1793*

(key to no. 103), 226 × 285 mm
1881-11-12-259

W. DENT

105 *Hell Broke Loose, or, The Murder of Louis*

etching, coloured, 247 × 336 mm, pub. 2(5?) Jan. 1793 by J. Aitken
1948-2-14-450

Though more comical than pathetic, this print has the distinction of being almost certainly the first response by a caricaturist to Louis XVI's execution.

ISAAC CRUIKSHANK

106 *The Martyrdom of Louis XVI, King of France*

etching, coloured, 248 × 204 mm, pub. 1 Feb. 1793 by S. W. Fores
Mm15-7; Banks Collection
INSCRIBED 'I Forgive my Enemies, I Die Innocent!!!'
LITERATURE BMC 8297

Another early response to the execution, which also shows the difficulty caricaturists had in dealing with an event for which satire was self-evidently inappropriate.

106

107

R. DIGHTON

107 *The Unfortunate Louis XVIth*

etching, coloured (cut and damaged)
Lent by The Lewis Walpole Library, Farmington, Conn.
INSCRIBED 'The Unfortunate LOUIS XVIth the minute before his DEATH. "To thee, O God, I commend my Soul! I Forgive my enemies – I DIE INNOCENT."'

The print has lost its address and date but it must date from about the period of Cruikshank's print (no. 106), to which it may be indebted. This impression appears to be unique, though intended for a large audience. The claim that it was taken 'from a sketch sent from Paris' should not be taken seriously.

JAMES GILLRAY

108 *The Zenith of French Glory; – The Pinnacle of Liberty*

etching, coloured, 351 × 248 mm, pub. 12 Feb. 1793 by H. Humphrey
1851-9-1-643; Smith Collection
INSCRIBED 'Religion, Justice, Loyalty, & all the Bugbears of Unenlighten'd Minds, Farewell!'
LITERATURE BMC 8300

Gillray characteristically uses the language of satire to set the execution within a context of the destruction of legal and spiritual authority by the sans-culottes, who are shown as massed around the scaffold, delineated almost entirely by their *bonnets rouges* and cockades. A 'typical' sans-culotte sits on a lantern outside a church, from which a bishop and two monks dangle, watching the execution scene below.

ISAAC CRUIKSHANK

109 *The Martyr of Equality*

etching, coloured, 242 × 212 mm, pub. 12 Feb. 1793 by S. W. Fores
1871-8-12-2930
INSCRIBED 'Behold the Progress of our System'
LITERATURE BMC 8302

This print, published shortly after no. 106 above, expresses retrospective shock at the fact that the Duke of Orleans, or Philippe Egalité (hence the pun in the title), was a signatory to his cousin Louis XVI's death sentence.

110 *Jug printed in red with 'The Martyr of Equality' after Isaac Cruikshank*

creamware, Staffordshire, H. 245 mm
Lent by Royal Pavilion, Art Gallery and Museums, Brighton, Willett no. 373
LITERATURE Willett cat. 1899, no. 373

Presumably copied from Cruikshank's print (no. 109) in 1793 or shortly after. AD

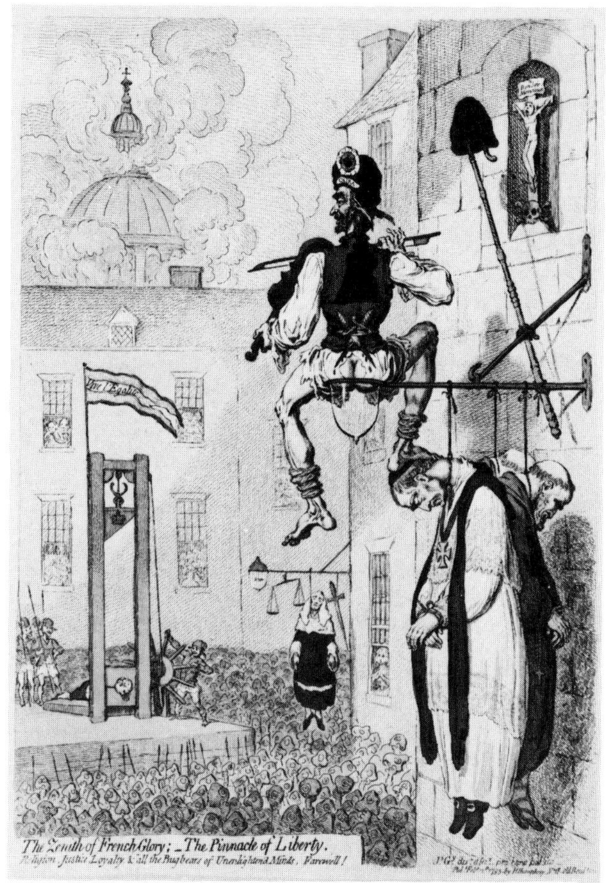
The Zenith of French Glory; _ The Pinnacle of Liberty.

108

The MARTYR of EQUALITY
Louis 16th Guillotined
January 21. 1793.

109

The MARTYR of E

110

Exact representation of that Instrument of French refinement in Assassination the GUILLOTINE
the Gentlemen of the Phalanx" & other well wishers to the King & Constitution of Great Britain,
by their devoted
The Assassins of the King of France
Whither, — O whither shall my Blood ascend for Justice! — my Throne is seized on by my Murderers; my Brothers are driven
into exile; — my unhappy Wife & innocent Infants are shut up in the horrors of a Dungeon; — while Robbers & Assassins are sheathing
their Daggers in the bowels of my Country! — Ah! ruined, desolated Country! dearest object of my heart! whose misery was to me the
sharpest pang in death! what will become of thee? — O Britons! vicegerents of eternal Justice! arbiters of the world! — look
down from that height of power to which you are raised, & behold me here! — deprived of Life & of Kingdom, see where
I lie; pull low, festering in my own Blood! — which flies to your august tribunal for Justice! — By your affection for your own
Wives & Children — rescue mine; — by your love for your Country, by the blessings of that true Liberty which you possess; by the
virtues which adorn the British Crown — by all that is Sacred, & all that is dear to you — revenge the blood of a Monarch most
undeservedly butchered, — and rescue the Kingdom of France from being the prey of Violence, Usurpation & Cruelty.
Pubd. Feb. 16th 1793. by H. Humphrey No 18. Old Bond Street
The Blood of the Murdered crying for Vengeance.
J. Gy. desr. et fect. pro bono publico

111

JAMES GILLRAY

111 *The Blood of the Murdered crying out for Vengeance*

etching, coloured, 350 × 260 mm, pub. 16 Feb. 1793 by H. Humphrey
1868-8-8-6277
LITERATURE BMC 8304

This highly emotional print in its dedication at the top, 'This Exact representation of that Instrument of French refinement in Assassination, the GUILLOTINE is submitted to the Gentlemen of *the Phalanx*, & other well-wishers to the King & Constitution of Great Britain, by their devoted Servants at Command The Assassins of the King of France', seems to refer back ironically to Lane's print of the execution (no. 102), but the powerful central image of the blood of the victim crying for vengeance derives from the biblical account of Cain's murder of Abel (Gen. 4: 10): 'the voice of thy brother's blood crieth unto me from the ground. And now art thou cursed from the earth . . . Therefore whosoever slayeth Cain, vengeance shall be taken on him sevenfold'. This derivation also accounts for the blood's address to the British public, 'by all that is Sacred, & all that is dear to you – revenge the blood of a Monarch most undeservedly butchered, – and rescue the Kingdom of France, from being the prey of Violence, Usurpation & Cruelty'.

RICHARD NEWTON, AQUATINT BY J. HASSELL

112 *Execution of Louis the XVI in the Square of Louis XV now called Place de la Revolution*

etching and aquatint, 500 × 603 mm, pub. 20 Feb. 1793 by W. Holland
Lent by Musée Carnavalet, Paris
LITERATURE Vovelle 1986, III, pp. 192-3

This print, of which this is the only known impression, is remarkable for giving a comprehensive and relatively accurate view of the Place de la Révolution filled with an immense crowd of soldiers, though like the work of other caricaturists, with the exception of Gillray, it hardly matches the pathos of the occasion.

112

115 left, 113 right

113 *Mug printed in blue-black with 'La Guillotine'*

pearlware, probably Staffordshire, H. 92 mm
Pot. Cat. H. 59
LITERATURE *Pot. Cat.* H. 59

The design derives from William Lane's popular woodcut (no. 102). The print shows the act of execution watched by two onlookers and is inscribed 'View of LA GUILLOTINE or the modern beheading machine at PARIS by which LOUIS XVI late king of France suffered on the Scaffold Jan 21 1793'. At either side of the grooved handle is a printed flower; the handle is decorated with stylised leaves, and inside the rim is a (poorly applied) printed trellis and flower design. AD

114 *Jug printed in blue with 'La Gullotine [sic] or the modern Beheading Machine'*

pearlware, probably Staffordshire, H. 174 mm
Lent by Manchester City Art Galleries, 1923–932

The design also derives from William Lane's woodcut (no. 102). The print, at either side of which are flower sprays, shows the act of execution watched by two onlookers and is inscribed 'View of LA GULLOTINE [*sic*] or the modern Beheading Machine at PARIS. By which LOUIS XVI late King of France was Beheaded Jan, 21 1793'. The border is printed with a cell pattern. AD

115 *Mug printed in black with the 'Massacre & Execution of Louis XVI, King of France'*

creamware, probably Staffordshire, H. 122 mm, print signed 'J Aynsley Lane End'
1988, 12-1, 1; from the collection of Sir Lincoln Hallinan, Cardiff

The print, within an oval line, depicts the moment after the execution when the king's head is held up by the second executioner, in the presence of the Commandant General and the king's Confessor. Parts of the scene and each figure are identified by numbers. Below the scene is inscribed 'MASSACRE & EXECUTION of LOUIS XVI, KING of FRANCE. Jan.y 21 1793. Aged 38 Years 4 Months – An Event most Wonderfull in the History of the World, 1 the Guillotine – 2 The Ax – 3 The King – 4 De Fermand His Confessor – 5 One of the Executione [*sic*] Drawing up the

114

Ax immediately after the Execution – 6 the other Executioner holding up the Head of the King & proclaiming Behold the Head of a Tyrant – 7 The Basket for the Head – 8 The long Basket for the Body – 9 De Santere the Commandant General – 10 The Way by which the unfortunate Monarch ascended the Scaffold'. John Aynsley (fl. 1780–1809) was in business at Lane End, Staffordshire, from about 1780 and marketed transfer-printed wares in the late 1780s. It is not clear whether he was a potter or merely a merchant, and it is likely that this print was engraved and printed by someone else. AD

CONRAD HEINRICH KÜCHLER

116 *Medal, Execution of Louis XVI*

silver, 51 mm
George III French Medals 69
LITERATURE Pollard 1970, pp. 262, 264, 270

The double portraits on the obverse are the same as those used for no. 99. The reverse is signed P, presumably by the engraver (probably Ponthon) of whom Boulton wrote on 13 March 1793, 'I have one medal die engraver in my employ . . . [who] is now engraving a die with a View of the execution of Louis 16th upon a scaffold with the Guards and a great crowd of people . . .'. That Küchler re-engraved the die seems likely, since he charged Boulton for making a pair of dies for this medal and shared the profits from it with him. MJ

JOHN WARREN, ENGRAVED BY I. GODEFROY

117 *Louis XVI attended by Religion, & Charity, enters the Elysian Fields*

engraving, 280 × 369 mm, pub. 5 Sept. 1793 by M. Parr
Lent by Her Majesty the Queen
INSCRIBED 'LOUIS XVI attended by Religion, & Charity, enters the Elysian Fields, CHARLES I. presents him the Palm of Martyrdom, SOCRATES, gives him the Crown of Immortality DIOGENES blows out his Lantern MUCIUS CURTIUS, discovers the Hero the instant he appears.'

The conceit of the dead hero greeted by his immortal forebears in the Elysian fields is not unfamiliar in France: there are prints of Voltaire and Mirabeau of a similar type. The author John Warren was clearly a gentleman amateur, while Godefroy (1771–1839) was an important

117

RÉCEPTION DE LOUIS CAPET AUX ENFERS.
PAR GRAND NOMBRES DE BRIGANDS CI-DEVANT COURONNÉS.
Aux Républicains Français

118

Anglo-French engraver, born in London to French parents, who worked in both England and France, settling in the latter in 1797 (*French Printmaking*, 1984–5).

ENGRAVED BY VILLENEUVE

118 *Réception de Louis Capet aux Enfers*

aquatint, coloured, 268 × 363 mm, 1794?
Lent by Musée de la Révolution Française, Vizille
LITERATURE de V 5228; Vovelle 1986, III, 200

The contrast with the previous print is intriguing, for it looks at first as if one is an answer to the other. It seems clear that the Godefroy print must be earlier for its date precedes the execution of Marie Antoinette, while Villeneuve appears to show her headless in the background. It is unlikely that the Godefroy print could have been known in Jacobin circles in Paris so the relationship is probably coincidental, based on mutual borrowing of a common French pictorial idea. Louis arrives in Hell headless, where he is presented by his tyrannical forebear Charles IX to Charles I who clutches his own head in recognition. They are surrounded by groups of counter-revolutionaries past and present, while outside people dance around a Liberty tree. This fine coloured impression was formerly in the collection of Soulavie, a contemporary who formed a great collection of revolutionary material (see Lugt, under Soulavie).

ANON.

119 *The Will of Louis the Sixteenth*

broadside with engraving of Louis XVI by Stevenson, engraved by I. Barlow, 562 × 385 mm, pub. 1793? by William Lane
1856-7-12-1099

The will of Louis XVI, which shows him in a charitable light, was printed in very large numbers in the period after his execution. For William Lane see no. 102.

ANON.

120 *A List of Regicides*

broadsheet, 870 × 480 mm, pub. by S. W. Fores
1932-2-26-5
LITERATURE BMC 8514

The reference to the fall of Robespierre dates this list from after 28 July 1794, and the reference in the design at the top to Collot d'Herbois, Barrère, Merlin and Tallien, who are crushed under fortune's wheel, suggests a date before the end of the year, when all these figures were under threat for complicity in the Terror.

121 *Patchbox painted in colours with the execution of Louis XVI*

enamel on copper, metal mount, mirror on inside of cover, probably Staffordshire, L. 55 mm
1987, 7-8, 1

The scene, which derives from William Lane's broadside (no. 102) entitled 'La Guillotine', is inscribed 'He died lamented by all good men' and shows a man under the guillotine, his head rolling into a basket, watched by two onlookers. It is a rare subject on enamel boxes such as this one, which probably held black patches, or beauty spots.

AD

122 *Medal, Mourning and vengeance*

tin, 31.5 mm
1906-11-3-803; presented by F. Parkes-Weber

This medal, with its legends in French reading 'Louis XVI, King of France, immolated by the factious/mourn and revenge him', was probably engraved by William Mainwaring. It exactly imitates a medal issued by the Prussian Court medallist Daniel Friedrich Loos.

MJ

5 The second year of equality: France under the guillotine, June 1793–July 1794

The confused period known as the Terror which followed the defeat of the Girondins by the Montagnards under Robespierre and Danton effectively began in early June 1793 and lasted until the end of July 1794. The period was characterised by economic and social conflict, inside and outside France, increasingly regulated by the extensive use of the guillotine to eliminate those suspected of treachery to the Revolution, at every level of society. Institutionalised xenophobia led to foreigners, even those sympathetic to the Revolution, being imprisoned or interned, with the result that information received in England was not always accurate, though those with

123

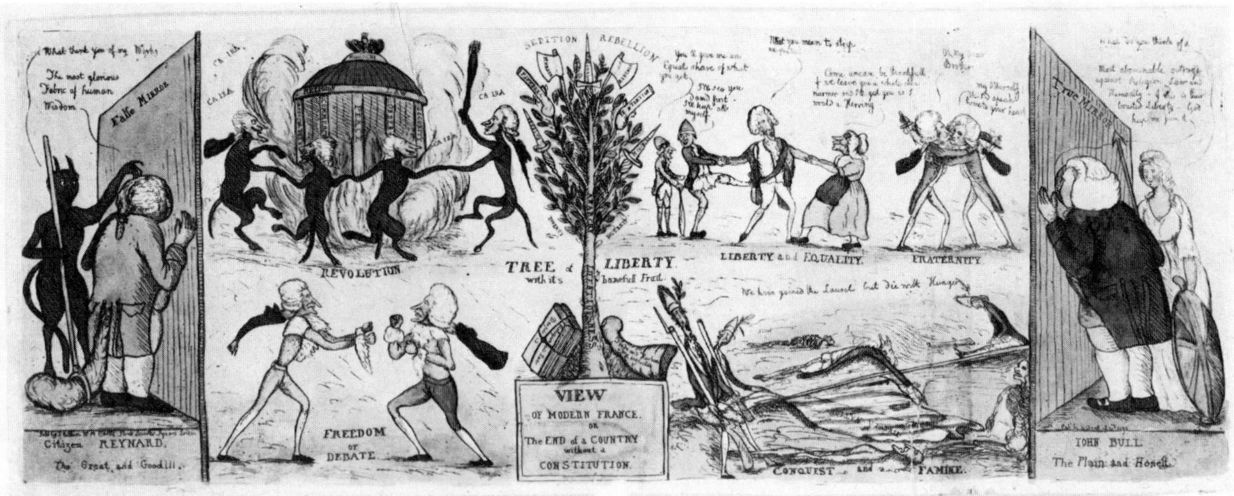

124

government connections like Joseph Farington did receive news. As he wrote on 16 November 1793: 'The events which are succeeding each other in France, and which posterity will consider with Horror & almost doubt of from their atrocity, are received here as the news of the day; so habituated are we, by repetition, to the shocking accnts received, that the natural effect of a first emotion is weakened' (Farington, vol. 1, pp. 94–5). The event which attracted most attention was the assassination of Marat by Charlotte Corday on 13 July 1793: this contributed greatly to the atmosphere of near panic in Paris which lay behind much of the vehemence against royalists and traitors, and the execution of Marie Antoinette on 16 October 1793.

The Montagnard Republic, June–November 1793

P. M. ALIX AFTER BOISSIER

123 *Le Triomphe de la République*

colour print, 718 × 520 mm, pub. 27 July 1794 (9 Thermidor l'an 2e de la Rép. F.) by Bance
1925-7-1-96; presented by the Earl of Crawford and Balcarres
LITERATURE *Fonds Français*, I, Alix, no. 38

Some impressions of this print are dated 10 August 1793, and it was paired with *Le Despotisme foudroyé*. As an allegory of the Republic it reveals with exceptional clarity the embattled mentality which lay behind the Terror of l'an II. The new Republic is seen as a mountain fastness in which the people rejoice in their new liberty and equality, symbolised by the dance around the Tree of Liberty, while surrounded by 'furious monsters' who are defeated by the lightning which emanates from the twin tablets of the Rights of Man and the Republican constitution. The mountain storms which the forces of despotism have called up are now turned upon themselves leading to their eternal destruction. Discord is struck on the forehead by lightning, and a drowning figure, symbolising religious superstition, vainly carries a cross aloft.

W. DENT

124 *View of Modern France. or The End of a Country without a Constitution*

etching, coloured, 199 × 550 mm, pub. June(?) 1793 by J. Aitken
1988-10-1-3

In some ways an English counterpart to the print above, presenting a total view of the Jacobin Republic, and employing some of the same symbolism to the opposite effect. At the same time it strikes a blow at Charles James Fox ('Citizen REYNARD'), who is shown on the left observing France through a 'False MIRROR' at the behest of the Devil, while John Bull ('The Plain and Honest') looks through a 'True MIRROR' and sees the 'most abominable outrage against Religion, Law and Humanity'. The Tree of Liberty with its malign fruit, Revenge, Extortion, Plunder, etc., derives from popular prints showing the Tree of the Knowledge of Good and Evil.

ANON.

125 *The Execution of the Famous Brissot*

etching, 176 × 248 mm, pub. 20 Nov. 1793 by I. Evans
1956-8-14-3

This crude print is of the type that was often produced rapidly for insertion in periodicals like the *Gentleman's Magazine* as a supplement to a news report. Evans appears to have been a specialist in this genre. The execution of

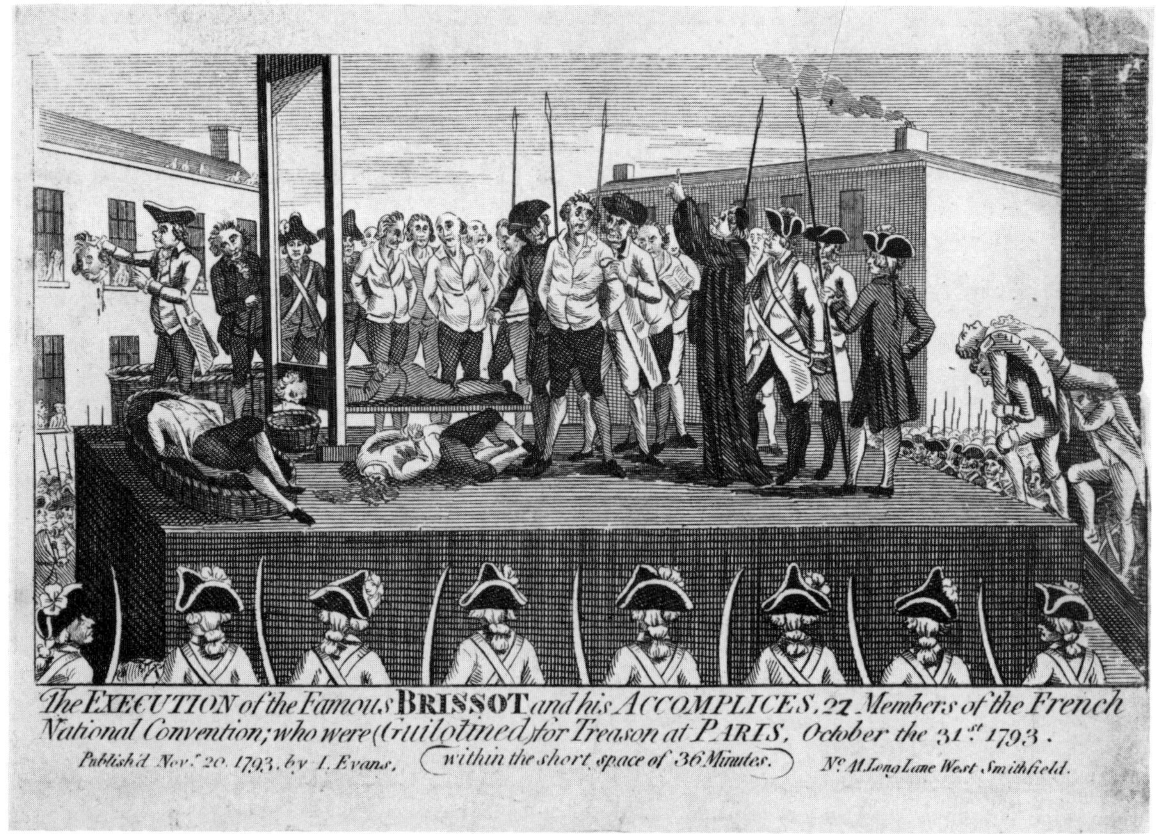

125

the Girondin deputies in the Convention, or Brissotins as they were usually known in England, meant the final destruction of the liberal opposition to the Montagnards who had seized power from them on the *journée* of 2 June 1793. The execution of the Girondins was followed rapidly by those of other sympathisers, like Philippe Egalité on 7 November, Madame Roland the next day, and Bailly, the first Mayor of Paris, on 11 November. The brutal dispatch of Robespierre's political opponents in the Convention became, even after the fall of Robespierre in July 1794, the principal example raised by British loyalists of the horrifying consequences for Britain which would follow from a successful French invasion.

The Republican martyr: the death of Marat, 13 July 1793

Jean-Paul Marat, the radical journalist, belonged to the Montagnard wing of the Convention in the period after the death of Louis XVI and was notorious for his strident denunciations of the Girondins. He was assassinated in his bath, which he used to relieve a skin disease, by Charlotte Corday, a Norman Girondin sympathiser, on 13 July 1793. She was guillotined herself after a trial on 17 July, and her composure and beauty brought forth instantly in England extravagant comparisons with the heroines of myth.

For English caricaturists Marat was, of course, the blackest of demons, and Charlotte Corday in the line of biblical heroines who had similarly disposed of tyrants. She remained a figure of unique glamour through the nineteenth century. In France, on the other hand, Marat instantly became the object of a cult, initially organised by Jacques-Louis David, who was responsible for the elaborately staged funeral ceremony and the celebrated painting of his death which hung in the Convention (Brussels, Musées Royaux des Beaux Arts). He was joined by other martyrs to the Revolution like Lepeletier de Saint-Fargeau and the boy Barra. Marat's glorified image was a presence in all the institutions and courts in the period before the fall of Robespierre, as well as in popular prints and propaganda, and correspondingly an object of execration after it.

Marat himself had interesting English connections: he had trained as a doctor in St Andrews and had practised in Newcastle in the 1770s where he may have come into contact with radical circles and possibly have known Thomas Spence (see nos 205–6). When he came to London in the early 1780s, according to Farington (27 October 1793 and 6 December 1793), he lodged, along with the painter William Hamilton, in the house of the painter Antonio Zucchi (see no. 136). 'He was called Doctor Marat, and never professed himself to be in any but the *Physical line*.' It appears that Marat boasted to Brissot (see his *Memoirs*, I, p. 336, and no. 125 above), of having seduced Angelica Kauffmann who married Zucchi on 14 July 1781 (P. Walch, 'Angelica Kauffmann', Ph.D. thesis, Princeton University, 1968, p. 76). Farington (27 October 1793) notes that Marat accompanied Zucchi on visits to Angelica while Zucchi was courting her. D. M. Meyer (*Angelica Kauffmann*, London, 1972) reproduces a copy of Marat's *Découvertes sur le feu, l'électricité et la lumière*, 1779, inscribed by the author in Italian to Angelica.

JACQUES-LOUIS DAVID, ENGRAVED BY J. L. COPIA

126 *Head of Marat, taken shortly after death*

etching and engraving, 380 × 317 mm
1898-5-27-289; presented by Monsieur F. Chèvremont
INSCRIBED 'A Marat l'ami du peuple David. Ne pouvant me corrompre, ils m'ont assassiné.'
LITERATURE de V 5313; Carnavalet 1977, no. 220

Copied from a drawing by David in the Musée de Versailles. This print, like David's famous painting in Brussels of *The Death of Marat*, was part of the attempt by the Convention under Robespierre, of which David himself was a prominent member, to elevate Marat as a martyr and victim of faction and royalism. This print belongs to a collection of 294 portraits of Marat that was presented to the British Museum in 1898 by F. Chèvremont, who had published it in his *Marat, index du bibliophile et de l'amateur de peintures, gravures . . .*, Paris, 1876. The collection also contains the original copper plate for this portrait.

PHILIPPE CURTIUS OR MADAME TUSSAUD

127 *The Death of Marat*

wax model of head and shoulders set in tin bath, H. 1230 mm
Wookey Hole Caves
LITERATURE J. Adhémar in *Gazette des Beaux Arts*, 1978, vol. 92, p. 203

This celebrated object has been recorded in the possession of Madame Tussaud since 1803, and it is safe to assume that the moulds from which the head and shoulders were cast were brought over in 1802 from Paris. In fact the head and shoulders have been cast from the moulds up to the present day, and earlier twentieth-century photographs suggest that the bath has been replaced at least once in the present century, perhaps in imitation of an eighteenth-century type, though it is not impossible that the present version survived the fire of 1925. There are no nineteenth-century pictures of the present work known to be in existence. A reference to a full-length figure of Marat in his bath after his execution can be found in posters advertising the wax display as early as 1810 (see no. 230a): 'Marat in the agonies of Death, immediately after receiving the fatal wound'), and in the 1822 Manchester Tussaud catalogue it was placed with the equally celebrated wax heads of Robespierre and others (see no. 225) in a separate room, now described as having been 'Taken immediately after his Assassination, by order of the National Assembly'. In her *Memoirs*, London, 1838, pp. 340–1, Madame Tussaud claims that she 'was brought to the scene of action a short time after it had happened, and took the cast from the demon's features, some gens d'armes attending her to keep off the crowd', but this account must be looked upon with suspicion. Even so there is every reason to suppose that the mould of the head

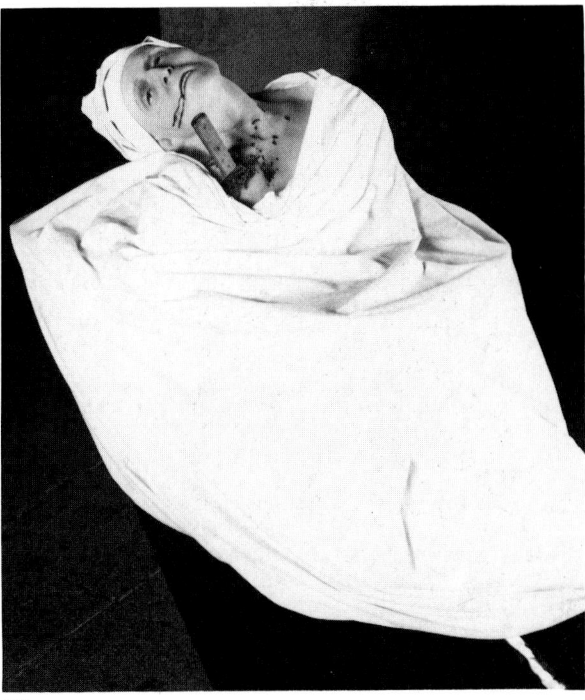

127

and shoulders is contemporary, and that the work was made originally to commemorate Marat's death as a revolutionary martyr, and displayed shortly afterwards in Curtius's waxworks. Though it has been claimed that it acted as a model for Jacques-Louis David's *Death of Marat* painting (Brussels Museum), it is more likely, as Adhémar suggests, that it derives partly from the painting. Adhémar (1978, p. 213) has tentatively attributed to Madame Tussaud an image of Marat writing, which was displayed underneath the Place du Carrousel shortly after his death. As Curtius was still alive at the time of Marat's death, he might have modelled the present piece rather than his niece. Dickens in *All the Year Round*, 7 January 1860, p. 253, mentions the present figure in his account of the visit to the Chamber of Horrors: 'What shall be said of the man who could stand at the door of the Chamber of Horrors *eating a pork pie*? Yet such a man there was – your Eye-witness saw him; a young man from the provinces; a young man with light hair, a bright blue neckcloth, and a red and beef neck. His eye was on the model of Marat, assassinated in a bath, and with this before him he could eat an underdone pork pie'.

P-M. ALIX AFTER GARNERAY

128 *Jean Paul Marat*

colour aquatint, 378 × 278 mm, pub. 1793–4 by Drouhin
1898-5-27-21; presented by Monsieur F. Chèvremont
LITERATURE *Fonds Français*, I, Alix no. 44

From the *Collection des Grands Hommes* by Garneray, a pupil of David, along with Lepeletier de Saint-Fargeau and (curiously) Charlotte Corday. The print of Marat was finished in January 1794. It is a particularly fine example of the many prints that were produced under Robespierre of revolutionary martyrs.

D. PELLEGRINI, ENGRAVED BY N. SCHIAVONETTI

129 *The Death of John Paul Marat*

stipple engraving, 383 × 300 mm, pub. 10 Feb. 1794 by Colnaghi
1988-12-10-1; presented by David Alexander
LITERATURE de V 5295

The news of the assassination of Marat reached England by 22 July and Charlotte Corday became an instant celebrity, but the fact that Marat was stabbed in his bath seems not to have been universally known at the time, though Gillray mentions it in the title to no. 132. In this version Marat is stabbed on an elegant sofa, and in Cruikshank's print (no. 130) apparently on the floor.

ISAAC CRUIKSHANK

130 *A Second Jean D'Arc or the Assassination of Marat by Charlotte Corde of Caen in Normandy on Sunday July 14 1793*

etching, coloured, 246 × 350 mm, pub. 26 July 1793 by S. W. Fores
1851-9-1-657; Smith Collection
LITERATURE BMC 8335

Here Charlotte Corday, to whom was attributed not only heroism in the highest degree but also compelling beauty, is identified with Joan of Arc.

(illus. in colour)

131 *Pottery figure group, 'The Assassination of Marat, by Charlotte Corde, of Caen, in Normandy 1793'*

lead-glazed earthenware, decorated in overglaze colours, impressed LAKIN & POOLE, H. 345 mm
Lent by Fitzwilliam Museum, Cambridge, Glaisher Collection, no. 939
LITERATURE G. W. and F. A. Rhead, *Staffordshire Pots and Potters*, London, n.d., illus. p. 266; B. Rackham, *Catalogue of the Glaisher Collection of Pottery and Porcelain in the Fitzwilliam Museum*, Cambridge, 1935, no. 939, pl. 66A

Surprisingly this delicate and touching object seems to be based on Cruikshank's rather inept caricature (no. 130).

The group is inscribed on the 'marbled' plinth 'The Assassination of MARAT, by CHARLOTTE. CORDE, of Caen, in Normandy. 1793'. It is adapted from the previous print (no. 130), was made at Thomas Lakin and Robert Poole's factory at Burslem, Staffordshire, and is one of the most

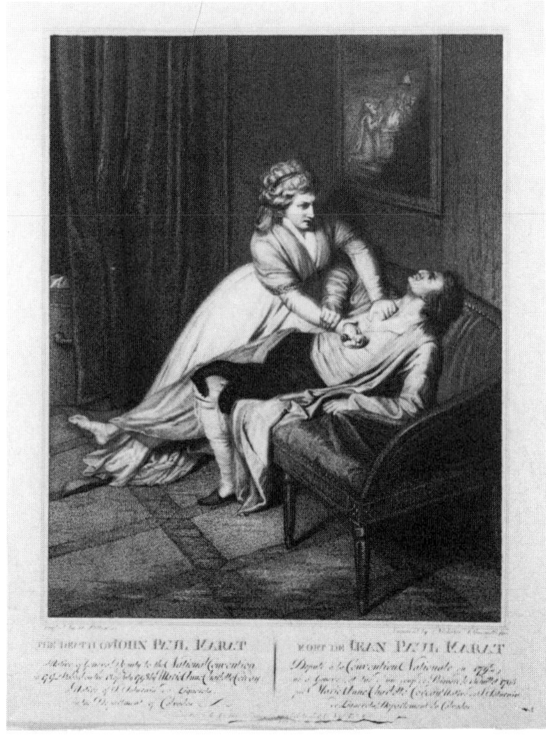

129

dramatic of all English pottery figure groups. There is a damaged example in the Hanley Museum, Stoke-on-Trent. A pottery bust of Charlotte Corday was also made by an unknown factory, after an engraving by J. J. Hinchcliffe after D-A. Raffet of Corday on her way to execution. AD

JAMES GILLRAY

132 *The heroic Charlotte la Corde, upon her trial, at the bar of the Revolutionary Tribunal of Paris, July 17th 1793*

etching, coloured, 310 × 358 mm, pub. 29 July 1793 by H. Humphrey
1868-8-8-6304
LITERATURE BMC 8336

A characteristically extreme Gillray view of Charlotte Corday's trial, in which she is presented as the biblical Judith ridding her country of a tyrant, facing a brutish judge and jury with judicial wigs under their hats and bonnets. The body of Marat, with leprous skin, lying on a bed may, as Mrs George suggests, be a satirical reference to Marat's funeral ceremony.

Down down to Hell & say A Female Arm has made one bold attempt to free her Country
A Second Jean D'Arc or the Assassination of MARAT by Charlotte Cordé of Caen in Normandy on Sunday July 14 1793.

130

The Assassination of MARAT.
by CHARLOTTE. CORDE.
of Caen, in Normandy.
1793

131

The heroic Charlotte la Cordé, upon her Trial, at the bar of the Revolutionary Tribunal of Paris, July 17th 1793. for having rid the World of that monster of Atheism and Murder the Regicide MARAT, whom she Stabbed in a bath, where he had retired on account of a Leprosy, with which, Heaven had begun the punishment of his Crimes.
"The noble enthusiasm with which this Woman met the charge, & the elevated disdain with which she treated the self created Tribunal, struck the whole assembly with terror & astonishment."

132

The fate of Marie Antoinette and the royal family

Marie Antoinette was an inevitable victim of the new atmosphere to prevail in France in the months after the Montagnard triumph of June 1793. Under threat from all sides – Britain and its allies, the revolt in the Vendée and pressure for dramatic results from the sans-culottes – almost anybody, even the most committed Montagnards, could fall under suspicion of harbouring Royalist sympathies or promoting counter-revolution by their actions. 'La veuve Capet' had often been accused of inciting her weak-willed husband to covert rejection of the Revolution he had claimed to accept, and she was potentially the focus of Royalist attacks on the Republic.

(illus. in colour)

D. PELLEGRINI, ENGRAVED BY L. SCHIAVONETTI

133 *The Dauphin taken from his Mother*

stipple and aquatint, printed in colours, 388 × 478 mm, pub. March 1794 by Colnaghi
1988-3-5-22

This print is quite different from the version of the subject published by Bovi, perhaps also after Pellegrini, on 1 March 1795. The scene proclaims with equal force the maternal feelings of the queen and the heartlessness of the Committee which had ordered the separation in July 1793 as a prelude to moving the queen to the Conciergerie. This subject was especially popular with Victorian painters: for a surprising example see no. 234.

D. PELLEGRINI, ENGRAVED BY M. BOVI

134 *The Persecuted Queen hurried at the Dead of Night into a Common Prison*

engraving, 463 × 542 mm, pub. 1 March 1795 by M. Bovi
1917-12-8-999; Lucas Collection

On 2 August 1793 the queen was moved from the Temple to the Conciergerie to await her trial. This scene shows her entering the prison with dignity, at the moment when she was suddenly struck with terror by the barking of a mastiff. Her queenly dignity while surrounded by barbaric oppressors was also a common theme of nineteenth-century representations of Marie Antoinette.

D. PELLEGRINI, ENGRAVED BY M. BOVI

135 *The Trial of Marie Antoinette Queen of France October 14, 1793*

engraving, 470 × 542 mm, pub. Sept. 1796 by M. Bovi
1870-10-8-2928

The scene shows Marie Antoinette's dignified reply to Hébert's charge of incest with the young Dauphin: 'If I have not answered you it is because Nature refuses to answer such an incrimination made to a Mother (here the accusers appeared violently confounded) but appeal it to all mothers who may be found here present.' Marie Antoinette is shown to display common humanity as well as queenly dignity. This subject may derive from an engraving dated 1794 by the French artist Bouillon, which it closely resembles.

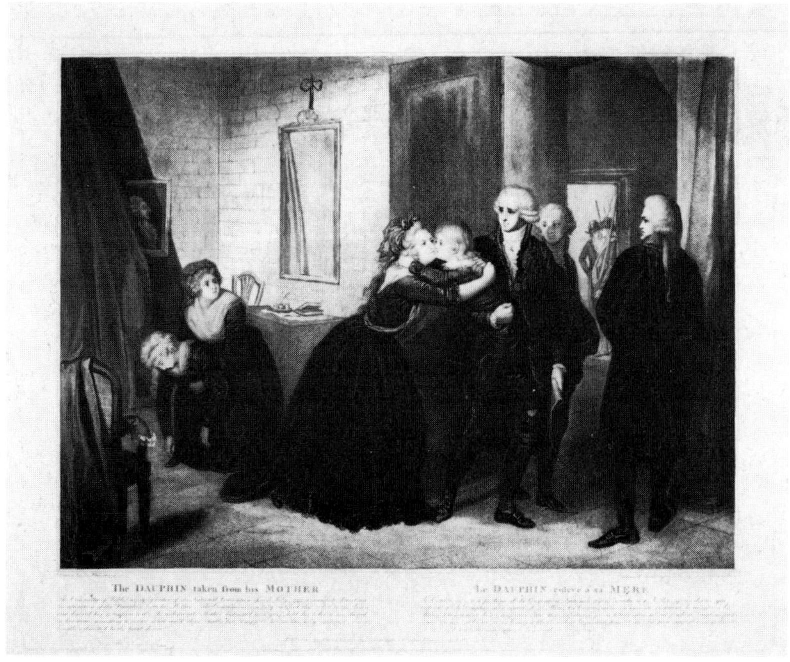

133

The PERSECUTED QUEEN hurried at the Dead of Night into a COMMON PRISON.
La REINE est trainée en PRISON au MILIEU de la NUIT.

134

THE TRIAL OF MARIE ANTOINETTE QUEEN OF FRANCE OCTOBER 14.1793.
PROCES DE MARIE ANTOINETTE REINE DE FRANCE OCTOBER 14.1793

135

136

WILLIAM HAMILTON

136 *Marie Antoinette leaving the Conciergerie*

oil on canvas
1970 × 1520 mm
Lent by Sutton Place Foundation

Perhaps the most impressive British painting of a French Revolution subject to have survived from the period. It shows Marie Antoinette as a Christian martyr accompanied by a priest, leaving the Conciergerie on the way to execution on 16 October 1793. It was engraved and published by Anthony Cardon in 1800. Though Marie Antoinette is confronted by soldiers of the Guard and ordinary people, there is no more than a hint of caricature in the faces, especially if compared to Zoffany's more obviously Hogarthian painting of the invasion of the Tuileries (see no. 46). The dramatic isolation of Marie Antoinette is achieved by the luminosity of her white dress against the darker tones which surround her, and the figures are slightly elongated in the manner of Fuseli (see no. 159). The scale and historical style of the painting resemble paintings made for the Boydell Shakespeare Gallery, to which Hamilton was a prominent contributor.

Hamilton appears not to have been a sympathiser with the French Revolution but he was well known to have been, by chance, a close acquaintance in his youth in the 1770s of Jean-Paul Marat (see p. 146), at that time practising in London as a physician. According to Farington (27 October 1793, p. 74), who knew Hamilton well, Marat lodged with Hamilton's master Antonio Zucchi about 1775, borrowed money from him, and suggested classical subjects for him to paint. Hamilton clearly dined out on his knowledge of Marat in the years of the latter's notoriety.

CONRAD HEINRICH KÜCHLER

137 *Medal, Execution of Marie Antoinette, 1793*

silver and copper, 48.5 mm
M2593 and M2594
LITERATURE Pollard 1970

Küchler was already working on this medal in December 1793 and had finished the dies by 27 March 1794. Like those for the Last Interview and the Execution of Louis XVI this was a joint speculation by Boulton and Küchler.

MJ

137

139

141

ANON.

138 *The Unfortunate Marie Antoinette Queen of France at the place of Execution, October 16th, 1793*

mezzotint, 352 × 250 mm, pub. 12 Dec. 1793 by J. Fairburn
1871-8-12-5267
LITERATURE BMC 8354

Though crude in execution, this anonymous print is a good example of the kind of reportage which conveyed a picture of events in France shortly after they happened. It conveys the idea of Marie Antoinette's queenly nobility and composure at the end, as if to obliterate the scurrility with which she had been treated in former years by caricaturists.

139 *Medal, Execution of Marie Antoinette, 1793*

tin, 33 mm
1928-8-13-13; presented by H. Garside

Probably engraved by William Mainwaring as a sequel to his medal for the Execution of Louis XVI (no. 122). MJ

140

CHEVALIER OR CAROLINE DE RIGNY, ENGRAVED BY BARTOLOZZI (AND MOLTENO?)

140 *Helas Voyés*

mezzotint, coloured and colour printed, 488 × 333 mm, pub. 26 Oct. 1794 by Anthony Molteno
1988-12-10-2; presented by David Alexander

The Chevalier de Rigny exhibited landscapes and portraits at the Royal Academy in 1795–9. A Caroline de Rigny was also active at this time and author of a print also engraved by Bartolozzi, *Il ne leur reste, que l'espérance* (pub. 7 Feb. 1796, BM 1917-12-6-1895). The Princess Elizabeth was Louis XVI's younger sister and was kept with the rest of the royal family in the Temple. She was particularly close to the *émigré* Comte d'Artois and this was the ostensible reason behind her execution on 10 May 1794. She is seen raising the curtain on urns containing the ashes of Louis XVI and Marie Antoinette; her own urn is set discreetly behind them. This print is a typical *émigré* production, and is dedicated to Charles IV of Spain by 'two Emigrant French Gentlemen' (see p. 35).

141 *Medal, Louis XVII, 1793*

tin, 32 mm
M9000
LITERATURE William Frazer, 'The medallists of Ireland and their work. No. 1 – the Mossops', *Journal of the Royal Historical and Archaeological Association of Ireland*, VII (1886), p. 450

The obverse of this medal, which like nos 100 and 139 is probably by Mainwaring, reads 'Louis XVII Roi de France', while the reverse confusingly comments 'Si tôt/ qu'il hait un roi/doit on cesser de l'être?' over the date 1793. MJ

WILLIAM HAMILTON, ENGRAVED BY C. LASINIO

142 *Apotheosis* (of the Dauphin)

engraving, 555 × 410 mm, pub. 21 Jan. 1799 by W. Dickenson
1875-7-10-560

The Dauphin, who died on 8 June 1795, is shown receiving his first glimpse of his deceased family in heaven, above the city of Paris. The small child on Marie Antoinette's lap is presumably the earlier Dauphin who died in 1781, while Princess Elizabeth, guillotined on 10 May 1794, receives the martyr's crown. There is another

142

144

version of the same subject, entitled *L'heureuse Réunion*, by L. Schiavonetti after D. Pellegrini, published on 2 January 1800 (see *Louis XVI et son image*, 1986).

143 *Prattware jug, moulded with portraits of the Duke of York (once identified as Lafayette) on one side, and Louis XVI, Marie Antoinette and the Dauphin on the other*

pearlware, coloured underglaze enamels (orange, olive green, brown, blue), H. 188 mm
Lent by Victoria and Albert Museum, C. 63-1952
LITERATURE Lewis 1984, pp. 129–30

The portrait has been identified as Frederick Augustus, Duke of York (1763–1827) after an engraving by I. Pass. The original naming of the portrait as Lafayette may have been done for the North American market. AD

144 *Prattware plaque moulded with portraits of Louis XVI, Marie Antoinette and the Dauphin in profile*

pearlware, coloured underglaze enamels (blue, green, yellow, brown), H. 261 mm
Lent by Harris Museum and Art Gallery, Preston, no. 229 (H393)
LITERATURE S. H. Pavière, *Catalogue of the Houghton Bequest of English Pottery*, Preston, 1929, no. 229; Lewis 1984, pp. 131–2

This group portrait, based on a medal by B. Duvivier struck to celebrate the birth of the Dauphin in 1781 with the child's head added, is known as 'the Royal Sufferers' from a jug sold in 1971 pencilled with this title (probably by its one-time owner). AD

145 *Mug printed in blue with 'A New Puzzle of Portraits'*

pearlware, probably Staffordshire, H. 90 mm
Pot. Cat. H. 60
LITERATURE *Pot. Cat.* H. 60

The 'puzzle' consists of (left) emblems of the British crown: a rose, a thistle, and the royal crown resting on an architectural structure; and (right) emblems of the French throne: tangled roots, a fleur-de-lis, a broken crown and sceptre. Inscribed below 'Striking Likeness[es] of the King & Queen of England and the late King & Queen of France'. The handle is printed with a stylised floral design.

The design derives from an engraving published by Orme on 18 January 1794 (Banks Collection J 11-126).

AD

145

Left Engraving pub. by Orme, 18 Jan. 1794 (Banks Collection J 11-126).

ANTOINE, ENGRAVED BY F. JUKES

146 *Arrival of the Princess Maria Theresa Charlotte Daughter of Lewis XVI, at Basle Decr 26th 1795*

etching and aquatint, 294 × 366 mm, pub. 23 March 1796 by Chr. de Mechel of Basle
1925-6-15-132

This poignant image shows the freeing of the one royal prisoner in the Temple to survive, Louis XVI's daughter and the Dauphin's elder sister, the Princess Marie-Thérèse Charlotte, later Duchess of Angoulême. She and her entourage were freed in exchange for French deputies and ministers held in Germany. She was married in 1799 to her cousin, the Duke of Angoulême, and lived on until 1851, courted incessantly by false Dauphins claiming to have escaped from the Temple. Her memoirs, the most convincing account of the last days of the royal family in the Temple, were first published in England by John Murray in 1817. This print seems to have been a speculation by a Swiss publisher from Basle, where the exchange took place.

Life under the Terror, November 1793–July 1794

W. DENT

147 *The French Feast of Reason, Or The Cloven-foot Triumphant. Nov 10, 1793*

etching, coloured, 270 × 368 mm, pub. 5 Dec. 1793
Lent by Andrew Edmunds
LITERATURE BMC 8350

Despite the grotesque caricature Dent's print shows knowledge of the ceremony held on 10 August 1793 (the anniversary of the attack on the Tuileries, one of the great *journées*), to deconsecrate Notre Dame in the presence of members of the Convention and establish it as a Temple of Reason. In the real ceremony Liberty was played by a well-known singer. The ceremony was part of a series of events held on the same day to celebrate the promulgation of the constitution of l'an I. Such *fêtes révolutionnaires* had been held in France since the Fête de la Fédération, and were to culminate in the Fête of the Supreme Being on the Champ de Mars on 8 June 1794, presided over by Robespierre. Though the details of such *fêtes* were well known in England, they rarely attracted the attention of caricaturists.

Drawn by Juleau. Engraved by Francois Jules.

ARRIVAL of the PRINCESS MARIA THERESA CHARLOTTE Daughter of LEWIS XVI. at BASLE Dec. 26th 1795

To be exchanged for the Deputies and French Ministers, Prisoners in Germany, in all 21 Persons including Servants. This Princess Born 19 Dec. 1778, left Paris 19 Dec. 1795 at 4 o'Clock in the Morning, accompanied by Madame de Soucy, Daughter of Madame de Mackau, Governess to the Royal Children, her Son Mr. Hue, formerly Valet de Chambre to Lewis 16th, a Captain of Cavalry, an Old Femme de Chambre, and Caron a Footman. She was delivered by Mr. Bacher, first Secretary to the French Ambassador in Switzerland & a Commissioner named for this exchange to the Prince de Gavres, & Mr. Le Baron Degelmann the Imperial Minister in Switzerland, both of whom had been previously named for this purpose by His Imperial Majesty. After which Mr. Le Baron de Degelmann remitted a discharge to Mr. Bacher, the French Prisoners were immediately set at Liberty & the Princess pursued her Journey to Vienna.

London, Published March 29, 1796, by Chr. de Mechel, of Basle in Switzerland to be had of his Agent C. Geisweiler No. 9 Jermyn Street St. James's.

146

CONTRAST this with HAPPY ENGLAND Where a Man may serve God without offending his neighbours and where Religion and Law secure real Peace and true Liberty

NO RELIGION

Death is only eternal Sleep

TORCH or VOLCANO of TRUTH Diffusing the LIGHT of REASON to the Surrounding Departments

PANDORA'S BOX

CHURCH PROPERTY

The French Feast of Reason, Or The Cloven-foot Triumphant. Nov. 10 1793. The People of Paris, supported by a Decree of the Convention, having resolved to abolish all Religious Ceremonies whatever, all Priesthood — and to acknowledge none but the God of Nature — the ceremony took place in the ci devant Church of Notre Dame now called the Temple of Reason where they placed a Woman in the dress of Liberty and worshiped her as their Divinity — of which the above Print is, tho' a satyrical, a just representation, for however pleasing the Figure and Decrees of those Hypocritical Monsters might appear there unblinded by enthusiasm could view them in no other light than they are here too truly delineated.

147

148 *Beau*

ISAAC CRUIKSHANK

148 *A Republican Beau and Belle. A Picture of Paris for 1794*

2 etchings, coloured, 250 × 175 mm and 250 × 173 mm, pub. 10 March 1794 by S. W. Fores
1868-8-8-6342 and 1851-9-1-677; Smith Collection
LITERATURE BMC 8435-6

A satire based upon fashion plates of the period, showing sans-culottes now given the guillotine as an attribute. It is in the background of the *Beau* and worn as fetching jewellery by the *Belle*, and there are explicit references to the cult of Reason. Striped trousers, as worn by the *Beau*, were a feature of sans-culotte dress.

J. SAYERS (*illus. p. 47*)

149 *Illustrious Heads designed for a new History of Republicanism in French & English dedicated to the Opposition*

volume of etchings, with additional slip of *bonnet rouge*, hand coloured, 210 × 177 mm (approx.), pub. 12 May 1794 by H. Humphrey
Y 10-1; Banks Collection (album 298 d 3*)

This bizarre volume consists of a frontispiece and eight portrait etchings of members of the Whig Opposition, but they are all captioned with the names of French revolutionary leaders. In the prints shown the head of Fox is given the name Robespierre, and the Duke of Grafton, a

148 *Belle*

descendant of Charles I, that of '[Philippe] Egalité ci devant noble', for his support of a peace treaty with France. In addition purchasers of the volume were given a slip with a *bonnet rouge* to place on the heads in accordance with the instruction of the satyr on the title-page 'If the Cap fit put it on'. At the end of the title is the note 'NB The Work will not be compleat till all the heads are taken off'. The other portraits are Sheridan as Barère, Earl Stanhope as Anacharsis Cloots 'l'Orateur du Genre humain', Lauderdale as Brissot, Courtenay as Desmoulins, Philip Francis as Philippeaux and Lansdowne as Chauvelin.

T. SNAGG, ENGRAVED BY PETER MAZELL

150 *The Prison of the Orphalins at Arras with English prisoners in 1794*

engraving, 380 × 522 mm, pub. 5 Nov. 1802 by Peter Mazell
1850-2-11-58
INSCRIBED 'To the Friends of Freedom and to the English who were imprisoned during the French Revolution: This Plate is most humbly dedicated by their obedient servants Thos. Snagg & Peter Mazell'

Thomas Snagg (1746–1812) was an Irish painter, and Peter Mazell a minor professional engraver who worked in London in the late eighteenth century. The detention of these British prisoners was presumably a consequence of

150

Saint-Just's decree of 26 February 1794 (8 Ventose, l'an II) to allow the confiscation of the property of suspects in favour of the poor. At the same time the power of identifying suspects had been devolved to local communities, in this case Arras, and there was a tendency, in the nervous and faction-ridden days of early 1794, to see all foreigners as suspects. It was in this period that foreign sympathisers like Tom Paine and Helen Maria Williams were imprisoned under threat of execution.

RICHARD NEWTON *(151a illus. in colour)*

151 *Desmoulins in Prison*

(a) pen and watercolour, 252 × 284 mm
1871-8-12-1675
(b) etching on broadside, 546 × 350 mm, pub. 10 June 1795 by W. Holland
1948-2-14-377

In both watercolour and etching Camille Desmoulins is seen as the very embodiment of aristocratic sensibility, looking through the bars of his cell towards nature and weeping for his beloved. In the watercolour a brutish sans-culotte guard looks on with hatred. The letters referred to in the broadside were written by Desmoulins to his wife Lucile before he was guillotined on 5 April 1794 after his denunciation by Saint-Just. Lucile herself was guillotined a week later. Despite the touchingly romantic quality of his letters Desmoulins hardly fits the stereotype of innocent victim of Jacobin cruelty which Newton has created. He was perhaps the best journalist of the revolutionary period, and from the start he leaned towards the radical wing of the movement that became the Montagnards and he was close to Danton. He voted for the death of the king but had little stomach for the use of the guillotine on the Girondins and as an 'indulgent' argued for humane treatment of the opposition and the general release of prisoners in early 1794.

151a

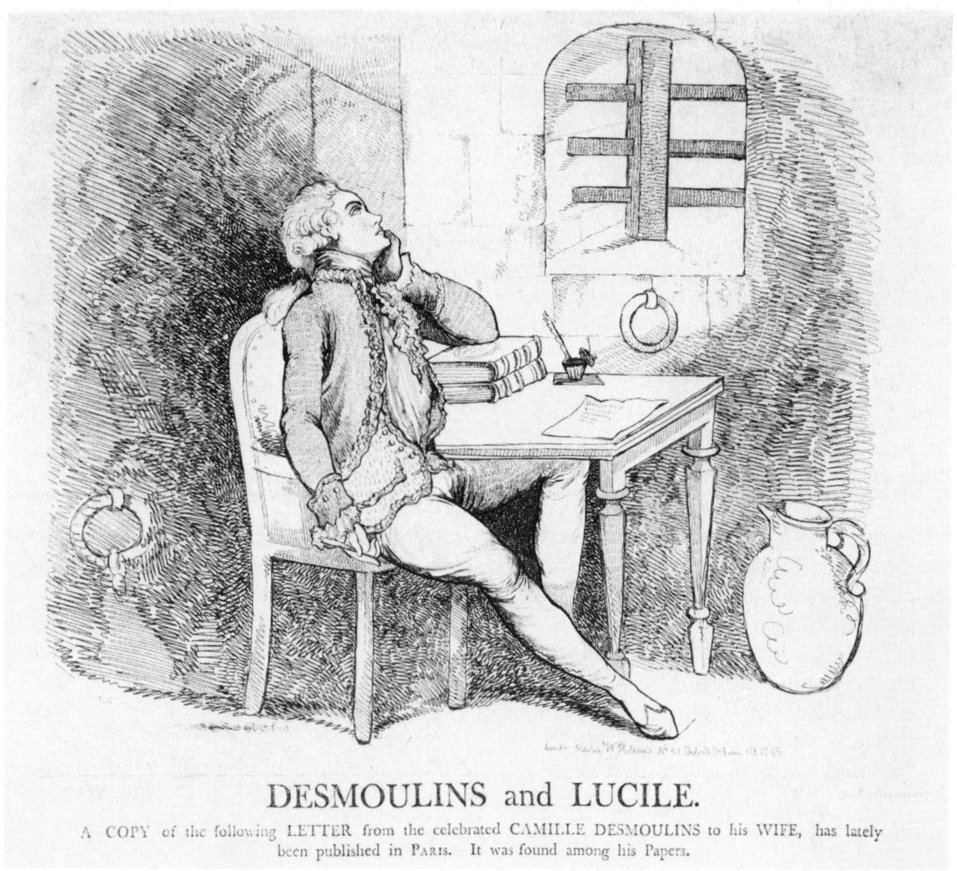
DESMOULINS and LUCILE.
A COPY of the following LETTER from the celebrated CAMILLE DESMOULINS to his WIFE, has lately been published in PARIS. It was found among his Papers.
151b

152

G. P. BARBIER, ENGRAVED BY MICHAEL SLOANE

152 *Apprehension of Roberspierre* [*sic*] *July 27. 1794*

engraving, 521 × 640 mm, pub. 1 April 1796 by Colnaghi
1870-10-8-2930

The scene is the final apprehension of Robespierre on 27 July 1794 (9 Thermidor) in the Hôtel de Ville, where he had fled after being refused permission to address the Convention. He had apparently hoped to gather forces for his defence in the Hôtel de Ville, but troops loyal to the Convention were able to break in, and in a scuffle he was shot in the jaw but not fatally (see the wound on Madame Tussaud's wax head, no. 225). He and his supporters were guillotined the next day, and with his death ended the phase of government known as the Terror, though France continued, under the Thermidorean regime and the Directory which followed, to be a Republic based on revolutionary principles. G. P. Barbier was a painter of French origin who exhibited at the Royal Academy, 1792–5 (Waterhouse 1981).

The Committee of Public Safety hits back: French caricatures of the British in Year II

The invitation by the Committee of Public Safety to Jacques-Louis David in September 1793 to produce caricatures which would 'awaken public sentiment and reveal the turpitude and absurdity of the enemies of liberty and the Republic' may be seen as a back-handed compliment to Gillray and other British caricaturists. Gillray's caricatures, though not designed for the French market at all, were undoubtedly known in France, and their value in awakening public sentiment in England would have been evident. A great many caricatures of English leaders were produced in France dating from the first Continental campaign under the Duke of York, of the Duke himself, of Pitt, who was declared by the Convention in August 1793 to be 'the enemy of the human race', and of George III and his family.

The caricatures in this section were all commissioned by the Committee of Public Safety under Carnot, and were placed under the general supervision of Jacques-Louis David, the most highly placed artist in the government and a supporter of Robespierre. (See Hould in Vovelle 1988, pp. 29–37.)

ANTOINE-DENIS CHAUDET

153 *Le Charlatan Politique ou le Léopard Apprivoisé* ('The political charlatan or the leopard tamed')

etching, coloured, 480 × 595 mm
1861-10-12-157; H. W. Martin Collection
LITERATURE de V 4388; Hould in Vovelle 1988, pp. 31, 37

On 27 March 1794 (7 Germinal) the Committee of Public Safety bought from Chaudet, best known as a sculptor, a number of examples of his print representing 'British power as a ridiculous structure on the point of collapse, under the emblem of a tamed leopard, ridden by George's family and directed by Pitt'.

DUBOIS

154 *La Grande Aiguiserie Royale de Poignards Anglais* ('The great royal grindstone for English daggers')

etching, coloured, 364 × 544 mm
1861-10-12-168; H. W. Martin Collection
INSCRIBED 'Le fameux Pitt aiguisant les poignards avec lesquels il veut faire assassiner les defenseurs de la liberté du peuple, le gros Georges Dandin tournant la roue, en chien remouleur' ('The famous Pitt sharpens the daggers with which he proposes to assassinate the defenders of the people's liberty, fat George Turkey turns the wheel in the dog grinder').
LITERATURE BMC 8464; de V 4386; Hould in Vovelle 1988, pp. 33, 37

153

EXPLICATION.
Nº 1. George Roi d'Angleterre commande en personne l'élite de son Armée Royal-Cruche Nº 2. Il est conduit par son Ministre Pitt ou Milor Dindon Nº 3 qui le tient par le Nez pour mieux lui prouver son attachement. L'avant-Garde de la Royal Armée Nº 4. reçoit un échec à la porte de la Ville Nº 5. qui est occasioné par la colique de quelques Sans-Culottes placés au haut de la Porte Nº 6. L'avant-Garde dans sa défaite brise les cruches, dont il ne sort que toutes sortes de Bêtes venimeuses Nº 7. qui est l'esprit qui les anime. Fox ou Milord Oie Nº 8 ferme la marche monté sur sa Trompette Angloise et qui témoin de l'échec sonne un rappel en arrière par prudence. Artillerie Angloise nouvelle Nº 9. qui a la vertu d'éteindre les incendies et de délater les fortifications.

155a

Nº 1. Gouvernement Anglois
EXPLICATION.
Nº 2. l'Anglois né Libre.
Ce Gouvernement est représente sous la figure d'un Diable écorché tout vif, accaparant le Commerce et revêtu de toutes les décorations Royal, le Portrait du Roi se trouve au derriere du Gouvernement lequel vomit sur son Peuple une multitude d'impôts avec lesquelles il le foudroye. Cette prérogative est attaché au Sceptre et à la Couronne.

155b

JACQUES-LOUIS DAVID, ENGRAVED BY V. DENON?

155 (a) *'l'armée de cruches'* ('army of jugs'); (b) *'le gouvernement anglais sous la forme d'une figure horrible et chimérique'* ('The British government in the form of a wild and horrible figure')

etchings, coloured, 395 × 542 mm and 334 × 445 mm
1882-8-12-472 and 1882-8-12-471
LITERATURE BMC 8462-3; (a) Vovelle 1986, II, no. 337; Hould in Vovelle 1988, pp. 31, 37

These two caricatures are unambiguously attached to the name of the great Neoclassical painter by a minute of the Committee of Public Safety of 27 March 1794 (7 Germinal), which states that David presented 'two caricatures of his composition, one showing an army of jugs, commanded by George [III], led by a turkey, the other represents the English government in the form of a wild and horrible figure, dressed in all his royal insignia'. While there is no clinching evidence of David's participation in their composition, there is no reason to doubt it either. They stand out from the others in the group in their use of excretory imagery, and the Englishness of their vulgarity may have been David's tribute to Gillray. Certainly they show a knowledge of English caricature, especially in the idea in '*Gouvernement Anglois*' of the destructive effects of taxation on the British people.

6 British artists and writers and the Revolution

This section is concerned with the work of certain artists and writers in the light of their changing attitudes towards the French Revolution. Blake, Fuseli, Barry and Romney, for example, were deeply involved in the French Revolution, yet rarely allude directly to the events of the Revolution in their work. Other artists like Thomas Banks who achieved some notoriety as 'a violent Democrat' (Farington, 16 Januarv 1794) and Thomas Girtin were assumed to have radical sympathies, but their work is hard to read in the light of their political convictions.

For many of the painters and some of the poets their responses to the French Revolution were able to coalesce around the figure of the seventeenth-century poet John Milton, who had himself lived through revolutionary times under Cromwell, and whose figure of Satan seemed to embody the ambivalence that an artist or poet must feel towards a revolution in which hope and despair were so strongly intertwined. Several artists embarked upon schemes to illustrate Milton in the 1790s, and a small group of their works is presented below with associated material bearing on their attitudes towards the Revolution.

Themes from Milton's *Paradise Lost*

Subjects from *Paradise Lost* had been attempted by painters since the 1730s, but there is a definable increase in paintings of such subjects and illustrated editions of the book in the 1790s. Milton had the reputation of a great British poet who had produced an epic to rival Homer and Virgil, but well before the French Revolution his support of the Commonwealth had attracted radical authors like Thomas Hollis, and drawn the suspicion of conservatives like Dr Johnson. The heart of the matter was the character of Satan whose heroic defiance of the Almighty could be taken as a model of resistance to a distant and arbitrary power and of the necessity to destroy the old order. The French Revolution, especially as it passed beyond the stage when English radicals could regard it as a new dawn for humanity, began to appear even more Miltonic, as destruction, chaos and envy seemed to attend it as they did Satan in his travels across the universe. Milton could be seen, depending upon one's degree of revolutionary commitment, as a prophet of Revolution, who had foreseen its inevitable collapse into tyranny, or alternatively had witnessed its hard and painful progress before it could achieve its aims.

JAMES BARRY

156 *Satan and his Legions hurling defiance toward the Vault of Heaven, Paradise Lost,* Book 1, 615

pen, ink and black chalk, 689 × 494 mm, *c.* 1792–5
1868-6-12-2143
SIGNED J. Barry RA PP [Professor of Painting]

> But he who reigns
> Monarch in Heav'n, till then as one secure
> Sat on his Throne, upheld by old repute,
> Consent or custom, and his Regal State
> Put forth at full, but still his strength conceal'd
> Which tempted our attempt, and wrought our fall.
> Henceforth his might we know, and know our own
> So as not either to provoke, or dread
> New warr, provok't; (637–645)

LITERATURE Pressly 1981, D48; Pressly, *Barry* cat., no. 49

Satan's defiance of the Almighty is here seen at its most heroic, as he rises from defeat to rally his legions for battle. He is conceived of by Barry as a figure of sublime strength in the mould of Michelangelo, 'his form had yet not lost/ All her Original brightness'. The drawing is a finished sketch for a large etching (Pressly 1981, PR25) which was the first of a series illustrating *Paradise Lost* conceived in the years 1792–5, perhaps as a challenge to Fuseli's *Milton Gallery*. Barry was undoubtedly a 'violent Democrat' in temperament who might well have identified with Milton's Satan in his hatred of the political and artistic establishment of Britain, but his Catholicism made his attitude towards the French Revolution equivocal.

156

158

HENRY FUSELI, ENGRAVED BY M. HAUGHTON *(illus. p. 71)*

157 *The Vision of the Lazar House* after Picture XXIV of the *Milton Gallery*

stipple engraving, 599 × 690 mm, pub. 10 Oct. 1813 by Moses Haughton
Lent by Victoria and Albert Museum, no. 19954

Immediately a place
Before his eyes appear'd, sad, noisome, dark,
A lazar-house it seem'd, wherein were laid
Numbers of all diseas'd, all maladies.
Demoniac phrenzy, moping melancholy,
And moon-struck madness, pining atrophy.
Marasmus [consumption] . . . . . .
Dire was the tossing, deep the groans . . .
And over them triumphant Death his dart
Shook, but delay'd to strike, though oft invok'd.
(Book XI, 477–91, Fuseli's adaptation)

LITERATURE Schiff 1963, fig. 37 (drawing for lost painting)

Despite the date of 1813 the print is after a painting by Fuseli which is known to have been completed in 1794 as no. 24 of the *Milton Gallery*. The account of the Lazar House in *Paradise Lost*, Book XI, seems to parallel Fuseli's grim account of the essential circularity of the revolutionary process as one that will eventually reproduce the tyranny it supplants (see Introduction, pp. 71–2). Here the grim scene of self-laceration under an unseeing deity is persuasive as an image of France under the Terror, but Fuseli characteristically is not explicit in his allusions to contemporary events. Blake made a monotype of the same subject in 1795 (see Butlin 1981, nos 320–2).

GEORGE ROMNEY

158 *Fall of the Rebel Angels, Paradise Lost,* Book I, 41

pencil, pen and wash drawing, 540 × 391 mm
Lent by Fitzwilliam Museum, Cambridge, BV161

Him the Almighty Power
Hurld headlong flaming from th'Ethereal Skie
With hideous ruin and combustion down
To bottomless perdition, there to dwell
In Adamantine Chains and penal Fire,
Who durst defie th'Omnipotent to Arms.
(Book I, 44)

LITERATURE Jaffé 1977, no. 114

This drawing apparently dates from 1794 or slightly later, when Romney was suffering from deep melancholy brought about by bereavement and the collapse of his hopes for the world (see Introduction, pp. 73–4). Though Satan is shown, with Adam and Eve at the Fall, as still defiant, he too must fall further, along with his Legions.

HENRY FUSELI

159 *Thor battering the Midgard Serpent*

oil on canvas, 1310 × 910 mm, 1790
Lent by Royal Academy of Arts, London
LITERATURE Schiff 1963, no. 716; *Fuseli* cat., 1975, no. 125; *Goya*, Hamburg, 1980, no. 437

Fuseli's Diploma painting for the Royal Academy in 1790 – an unusual subject taken from northern mythology, in this case the *Edda* of Soemundus, known in England from Mallet's *Northern Antiquities II*, published 1770. Schiff (1963, p. 137) has drawn attention to the element of parody, particularly in the depiction of the giant Hymir in the boat and the comic figure of Wotan in the sky. Even so the figure of Thor is undoubtedly heroic as he wrestles with the great serpent of Midgard. Siegmar Holsten (*Goya*, Hamburg, 1980, p. 452) argues persuasively that the subject should be seen in the light of Fuseli's earlier paintings of William Tell as a struggle between freedom, represented by Thor, the god of the free peasantry and defender of men against the race of giants, and the enslaving power of the sea serpent Midgard. Thor's triumph over the age-old forces of repression may in the year 1790, when Fuseli was still full of enthusiasm for the French Revolution, have contained an implicit reference to events in France.

159

160

GEORGE ROMNEY

160 *Howard in the Lazaretto*

pen and wash, 359 × 495 mm
Lent by Fitzwilliam Museum, Cambridge, BV153
LITERATURE Jaffé 1977, no. 98

Romney probably began work towards a painting of *Howard visiting a Lazaretto* in 1790, after the news came through of the great prison reformer's death in Russia. Howard was enormously admired by William Hayley, the poet, with whom Romney had visited Paris in the months after the Fédération of 14 July 1790 (see p. 73). Howard is shown as a Jesus-like figure among the tormented victims, and the scene evokes all forms of incarceration, physical and spiritual. In the many drawings Romney made of Howard in the lazaretto he often showed a grim figure of a gaoler, in this case a monkish figure on the right, who represents superstition and despotism in contrast to the suffering humanity of the victims. In such images Howard acts as a link between the sentimental idealism of his mentor Hayley and the spirit of liberation represented in 1790 by the fall of the Bastille (see no. 24). This triumph of compassion may be compared with Fuseli's *Lazar House* (no. 157), where agony and torment under an oppressive god are seen as the conditions of earthly existence.

William Blake and the Revolution

WILLIAM BLAKE *(illus. in colour)*

161 *Albion Rose* (also known as *Glad Day*)

engraving, colour printed 272 × 200 mm
1856-2-9-417
(INSCRIBED on later state: 'Albion rose from where he laboured at the Mill with Slaves
Giving himself for the Nations he danc'd the dance of Eternal Death.')
LITERATURE Essick, *Separate Plates*, 1983, VII, 1A

The general design is thought to have originated as a line engraving in 1780. This impression was colour printed *c.* 1794–6, perhaps to be added at the end of a copy of *Europe*. It represents in its most complete form Blake's idea of the Redemption of the soul or spirit from the prison of the body, and in the political sense the state of revolutionary consciousness. It came to stand also for Britain, of which Albion was an ancient name, after she had exultantly thrown off the shackles of physical and spiritual oppression. Albion has, in a moment of divine perception, transcended the material state and rises up in his full humanity. Such a vision of redemption transcends earthly

161

revolution: hence this design remained part of Blake's repertoire even after his loss of faith in the French Revolution.

WILLIAM BLAKE *(illus. p. 68)*

162 *America a Prophecy*

hand-printed book with 18 relief etched plates, some touched with wash, 230 × 170 mm (approx.), 1793
copy F 1953-1-1-1
LITERATURE Bentley, *Blake Books*, 1977, no. 6; reproduced in full in Bindman, *Graphic Works*, 1978, pp. 146–63

America was the first of Blake's prophecies to appear, in late 1793, and it was followed the next year by *Europe*. Blake's aim was to bring the events of the new revolutionary age, which he saw beginning with the American Revolution, into the frame of universal history, for the American and French Revolutions were, for Blake, events of transcendental importance for humanity. They represented the promise of the fulfilment of biblical prophecy, as part of the process of final Apocalypse. Blake belonged broadly to the stream of millenarianism in England in the 1790s, which with varying degrees of commitment saw the Revolution as a stage in the process which would lead to the imminent end of the world (see J. F. C. Harrison, *The Second Coming*, London, 1979).

The action of *America* begins with the outbreak of the American Revolution and the freeing of Orc, or Energy, from his chains. Orc is Blake's emblem of revolution, youthful, fiery and destructive, who, in breaking his chains, visits destruction and the hope of liberation upon the world. Like Fuseli's Thor (no. 159 above) he grappled fearlessly with the dark forces of the Old Order, but as Blake realised by 1793 his progress contained the possibility that he might replace one tyranny with another.

WILLIAM BLAKE

163 *Europe a Prophecy*

relief etching; (a) proof of title-page, 240 × 176 mm; (b) final plate, 236 × 171 mm
1936-11-16-33; 1936-11-16-39
LITERATURE Bentley, *Blake Books*, 1977, no. 333; Bindman, *Graphic Works*, 1978, no. 168

The serpent is a highly ambiguous symbol in the context of Blake's prophecies. Here it is uncoiling, ready to strike after slumber, which suggests the idea of revolution as an awakening, yet with destructive consequences. The final plate is a less hopeful image of destruction based on the Prophecy page of *America*, where a family also flees from the ruins of a city. In *Europe* this image accompanies an allegorical account of the outbreak of the French Revolution. Orc, or Energy, is frequently referred to in Blake's prophecies as a serpent by the enemies of revolution.

163a

163b

165

WILLIAM BLAKE *(illus. p. 70)*

164 *The Pope and Lucifer in Hell* (Isaiah 14: 4–12)

engraving, 188 × 252 mm, *c.* 1793–4
1966-7-23-3
LITERATURE Essick, *Separate Plates*, 1983, x, 1A; Bindman, *Graphic Works*, 1978, no. 323A

One of two known impressions of this plate, dating from *c.* 1793–4; the other, colour printed, is in the Huntington Library. It illustrates a passage from Isaiah in which the King of Babylon is warned of his fate in Hell: 'Hell from beneath is moved for thee to meet thee at thy coming: it stirreth up the dead for thee, even all the chief ones of the earth; it hath raised up from their thrones all the kings of the nations.' This passage is one of the most uncompromising prophecies in the Bible against kingship and it was often alluded to by Protestant Dissenters in the seventeenth century (see D. Bindman, 'Blake and popular religious imagery', *Burlington Magazine*, October 1986, p. 712). Essick categorises it as a political print and takes it to refer to George III.

Radical artists and authors

The following section presents a portrait gallery of some of the more important artists, authors and political thinkers to have retained an involvement in the French Revolution after the distressing events of late 1792 and 1793, and a belief that it had some positive lessons for British society. Some, like Mary Wollstonecraft and Helen Maria Williams (not represented here by a portrait), actually spent long periods in Paris under the Revolution, where they formed part of a notable colony of British *emigrés.* Others, like Wordsworth, had gone to France at critical moments in the Revolution and had become caught up in the hopes of a new universal society.

JAMES GILLRAY

165 *New Morality; – or – The promis'd Installment of the High-Priest of the Theophilanthropes, with the Homage of Leviathan and his Suite*

etching, coloured, 274 × 622 mm, pub. 1 Aug. 1798 by J. Wright or *The Anti-Jacobin Review and Magazine*
1868-8-8-6762
LITERATURE BMC 9240; Hill, *Gillray*, 1965, pp. 71, 81

This extremely complex print is an illustration for *The Anti-Jacobin Review and Magazine* accompanying a poem by George Canning, at that point Pitt's Under-Secretary for Foreign Affairs. It is a characteristically learned and derisory attack on the French Theophilanthropists in France, who, under the Directory, sought to impose a 'Religion of Nature'. The scene is of Theophilanthropical service in a deconsecrated St Paul's after a successful French invasion of Britain, with a member of the French Directory, Larevellière-Lépeaux, acting as high-priest to a congregation made up of English sympathisers who include a great many poets ('the Jacobin muse') and radical political theorists. Though omitting Wordsworth, it refers to almost all those identified by the government as dangerously susceptible to the intellectual influence of the French Revolution. The members of the congregation who offer the fruits of nature to the Supreme Being before the altar of a highly travestied Justice, Philanthropy and Sensibility also include the usual Opposition Whigs led by

166

Fox. Heading the procession, offering a cornucopia inscribed 'Cornucopia of Ignorance', are the poets Southey, Coleridge, Charles Lloyd ('Todd') and Charles Lamb ('Frog'). Also in the group are Erasmus Darwin (with a basket on his head sprouting *bonnets rouges*), Joseph Priestley and Gilbert Wakefield, both clergymen sympathetic to the French Revolution. Also alluded to, mainly in the publications emanating from the cornucopia, are Mary Wollstonecraft, Horne Tooke, Thomas Holcroft, Thomas Spence and Helen Maria Williams. The giant figure of Leviathan arising from the sea is the Duke of Bedford, a member of the Whig Opposition and the particular object of Burke's hatred, and on his head is seated Thelwall. The crocodile in front with a pair of stays is Tom Paine and next to him is Holcroft. Hill (*Gillray*, 1965, p. 72) quotes a letter from Southey, who is depicted as an ass: 'I have seen myself Bedfordized, and it has been a subject of much amusement. Holcroft's likeness is admirably preserved. I know not what poor Lamb has done to be croaking there. What I think the worst part of *The Anti-Jacobin* abuse is the lumping together men of such opposite principles.'

JOHN RAPHAEL SMITH, ENGRAVED BY W. WARD

166 *John Horne Tooke*

mezzotint (proof), 644 × 456 mm, pub. 29 May 1811
by J. R. Smith
1890-4-15-241

Horne Tooke (1736–1812) spans the history of eighteenth-century radicalism, from the metropolitan extra-parliamentary campaigns of John Wilkes in the 1760s to the Treason Trials of 1794 in which he was tried and acquitted. He was a founder of the Society of Supporters of the Bill of Rights in 1769 and in the late 1780s he was partly responsible for the revival of the Society for Constitutional Information and for its sympathetic attitude towards the French Revolution. His main interest was parliamentary reform and his gifts were as a tactician, though his skills were overtaken by events in the 1790s. At a banquet of reformers, chaired by Lord Stanhope on 14 July 1790 to celebrate the fall of the Bastille, cockades were worn and a stone from the Bastille sat in the middle of the table, but Tooke argued that a toast should be offered to the British constitution as well as the French

Revolution (Goodwin 1979, p. 123). Though a supporter of the Revolution (he kept a stone from the Bastille in his study, unfortunately not visible in the print) and reform in Britain, he was not totally opposed to the hereditary principle nor was he anti-monarchist. His contribution was to bring urbanity and organisation to the radical movement and at the same time a powerful intellect which was applied most lastingly in his philological work *The Diversions of Purley*, 1786. He was little involved in politics after his acquittal in 1794, and this print from a pastel by John Raphael Smith shows him in old age, reclining in his study, working on the third volume of *The Diversions of Purley*.

THOMAS LAWRENCE

167 *William Godwin and Thomas Holcroft at 1794 Treason Trials*

pencil, 230 × 180 mm
Private Collection
LITERATURE Garlick 1964, p. 228, no. 2; Marshall 1984, p. 139

Holcroft is in front, lightly caricatured, while Godwin rests his head on his hand behind him. The particular occasion for the drawing seems to have been the moment during the Treason Trials at the end of October, when after the acquittal of Horne Tooke and Thelwall, Holcroft was discharged without trial and immediately went to sit next to Godwin who had been his chief supporter (Marshall 1984, p. 139).

Godwin and Holcroft were intimate friends, and though the former was a political philosopher and the latter a playwright and novelist, their ideas converged in most respects. Both had been deeply stirred by the French Revolution and they had helped to publish Paine's *The Rights of Man* in 1791. They attended such famous occasions as the Revolution dinner of 4 November 1791, at which Paine and Jérome Pétion, the future Mayor of Paris (see no. 89), were present. Holcroft became a prominent member of the Society for Constitutional Information in 1792 after achieving a considerable reputation as a playwright. Neither was strictly Painite, for they rejected ideas of the 'rights of man' and a government representing the general will, in favour of 'universal benevolence' which would eventually make law and government redundant. Their drift was strongly Utopian and based upon an idea of the infinite perfectibility of man, which if not hindered by riches, rank and power, would lead to the triumph of wisdom and virtue. Such ideas are expressed in Godwin's *Enquiry concerning the Principles of Political Justice*, 1793, a book of immense influence on the literary figures who met at the publisher Joseph Johnson's and on the Wordsworth–Coleridge circle but too learned to have the

167

popular impact of Paine's works. Holcroft expressed similar ideas to Godwin in his plays and novels, and their popularity may have made him appear more dangerous to the government than the more scholarly Godwin. Godwin's most important public intervention came during the Treason Trials of October 1794 when he succeeded in discrediting the idea of 'constructive treason' in the summoning of a constitutional convention by the radicals, and this undoubtedly contributed towards their acquittal.

JOHN OPIE

168 *Mary Wollstonecraft*

oil, 759 × 638 mm
Lent by Tate Gallery, N 01167
LITERATURE *John Opie*, Arts Council, 1962–3, no. 46

Mary Wollstonecraft's involvement with the French Revolution was more immediate than any other British writer, except perhaps Wordsworth and Helen Maria Williams, for she was actually resident in France from December 1792 to early 1795 and wrote a history of the French Revolution. In 1787 she began to work for the publisher Joseph Johnson and there met Paine, Blake, Godwin and Holcroft. By 1790 she had rejected Christianity and became a believer in human perfectibility, and was one of the first into print with a reply to Burke's *Reflections* in *A Vindication of the Rights of Men*, a rationalistic attack on 'the demon of property', rank and privilege. From the start of the Revolution she looked to France, and *A Vindication of the Rights of Woman* was dedicated to Talleyrand and designed to influence the Assembly in the direction of providing full education for girls and revolutionising the status of women. She apparently had an affair with the painter Fuseli and was proposing to visit France with him, but in the event she travelled alone, arriving in Paris in December 1792. At first she was shocked by conditions in Paris and wrote to Johnson that 'the turn of the tide has left the dregs of the old system to corrupt the new', but under the influence of her Girondin friends she recovered her rationalist belief in humanity, and her volumes of *An Historical and Moral View of the Origin and Progress of the French Revolution*, though written between late 1793 and April 1794, and fully mindful of 'the base, and nefarious assassinations', still reveal a belief that 'sincerity of principles seems to be hastening the overthrow of the tremendous empire of superstition and hypocrisy, erected upon the ruins of gothic brutality and ignorance'. The painting is the lesser

168

known of two versions of the portrait (the other is National Portrait Gallery, no. 1237) by John Opie, who seemed to have known the Johnson circle well without acquiring a reputation for radicalism. According to Farington (11 November 1796) there were rumours about that he was about to marry Mary Wollstonecraft, though in the end she married William Godwin.

ROBERT HANCOCK

169

(a) *Samuel Taylor Coleridge, 1796*
(b) *Robert Southey, 1796*
(c) *William Wordsworth, 1798*
(d) *Charles Lamb, 1798*

4 drawings, pencil and wash, in one frame, 320 × 820 mm: (a) 178 × 156 mm; (b) 171 × 146 mm; (c) 165 × 140 mm; (d) 171 × 146 mm

Lent by National Portrait Gallery, nos 452, 451, 450, 449 respectively

LITERATURE Walker, *Regency Portraits*, 1985, vol. 1, pp. 118–19, 469, 571–2, 303–4

These four drawings were commissioned by the radical Bristol publisher Joseph Cottle, who later published *Early Recollections; chiefly relating to the late Samuel Taylor Coleridge, during his long residence in Bristol*, 1837. The dates given above were probably written on the back by Joseph Cottle. The artist was Robert Hancock, chiefly known as a porcelain decorator for Worcester and other factories but in the 1790s resident in Bristol. The four writers were drawn together in the later 1790s by their radicalism which in each case in later life they repudiated. Though frequently stigmatised even into the nineteenth century as Democrats, the origins of their attitude to the French Revolution were varied. The question of these origins, the depth of their commitment and its relationship to their later Toryism have been endlessly discussed by literary historians in recent years, and all that can be offered below is the briefest summary.

Of the four writers Wordsworth's commitment to the French Revolution was the most sustained and the most intense, as is revealed in *The Prelude*. Wordsworth made two visits to France: the first about the time of Fédération in July 1790 and the second between November 1791 and December 1792. On the first trip he was merely passing through on his way to Switzerland but he was caught up in the joyful atmosphere of Fédération, crossing the country in the company of returning *fédérés*. Seeing 'the whole nation mad with joy' predisposed him to sympathy with the Revolution, and his visit the next year, when he went to learn French, was decisive in converting him to the cause. Though he had an introduction to a Deputy and watched debates in the Assembly in early December 1791, his destination was Orléans. It was here that he came under the influence of the ardent revolutionary aristocrat Michel Beaupuy, and it was in his company that he

169c

experienced the exultation of 'A people risen up/Fresh as the morning star' described unforgettably in *The Prelude*. There is no doubt at all that he was firmly converted to the Revolution, and his own youthful ardour may be compared with that of the more intellectual Girondins who were still in the ascendant in France in his time in Orléans. By the time he reached Paris at the end of October 1792 he was disturbed by the atmosphere of fear after the September Massacres, and this apparently made him cling more strongly to the Girondins with whom he may have made some tentative contact. He also made friends with James Watt, the Jacobin son of the great engineer, and he appears not to have met Helen Maria Williams though carrying a letter of introduction to her. He was forced to return to England unwillingly through lack of funds in late December 1792 and was, of course, unable to get back after the outbreak of war in February 1793. He reflected later that had he stayed in France he would have 'made common cause with some who perished', and it is a striking thought that had circumstances not thwarted his intention of remaining there he might well have found himself in danger of the guillotine, as did other foreigner sympathisers like Tom Paine and Helen Maria Williams.

He returned to England, then, a revolutionary in the French mould, and he produced in early 1793 *A Letter to the Bishop of Llandaff* in reply to an attack on the French Revolution which he wisely left unpublished: the strength of his own attack upon monarchy, nobility and the war against France would have labelled him in English terms as an extreme Jacobin, though in fact he was firmly opposed to French Sansculottism. He refused to condemn the execution of Louis XVI and he rejected the 'idle cry of modish lamentation, which has resounded from the Court to the cottage'. None the less, he was disturbed by the war and the situation in France, and he seems to have been encouraged by the fall of Robespierre into believing that the Revolution could once more 'march firmly towards righteousness and peace'.

Coleridge's radicalism, by contrast, was altogether more shallow, and it first emerged in 1793 when he was still an undergraduate at Cambridge. It was at its height in the years 1794–5 when he and Southey put together the idea of Pantisocracy ('the equal government of all') which involved a Utopian scheme to set up an ideal society on the banks of the Susquehanna; and he was inclined, like his friend Thelwall, to use what he later called 'flame-coloured epithets' and condemn rank and 'that leprous stain, nobility'. Like Blake his Christianity got in the way of his admiration for the French Revolution, and his ambition in the years 1795–8 to become a Unitarian minister drew him, like others, away from support of a regime which sought to relegate Christianity to the realm of myth.

The idea of Pantisocracy seems originally to have been thought up by Southey, who was, despite his later career as Poet Laureate and government apologist, a committed Democrat before Coleridge met him in June 1794. By the time Coleridge met Wordsworth in Bristol in autumn 1795 Pantisocracy had practically been abandoned and with it, temporarily, the friendship with Southey. The two friends had, however, before the end of 1794 written a high-flown drama called *The Fall of Robespierre*, and it was Southey who introduced Coleridge to Joseph Cottle which led to their both settling in Bristol to give lectures on historical and political matters, including a whole series by Coleridge on the French Revolution, and produce journals. Charles Lamb, despite his great friendship with Coleridge in the 1790s and his appearance in Gillray's *New Morality*, was not significantly involved in the excitement about the French Revolution.

G. DANCE

170 *Thomas Banks*

pencil drawing, 305 × 242 mm, dated 8 July 1794
1898-7-12-12
LITERATURE C. F. Bell, *Annals of Thomas Banks*, Cambridge, 1938, p. 100

Thomas Banks was one of the most notable sculptors of his day and the author of some of the most prominent monuments in St Paul's; yet he was also 'a violent Democrat' (Farington, 16 January 1794), a close friend of Horne Tooke (no. 166) and a long-standing member of the Society for Constitutional Information. He was even questioned by the Privy Council in late 1794 on the suspicion of high treason, but he was released before trial. After Horne Tooke's trial in November 1794, and his subsequent release, Banks joined Tooke for a celebration dinner. Despite such ample evidence of radicalism Banks still had an important role in the Royal Academy and was able to obtain commissions for naval monuments in St Paul's. He was on perfectly friendly terms with Farington, who described him, with Smirke, another radical Royal Academician, on 16 November 1795 as 'Crops and Democrats', including also the Duke of Bedford and Fox. This alludes to the fashion at this time among the Opposition for wearing hair unpowdered and close-cropped around the skull in veiled allusion presumably to Roman republican busts, especially of Brutus. In this drawing Banks's hair is not cropped so he must have adopted the fashion shortly afterwards, perhaps in response to the 'Gagging Acts' of late 1795.

171

G. DANCE

171 *Thomas Girtin*

pencil drawing, 316 × 254 mm, dated 28 Aug. 1798
1898-7-12-21
LITERATURE Girtin and Loshak 1954, p. 112

Thomas Girtin, the great landscape watercolour painter, is seen here as a 'Crop', and Girtin and Loshak (1954, p. 112) noted that there is evidence of the radical implications of his hairstyle in a letter dated 18 December 1798 from a friend, Abbé Ange Denis Macquin, to James Moore:

> But more of this when next we meet,
> As I hope soon in Stanford Street,
> We'll talk of Girtin's Brutus head,
> And curls not bigger than a bead.

7 Thermidor to Brumaire, July 1794–November 1799

The revolutionary government which followed the execution of Robespierre was known as the Thermidor regime after the month it took power, and it was followed on 26 October 1795 (4 Brumaire, l'an IV) until 10 November 1799 (19 Brumaire, l'an VIII) by a new and complex constitution by which executive power rested in the hands of a Directory of five, while the legislative power was in the hands of two chambers, the Council of Five Hundred and the Council of Elders. The Directory kept to an extremely difficult path, beset by the threat of Jacobins on one side and Royalists of all persuasions on the other. Though the Directory was regarded generally as weak and unstable, it governed over a period of remarkable revival, with real consolidation of the institutions of the Revolution and great military victories under General Bonaparte and others.

France under the Directory and the advent of Bonaparte

From the British point of view the collapse of the Terror with the fall of Robespierre brought relatively few practical changes, except for an incessant clamour for peace negotiations which the government had difficulty in quelling. Though the Thermidor regime and the Directory which followed were less repressive, the growing military success of the French generals made France ever more threatening, and the possibility of a French invasion became a real fear. From 1795 onwards the rise of Bonaparte can be traced in British caricature, until by the time of his *coup d'état* in 1799 he was a familiar figure in Britain.

POIRIER (DESIGNER), ENGRAVED BY J. B. LOUVION

172 *Le Neuf Thermidor ou la Surprise Angloise (Fructidor l'an 3e)*

etching, 285 × 365 mm, pub. Aug. 1795
1858-4-17-1554
LITERATURE BMC 8675; Jouve 1983, pl. 7

This print offers to the world a new image of France scarred by the recent experience of the Terror. France is seen as an ostrich which had first laid eggs that produced

172 detail

monsters, Marat, Carrier, Robespierre, etc., but has now laid a fresh batch containing emblems of peace which are offered to the nations. Britain, happily, is symbolised by a fat John Bull, taken from Gillray's famous print *French Liberty. British Slavery* (no. 84), who according to the caption 'revealing by his appearance a well-fed existence devoted to eating, expresses his surprise at this welcome change'. The idea for the design was that of a Dunkirk lawyer called Poirier, who was also responsible for the famous print *Les Formes Acerbes* (Carnavalet, 1977, no. 283), attacking the Terror in northern France.

JAMES GILLRAY

173 *French Habits:* (a) *Le Ministre d'Etat, en Grand Costume;* (b) *Les Membres du Conseil des Anciens*

etchings, coloured, 261 × 193 mm and 260 × 195 mm, pub. 18 April 1798 by H. Humphrey
1868-8-8-6720, 6721
LITERATURE BMC 9196-7

The set of plates called *Habits of New French Legislators, and other Public Functionaries* is a characteristic Gillray double satire. It shows in exaggerated form the costumes of the French Directory as worn for state occasions; but they are

173a

worn here by members of the Whig Opposition. Charles James Fox is represented as a paunchy unshaven figure wearing the costume of Le Ministre d'Etat trampling on the royal arms, while the Conseil des Anciens costumes are worn by the aristocratic Whigs Lansdowne, Norfolk and Grafton. The costumes of the Directory were published in England by E. and S. Harding in 1796 in an edition copied from J. Grasset de Saint-Sauveur's book. The idea behind these caricatures may have come from George Canning, the founder of *The Anti-Jacobin*, for he is known to have corresponded with Gillray about them.

J. GRASSET DE SAINT-SAUVEUR

173c *Dresses of the Representatives of the People*, 1796

printed book with colour plates, 195 × 120 mm, pub. E. and S. Harding,
Lent by British Library, 8122.b.134

Translated from the French edition, first published in 1795.

173b

CARLE VERNET, ENGRAVED BY DARCIS

174 *Les Incroyables*

stipple engraving, colour printed, 306 × 356 mm
1874-7-11-835

The years of the Directory saw the return of fashionable life in Paris and of extravagant display in dress which was much satirised. *Les incroyables* were young men noted for their long hair, wide collars, culottes and pointed shoes, all of which implied rejection of the austere values of Robespierre and of the spirit of l'an II. Their female counterparts were the *merveilleuses*, and they tended to wear the long white gowns familiar from Jacques-Louis David's paintings. In political terms they can be identified with the *jeunesse dorée*, counter-revolutionary thugs who sought to destroy the symbolic remains of the previous regime and attacked those associated with it. This print was copied in England at the time.

JAMES GILLRAY

175 *The Apotheosis of Hoche*

etching, coloured, 486 × 377 mm, pub. 11 [Jan.?] 1798 by H. Humphrey
1851-9-1-953; Smith Collection
LITERATURE BMC 9156; Hill, *Gillray*, 1965, pp. 68–9

The vigour of this print is all the more remarkable in being designed and evidently supervised by non-artists, J. H. Frere and the Rev. Walter Sneyd. It belongs to the period when Gillray was employed by a group of government supporters gathered around the young George Canning,

EQUALITY.
Thou shalt Murder
Thou shalt commit Adultery.
Thou shalt Steal.
Thou shalt bear false witness
Thou shalt covet thy Neighbours House & every thing that is his.
Renounce thy Father & thy Mother
The Apotheosis of HOCHE.

175

176

and close to Pitt himself, who ran *The Anti-Jacobin* periodical and saw themselves as the scourge of radicals and French sympathisers. It refers to the death of General Hoche on 18 September 1797, and in particular the spectacular funeral celebrations held in Paris and the overblown rhetoric which was applied to his death. Hoche was notorious for his brutal attempt to suppress the counter-revolution in the Vendée. The print was accompanied originally by a printed account of the apotheosis purporting to come from the *Rédaction*.

The print itself is an extraordinary transformation of elements from an apotheosis of a saint and a Last Judgement based on Italian models, in which Christian symbols are wittily and horrifically inverted.

ISAAC CRUIKSHANK

176 *The French Bugabo Frightening the Royal Commanders*

etching, coloured, 272 × 444 mm, pub. 14 April 1797 by S. W. Fores
1851-9-1-857; Smith Collection
LITERATURE BMC 9005

An early representation of Bonaparte before his physical characteristics were fixed by British caricaturists. The reference is to the triumphal Italian campaign of 1796–7 and the humiliation of the Pope who is seen underneath the monster. The royal commanders are the Archduke Charles of Austria and the Duke of York.

FRANCESCO VIERA, ENGRAVED BY F. BARTOLOZZI

177 *The sitting of the Council of Five Hundred . . . Novr 10th 1799*

etching and stipple engraving, 552 × 711 mm, pub. 1 Sept. 1800 by Bartolozzi and Vendramini
1917-12-8-3960; Lucas Collection

Bonaparte's *coup* on 9–10 November (18–19 Brumaire, l'an VIII) and the subsequent establishment of the Consulate to replace the Directory mark the effective end of the Revolution and the beginning of a new system based upon the personal ascendency of Bonaparte himself. The events behind the *coup* are complex but there can be little doubt that Bonaparte plotted, with Sieyès and Talleyrand, to overthrow the Directory which had suffered military reverses. The Councils of the Elders and Five Hundred had adjourned to Saint-Cloud in fear of a Jacobin rising but found that the Directory itself had resigned. Bonaparte, who was to be offered the military command to defend the Councils, on finding himself threatened by daggers in the chamber, called in troops to expel his opponents. The remaining members of the Councils then approved the new executive of three Consuls, Bonaparte, Sieyès and Ducos.

Viera was a Portuguese artist who spent time in London in the 1790s where he struck up a close association with Bartolozzi.

177

178

ANON. *(illus. in colour)*

178 *The Corsican Crocodile dissolving the Council of Frogs!!!*

etching, coloured, 255 × 346 mm, pub. Nov. 1799 by W. Holland
1868-8-8-12565
LITERATURE BMC 9427

A view of the same events as the previous print, combining the attack on Napoleon with his return with troops to overwhelm the Council. Napoleon had himself adopted the crocodile as a symbol after his return from Egypt, and he was often caricatured as such by British satirists. However, the scene appears to refer to the fable of the frogs who petitioned Jupiter for a king (Aesop, Fable II) and were sent a log, which they eventually rejected. In anger Jupiter sent a crane who proceeded to eat the frogs, an apt analogy for a people who had executed their king and had acquired Napoleon in his stead.

The threat of invasion and its imagined consequences

British government attempts from February 1793 onwards to keep up interest in the war with France were hindered by the lack of military success. The land campaign in Flanders and the siege of Valenciennes of late July 1793 produced a great many works of all kinds to commemorate the victory and the commander, the Duke of York, but the siege did not lead to permanent success. With Admiral Howe's celebrated naval victory on 1 June 1794 and the continual threat of naval invasion from northern France, the navy became the focus of patriotic imagery, and this reached an apogee with Nelson's victory at the Battle of the Nile in 1798. Heroic admirals and jolly tars, despite a series of naval mutinies in 1797, now abounded in all media, and caricatures were produced to emphasise the dangers of invasion and to whip up fear that the Opposition were plotting with their radical supporters to invite the French over in order to seize power themselves.

P. DE LOUTHERBOURG, ENGRAVED BY W. BROMLEY

179 *The Grand Attack on Valenciennes*

engraving, 584 × 802 mm, pub. 1 Dec. 1801 for V. and R. Green by R. Cribb
1877-6-9-1821
INSCRIBED 'The Grand Attack on Valenciennes, by the Combined Armies under the command of His Royal Highness the Duke of York, on the twenty-fifth of July 1793'
LITERATURE Joppien 1973, no. 64

The painting (Hesketh Collection, Easton Neston) was commissioned in 1793 and finished in 1794, in which year it was joined by Loutherbourg's painting of Lord Howe's victory of 1 June (see no. 181 below). Despite the immense popularity of both paintings publication of the print was delayed until 1801. As a military operation the attack on Valenciennes was a doubtful success, for the Duke of York was unable to press home a further attack on Dunkirk, giving the French time to regroup and defeat his Hanoverian allies, forcing the Duke in turn to retreat to the coast.

180 *Beaker painted in black with a verse for the Duke of York (1763–1827)*

creamware, probably Staffordshire or Yorkshire, H. 96 mm
1987, 7-5, 1

The verse, enclosed within a laurel leaf frame, reads 'May Success Attend/the DUKE of YORK/Wherever HE goes' and continues on the other side 'Blasted Be the FRENCH/& Confusion to All Inglish/JACKOBINS [*sic*]'.

The inscription is connected with the campaigns of 1793–5 against the French republican forces in which the Duke of York led the troops. AD

P. DE LOUTHERBOURG, ENGRAVED BY J. FITTLER

181 *The Glorious Victory obtained over the French Fleet by the British Fleet under the command of Earl Howe on the First of June 1794*

engraving, 587 × 808 mm, pub. 1 Jan. 1799 for V. and R. Green by R. Cribb
1859-7-9-1577
INSCRIBED 'The Glorious Victory, obtained over the French Fleet, under the command of Earl Howe, on the First of June 1794'
LITERATURE Joppien 1973, no. 65; *Earl and Countess Howe*, Kenwood, 1988, no. C15

One of several large-scale prints produced to commemorate the victory, it shows the encounter between the two flagships, the *Queen Charlotte* and *La Montagne*. The 'Glorious First of June' was the first major naval victory of the French war and it gave rise to an immense amount of celebratory material which was overshadowed only by Nelson's later triumphs. Howe was in charge of watching the Channel, and the French fleet was engaged in bringing grain from America. Howe destroyed and captured several ships, though he failed to stop the grain. Nevertheless, he was given a royal reception on his arrival.

180

182

ANON.

182 *Jack's return after Lord Howe's Glorious Victory*

mezzotint, 358 × 252 mm, pub. 1 Aug. 1794 by Laurie and Whittle
1981 U. 185

A characteristic celebration of Howe's victory, proclaiming it a national triumph, and enlisting the participation of the ordinary sailor (see Introduction, p. 65).

183

RICHARD NEWTON

183 *A Peep into Brest with a Navel Review!*

etching, coloured, 275 × 302 mm, pub. 1 July 1794 by R. Newton
Lent by The Lewis Walpole Library, Farmington, Conn.

A pun on the fact that the French fleet was blockaded in the harbour of Brest and was thought to be gathering for an invasion of Britain.

184 *Cap of liberty from French frigate Unité, captured off Ushant, April 1796, by Captain Francis Cole RN in the Révolutionnaire*

iron, H. 254 mm
Private Collection (on loan to Royal Naval Museum, Portsmouth)
LITERATURE Royal United Services Museum, exh. cat. 1961

The *Révolutionnaire*, as its name suggests, was a French boat captured shortly after she was built in late 1794. The *Unité* had the misfortune to meet a squadron of four ships under the command of Captain Sir Edward Pellew, and after a chase was captured by Captain Cole's ship. A similar cap taken from *La Cléopatre* captured in June 1793 is in a private collection.

184

186

MONSALDY

185 *Le Triomphe des Armées Françaises*

etching, coloured, 331 × 452 mm, pub. April 1797
Lent by Her Majesty the Queen

A graphic illustration of the remarkable conquests achieved by French generals in the years 1796–7, yet the achievements of the generals on the left, Pichegru, Moreau and Hoche, are minor compared with the enormous chunk of the map pulled off by the young General Bonaparte. In October 1797 Bonaparte was appointed Commander of the Army of Britain to prepare an invasion from Brest, but Duncan's victory at Camperdown, which confirmed Britain's naval superiority, put paid to such plans.

ANON.

186 *The Grand Republican Balloon*

etching, coloured, 488 × 278 mm, pub. 24 Feb. 1798 by J. Wallis
1868-8-8-6702

INSCRIBED 'Intended to convey the Army of England from the Gallic Shore, For the purpose of exchanging French Liberty! for English Happiness! Accurately copied from a PLAN presented to the EXECUTIVE DIRECTORY, BY CITIZEN MONGE.'

LITERATURE BMC 9176

Prints purporting to show fantastic rafts and other devices for transporting French armies to invade the shores of Britain were produced in large numbers in 1797–8, and this immense balloon is as much a satire on the genre of print and the alarmism it represented as on the French themselves. In fact the print is an altered state of *The Grand British Balloon*, 1784 (BMC 6710) with a French cock and guillotine in place of emblems of British power.

ANON. FRENCH

187 *Vent Contraire. ou Vaillans efforts du Beau Sexe Anglais pour empêcher la descente*

etching, coloured, 185 × 163 mm, pub. 1798? by Martinet
1868-8-8-6807
LITERATURE BMC 9165

The invasion fear from the French point of view. A group of Englishwomen wave their fans to turn the wind against the French fleet, while a British officer hides in terror beneath one of their petticoats. Mrs George dates the print to 1798 but there is a possibility that it refers to the invasion scare of 1803.

P. DE LOUTHERBOURG

188 *Allegorical design of the Battle of the Nile*

pen and sepia drawing, 514 × 381 mm
1880-2-14-303
LITERATURE Binyon 1902, III, p. 69; Joppien 1973, no. 67

Clearly a finished drawing for a patriotic publication celebrating British naval victories, of which the Battle of the Nile of 1 August 1798 was the most decisive before the end of the century, resulting in the loss of eleven French warships. This victory surpassed in importance even Howe's victory of 1 June 1794 (see no. 181) and virtually cut off Bonaparte's new possession of Egypt from France. The battle made Nelson a national hero and led to a flood of commemorative souvenirs, a large display of which can be seen in the National Maritime Museum. Loutherbourg made himself a specialist in the heroic depiction of British naval victories, and the great number of rival versions of each of his compositions testifies to his success. Here

188

189 Patriotic Regeneration, — viz. — Parliament Reformd, a la Françoise, — that is, — Honest Men (i.e. — Opposition) in the Seat of Justice. Vide Carmagnol Expectations

190 Promis'd Horrors of the French INVASION, — or — Forcible Reasons for negociating a Regicide PEACE. Vide, The Authority of Edmund Burke.

Nelson's victory is seen in terms of a British lion crushing the inflated pretentions of a French cock. For a companion drawing see no. 214 below.

JAMES GILLRAY

189 *Patriotic Regeneration, – viz. – Parliament Reform'd, a la Françoise, – that is, – Honest Men (i.e. Opposition) in the Seat of Justice. Vide. Carmagnol Expectations*

etching with aquatint, coloured, 309 × 454 mm, pub. 2 March 1795 by H. Humphrey
1868-8-8-10376
LITERATURE BMC 8624; Hill 1976, no. 1

A picture of the House of Commons according to the supposed objectives of the Whig Opposition which, according to Gillray, would lead to their installation in the seats of power. Fox is presiding judge while Pitt in his shirt, the white suggesting martyrdom, is arraigned before him. Stanhope, defence counsel in the Treason Trials of 1794 (see p. 193), reads the charges: '1st For opposing the Right of Subjects to dethrone their King. – 2d For opposing the Right of Sans-Culottes to Equalize Property, & to annihilate Nobility. 3d For opposing the Right of Free Men to extirpate the farce of Religion, & to divide the Estates of the Church.' The objectives of the Opposition are seen as the direct imposition of a British Terror in which Whig politicians act out the parts of members of the French Convention. The radical artisans and tradesmen who make up the jury are in the position of sans-culottes motivated by greed and hatred of their betters. This print was issued in unusually large numbers, suggesting that it was subsidised by government supporters.

JAMES GILLRAY

190 *Promis'd Horrors of the French Invasion, – or – Forcible Reasons for negociating a Regicide Peace*

etching, coloured, 303 × 421 mm, pub. 20 Oct. 1796 by H. Humphrey
1868-8-8-6554
LITERATURE BMC 8826; Hill, *Gillray*, 1965, p. 63

This extremely complex print presents a vision of London after the anticipated French invasion, which was much feared in 1796 after Bonaparte's Italian campaign. The scene is set among the gentlemen's clubs of St James, where a Liberty tree is fixed and a guillotine is actively in operation. The point is to show the Whig Opposition now in power with the aid of the French, wreaking their revenge like bloodthirsty sans-culottes upon the government and its sympathisers. Fox in the centre is seen chastising William Pitt, while the loyalist Edmund Burke is tossed by a bull representing the radical Duke of Bedford. The immediate occasion for the print was the prospect of peace negotiations between Pitt and the Directory, which were strongly denounced by Burke in his pamphlets *Thoughts on a Regicide Peace*.

JAMES GILLRAY (*illus. p. 62*)

191 *Consequences of a Successfull French Invasion. no. III, pl. 2nd, Me teach de English Republicans to work. – Scene. A Ploughed Field*

etching, coloured, 304 × 399 mm, pub. 1 March 1798 by James Gillray
1868-8-8-10381; Smith Collection
LITERATURE BMC 9182; Hill, *Gillray*, 1965, pp. 73–80

One of a set of four plates, all that were completed of a planned twenty commissioned by Sir John Dalrymple, a Scottish gentleman. The project, which is documented in surviving correspondence (British Library, Add. MSS. 27, 337), was conceived as a way of rousing 'all the People to an active Union against that Invasion; at a Time when above five Millions of Vultures, with Beaks and Claws, hover over them; when the Indolence and Divisions of the people themselves are more alarming than all foreign enemies' (quoted from Hill, *Gillray*, 1965, p. 74). Dalrymple himself laid down the content of the proposed plates, and this seems to have led to quarrelling with Gillray, who was notoriously touchy. Furthermore, Dalrymple hoped 'that so public Spirited an undertaking would have been supported by Government', but was disabused of this hope, with the result that Gillray was not adequately paid and refused to go on with the commission after four prints, of which this is the third, had appeared. In this print the radicals and complacent citizens who had welcomed the French invasion, or allowed it to take place, are not put in power by the French but are enslaved by them. The hoers in the field include John Bull himself, and also a manufacturer and a curate, both representing groups in society thought to be susceptible to republican ideas.

8 Sovereignty of the king and sovereignty of the people

Despite the massive preponderance of imagery upholding the established order developed in the years 1793–4, radicalism underwent a revival in 1794 in the face of desperate shortages of bread and other commodities. From the government's point of view more alarming kinds of activists were threatening to raise popular discontent. Though the government's laws against sedition and assembly were eventually successful in limiting radical expression, the Treason Trials of late 1794 resulted in the acquittal of all the accused. In this section there can be seen a number of 'seditious' prints, medals and tokens, which represent an alternative vision to the imagery of rustic contentment disseminated by loyalists. Contentment as defined by radicals is seen to precede or postdate the corrupt order of the present day, while satire, especially in the work of Thomas Spence, is used to point out the burdens imposed on the common people.

The Treason Trials, 1794

I. C-KS (ISAAC CRUIKSHANK?)

192 *A General Fast in Consequence of the War!!*

etching, 250 × 353 mm, pub. 14 Feb. 179(5?) by S. W. Fores
1868-8-8-6338
LITERATURE BMC 8428

The period 1794–5 was one of famine and misery among the labouring classes in both town and country, and it was commonly attributed to the needs of the war against France and to Pitt's determined prosecution of it. Here it is seen as the cause of social division between the feasting clergyman and the poor weaver of Spitalfields, whose

192

193

ruined manufactory can be seen through the window. On his walls are two subscription lists: the one for 'Familys in Distress in Consequence of the War' contains one signature, while the other 'A List of Subscription for Emigrant Clergy' is filled with signatures and has raised £10,000. The sense that such social distress did not affect the privileged classes undoubtedly helped the revival of radicalism in these years and strengthened its roots in the labouring classes, though it also attracted the indignation of middle class radicals like Coleridge. The fear that the famine of the years 1794–5 would lead to class hatred and the spread of Jacobin ideas was uppermost in the minds of the clergy themselves and led to popular attempts to counteract them through pamphlets and broadsides.

RICHARD NEWTON

193 *Soulagement en Prison; or, Comfort in Prison*

watercolour, 369 × 575 mm
Lent by The Lewis Walpole Library, Farmington, Conn.
LITERATURE Jouve 1983, p. 32

Study for an aquatint published 20 August 1793 by W. Holland and known through a photograph in the British Museum (BMC 8339). The numbers pencilled on the watercolour refer to a list of names beneath the print. The tall figure on the far left is Lord George Gordon of the Gordon Riots (see no. 4), who had been imprisoned in Newgate from 1788 until his death in 1793. The occasion for the drawing, the etching derived from this drawing, and the next etching seems to have been the imprisonment of Newton's publisher William Holland (no. 2 in the print and on the far left beneath Lord George Gordon in the watercolour). Holland was arrested in 1793 for publishing seditious tracts, and his prints in general are more radical than those of his chief rival Fores. Jouve (1983) suggests that Newton himself might also have been arrested and kept in Newgate, but there is no evidence that he was more than a visitor. Though many of the people in the drawing were imprisoned for sedition, it does not follow that all were inmates. Mrs George quotes Francis Place as saying that on the state side of Newgate political prisoners were 'comfortably accommodated, well provided for as to food, and had their friends not only to visit them but sometimes to dine with them'. Other radicals of interest depicted here are Daniel Isaac Eaton (see no. 195b), James Ridgeway, the publisher, and Charles Pigott, the journalist.

194

RICHARD NEWTON

194 *Promenade in the State Side of Newgate*

etching, 470 × 725 mm, pub. 5 Oct. 1793 by W. Holland
1867-3-9-777
LITERATURE BMC 8342

This print was made some two months after the previous watercolour and has a slightly different cast of characters with some interesting additions. On the far left (1) is Peter Pindar (John Walcot), the satirist of the Royal Academy, no. 9 in the left group is John Horne Tooke, and the bearded figure in the foreground talking to Lord George Gordon is Martin Van Butchell, a highly eccentric surgeon and radical.

TREASON TRIAL MEDALS, 1794

In 1794 Thomas Hardy, the Secretary of the London Corresponding Society, John Horne Tooke and John Thelwall were arrested for High Treason. Defended by Thomas Erskine and Vicary Gibbs, Hardy and Tooke were acquitted and the prosecution of Thelwall was dropped.

W. WHITLEY *(illus. p. 55)*

195a *Acquittal of Hardy, Horne Tooke and Thelwall*

tin, 37.5 mm
S. S. Banks, p. 18-15, and 1914-5-7-348
LITERATURE Brown 1980, no. 377

On the obverse are the profile portraits of Hardy, Horne Tooke and Thelwall; on the reverse portraits of their lawyers and the names of the juries which acquitted them. Engraved by Whitley, a die and seal engraver of Round Court, St Martins-le-Grand, this medal was advertised for sale by Mr Mousele, also of Round Court, for £1. 11*s*. 6*d*. in silver and 1*s*. 6*d*. in copper. The advertisement does not mention copies in tin; these would have been sold for a few pence. MJ

(illus. p. 55)

195b *The King v. Daniel Eaton*

copper, 40 mm
M5014
LITERATURE Bell, *Political Tokens*, p. 99

Early in 1794 Eaton was tried for selling Spence's *Hog's Meat, or Politics for the People*. Following his acquittal the London Corresponding Society passed a resolution thanking his jurymen, each of whom was presented with a silver example of this medal to commemorate the occasion.

The obverse shows a crowing cock, traditionally the emblem of France and here representing the 'Crow of Liberty' (see no. 206h), with the legend 'Struck by the order of the London Corresponding Society'. The reverse records the names of the jurymen who acquitted Eaton. MJ

(illus. p. 55)

195c *Thomas Hardy*

copper, 28.5 mm
M5013

The obverse shows Hardy in profile, with the inscription 'tried for High Treason, 1794' which is continued on the reverse: 'acquitted by his jury. Counsel Hon T. Erskine, V. Gibbs Esqr'. MJ

(illus. p. 55)

195d *Thomas Hardy*

copper, 32 mm
M5019
LITERATURE Bell, *Political Tokens*, p. 105

A three-quarters facing portrait of Hardy, with the inscription 'Thos. Hardy secretary to the London Corresponding Soci[ety]' which is continued on the reverse: 'by the integrity of the jury who are judges of law as well as fact'. The names of the jurymen are given. According to Bell the dies for this medal were engraved by Thomas and/or Peter Wyon in Birmingham. He adds that it was probably struck by Kempson, a Birmingham token manufacturer. MJ

(illus. p. 55)

195e *Thomas Hardy*

tin, 33.5 mm
M5021

The scales of justice are radiant above the Tower of London, where Hardy was held. The reverse again names the members of his jury. MJ

W. WHITLEY *(illus. p. 55)*

195f *Lord Stanhope*

tin, 41.5 mm, 1795
S. S. Banks, pp. 19-18

Lord Stanhope is described as 'The minority of one . . . the friend of trial by jury, liberty of the press, parliamentary reform, annual parliaments, habeas corpus act, abolition of sinecures, and of a speedy peace with the French Republic'.

Charles, Earl Stanhope (1753–1816) earned his title on 6 January 1795 when he found himself the sole supporter of his motion, in the House of Lords, against British interference in the internal affairs of France. On 4 February he chaired a meeting at the Crown and Anchor tavern to celebrate the acquittal of his sons' tutor Jeremiah Joyce at the previous year's treason trials. His speech to the meeting was published and widely circulated and it is likely to have been at this period that the medal was struck. MJ

(illus. p. 55)

195g *Daniel Eaton*

copper, 29 mm, 1795
T6469 and 1870-5-7-1308

A profile portrait of Eaton above the inscription 'Frangas non flectes' ('you may break but you will not bend'). The obverse inscription reads 'D. I. Eaton three times acquitted of sedition', the reverse 'Printer to the majesty of the people, London, 1795', around a depiction of pigs feeding on books while a cock crows above them – a reference to the publication *Politics for the people, or Hog Wash* for which he was tried. MJ

(illus. p. 55)

195h *Horne Tooke*

copper, 32 mm
1947-6-7-180; presented by the family of Dr S. Fairburn

The obverse portrait is signed by Jacobs, a die engraver who worked for a variety of London token manufacturers. The reverse shows the Old Bailey. MJ

(illus. p. 55)

195i *Token, London Corresponding Society*

copper, 30 mm, 1795
T6449 (presented by Miss S. S. Banks) and 1870-7-5-16240
LITERATURE Spence 1795, no. 213; Bell, *Political tokens*, no. 105

On the obverse an old man demonstrates to his sons that unity is strength. The legend 'London Corresponding Society' continues on to the reverse, 'united for a reform of parliament' around a dove carrying an olive branch. The reverse refers both to the peaceful intentions of the society and to the widespread demand for peace with France. MJ

The 'Gagging Acts', November–December 1795

ISAAC CRUIKSHANK

196 *The Royal Extinguisher or Gulliver Putting out the Patriots of Lilleput!!!*

etching, coloured, 317 × 483 mm, pub. 1 Dec. 1795 by S. W. Fores
1868-8-8-6487
LITERATURE BMC 8701

A satire apparently in favour of Pitt on the occasion of the joint Treasonable Practices and Seditious Meetings Bills of November–December 1795, the former of which effectively brought speech and writing within the scope of treason, while the latter put severe restrictions upon public meetings to raise grievances. The Lilliputian radicals under the extinguisher are girdled by a hoop inscribed 'Copenhagen', referring to the great radical meeting held by the London Corresponding Society in Copenhagen Fields on 26 October 1795, addressed by John Thelwall, who is presumably the figure raised aloft in the middle behind Fox. Pitt's lamp is inscribed 'For protecting his majesty's person', a reference to the attack on the king's coach in Westminster on 29 October, which had been attributed by the government to the inflammatory proceedings at Copenhagen Fields and to the seditious pamphlets on sale there (Goodwin 1979, pp. 386–7). Though Cruikshank here appears to approve of Pitt's acts there are many caricatures which saw them as gagging the 'Freeborn Englishman' (see no. 197). The 'Gagging Acts' provoked a number of public meetings all over the country before the bills became law on 18 December, including one on 16 November 1795, presided over by Fox, which was attended by Joseph Farington and Thomas Banks (see no. 170).

196

T. FRENCH

197 *A Freeborn Englishman, the Admiration of the World, the Envy of Surrounding Nations, &c, &c*

etching, coloured, 159 × 111 mm
1868-8-8-6328
LITERATURE BMC 8710

A crude caricature of a highly influential motif, copied by Thomas Spence, 1796 (see also Cruikshank's version, BMC 8711). The Acts of December 1795 attracted a number of hostile caricatures in which the idea of gagging or padlocking John Bull's lips was the central motif.

197

RICHARD 'CITIZEN' LEE

198 *King Killing*

broadside, 278 × 215 mm, sold by Citizen Lee, at the British Tree of Liberty, No. 98, Berwick-Street, Soho
Lent by British Library, 806.k.1 (124*)
LITERATURE Goodwin 1979, p. 392; *Wordsworth*, 1987, no. 1

This celebrated pamphlet was denounced in the House of Commons on 17 November 1795 as the kind of seditious tract which justified the proposed Treasonable Practices Bill, on the grounds of its content but especially its wide distribution at public meetings. It was claimed that Lee had been publisher to the London Corresponding Society, though in fact he had been expelled from it. The public impact of the work derives from the title which refers back to the famous seventeenth-century regicide tract *Killing no Murder*.

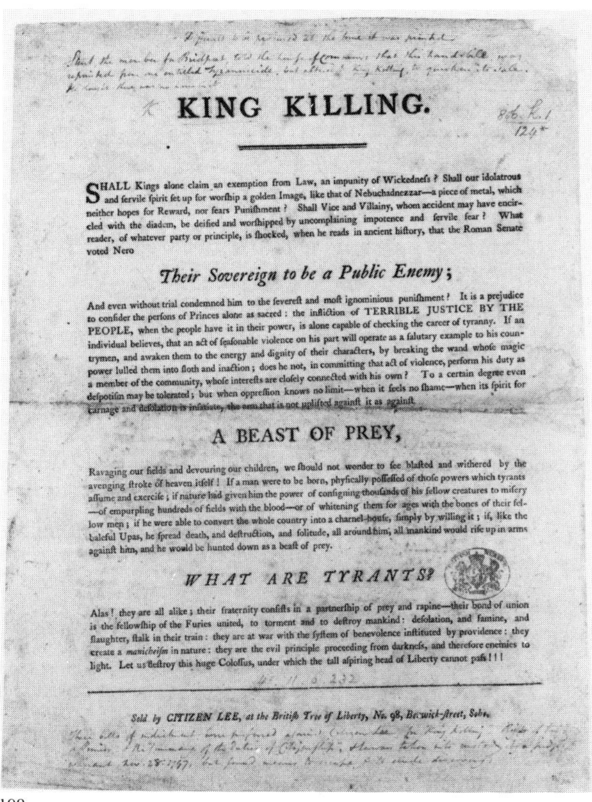

KING KILLING.

SHALL Kings alone claim an exemption from Law, an impunity of Wickedneſs ? Shall our idolatrous and ſervile ſpirit ſet up for worſhip a golden Image, like that of Nebuchadnezzar—a piece of metal, which neither hopes for Reward, nor fears Puniſhment ? Shall Vice and Villainy, whom accident may have encircled with the diadem, be deified and worſhipped by uncomplaining impotence and ſervile fear ? What reader, of whatever party or principle, is ſhocked, when he reads in ancient hiſtory, that the Roman Senate voted Nero

Their Sovereign to be a Public Enemy ;

And even without trial condemned him to the ſevereſt and moſt ignominious puniſhment ? It is a prejudice to conſider the perſons of Princes alone as sacred : the infliction of TERRIBLE JUSTICE BY THE PEOPLE, when the people have it in their power, is alone capable of checking the career of tyranny. If an individual believes, that an act of ſeaſonable violence on his part will operate as a ſalutary example to his countrymen, and awaken them to the energy and dignity of their characters, by breaking the wand whoſe magic power lulled them into ſloth and inaction ; does he not, in committing that act of violence, perform his duty as a member of the community, whoſe intereſts are cloſely connected with his own ? To a certain degree even deſpotiſm may be tolerated ; but when oppreſſion knows no limit—when it feels no ſhame—when its ſpirit for carnage and deſolation is inſatiate, the arm that is not uplifted againſt it as againſt

A BEAST OF PREY,

Ravaging our fields and devouring our children, we ſhould not wonder to ſee blaſted and withered by the avenging ſtroke of heaven itſelf ! If a man were to be born, phyſically poſſeſſed of thoſe powers which tyrants aſſume and exerciſe ; if nature had given him the power of conſigning thouſands of his fellow creatures to miſery—of empurpling hundreds of fields with the blood—or of whitening them for ages with the bones of their fellow men ; if he were able to convert the whole country into a charnel-houſe, ſimply by willing it ; if, like the baleful Upas, he ſpread death, and deſtruction, and ſolitude, all around him, all mankind would riſe up in arms againſt him, and he would be hunted down as a beaſt of prey.

WHAT ARE TYRANTS?

Alas ! they are all alike ; their fraternity conſiſts in a partnerſhip of prey and rapine—their bond of union is the fellowſhip of the Furies united, to torment and to deſtroy mankind : deſolation, and famine, and ſlaughter, ſtalk in their train : they are at war with the ſyſtem of benevolence inſtituted by providence : they create a *manicheiſm* in nature : they are the evil principle proceeding from darkneſs, and therefore enemies to light. Let us deſtroy this huge Coloſſus, under which the tall aſpiring head of Liberty cannot paſs ! ! !

Sold by CITIZEN LEE, *at the Britiſh Tree of Liberty, No. 98, Berwick-ſtreet, Soho.*

198

200

RICHARD 'CITIZEN' LEE, PUBLISHER *(illus. p. 59)*

199 *A Cure for National Grievances. Citizen Guillotine, A New Shaving Machine*

etching on printed broadside, 286 × 138 mm
Lent by British Library, 648. c. 26, no. 70
LITERATURE BMC 8365; Dickinson 1985, no. 55

This undeniably seditious print was printed for 'Citizen' Lee, and though Mrs George dates it 1793?, a date of late 1795 seems preferable, on the grounds of its closeness to no. 198 above. Wilberforce noted on 29 October 1795 that 'Papers are dispersed against property. Prints of guillotining the King and others' (BMC 1793, p. 52). An unexpected confirmation of a 1795 date comes from the unmistakable reference to George Packwood's advertising campaign for his razor strop: on 10 April 1795 he published a report of his 'NEW INVENTION' and claimed to have accomplished his ambition 'TO SHAVE THE NATION' (see Neil McKendrick, 'George Packwood and the Commercialisation of Shaving' in N. McKendrick, J. Brewer and J. Plumb, *The Birth of a Consumer Society*, Cambridge, 1983, p. 157).

ANON.

200 *Farmer Looby manuring the Land*

etching, coloured, 280 × 200 mm
1868-8-8-6380
LITERATURE BMC 8515

Such ephemeral and unregistered prints are impossible to date accurately, but if, as Mrs George suggests, 'Kate' is Catherine II of Russia, then it must date from before her death in November 1796, and perhaps from the same period as no. 199 above.

ANON.

201 *A Warning Voice to the Violent of all Parties, November 6, 1795*

printed broadside, 375 × 245 mm
Lent by Guildhall Library, Broadsides 8.131

Thelwall's lecture is dated the very day that the Treasonable Practices Bill was introduced into the House of Lords, and it appears to be a response to the government's attempt to tie the attack on the king's coach on 29 October to the effect of the speeches at the famous Copenhagen Fields meeting of 26 October, one of which was given by Thelwall. Thelwall, as a protégé of Horne Tooke, had become a leader of the London Corresponding Society in early 1794. His chief fame came through his lectures which he used to raise funds for the Society, but which

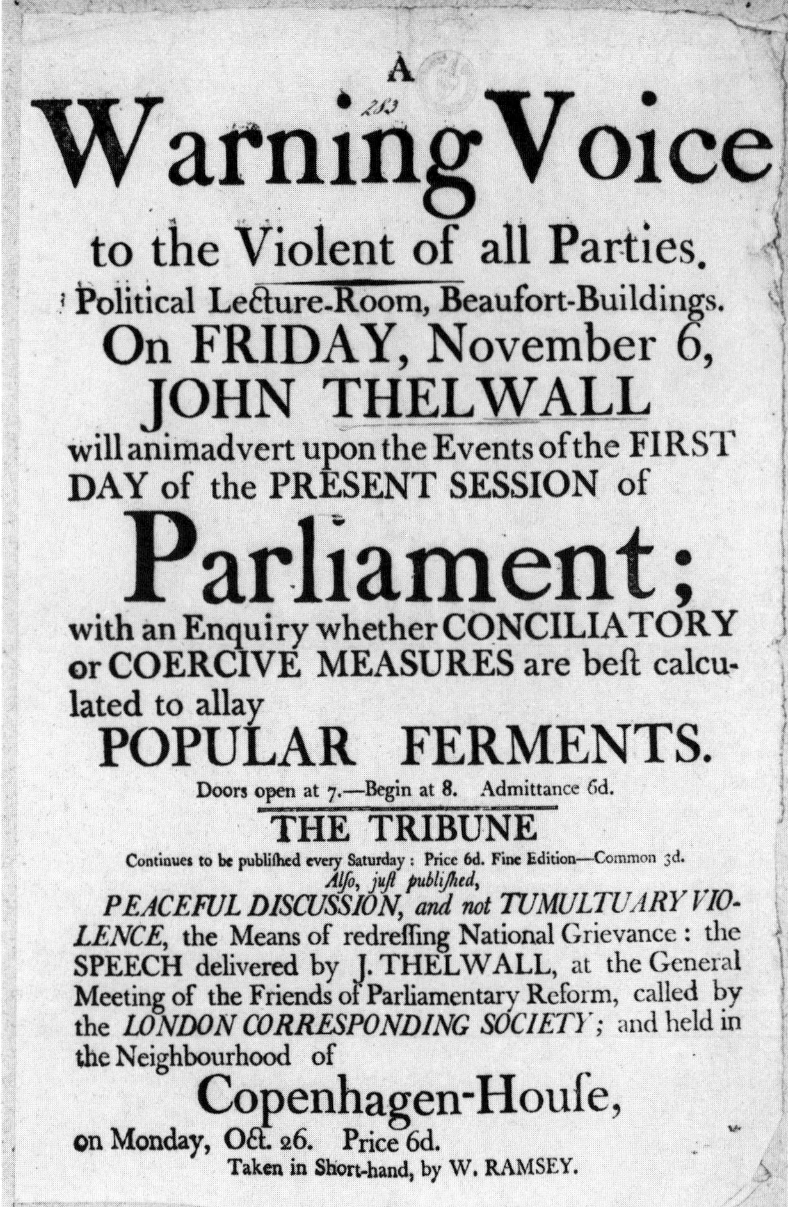

A
Warning Voice
to the Violent of all Parties.
Political Lecture-Room, Beaufort-Buildings.
On FRIDAY, November 6,
JOHN THELWALL
will animadvert upon the Events of the FIRST DAY of the PRESENT SESSION of
Parliament;
with an Enquiry whether CONCILIATORY or COERCIVE MEASURES are beſt calculated to allay
POPULAR FERMENTS.
Doors open at 7.—Begin at 8. Admittance 6d.
THE TRIBUNE
Continues to be publiſhed every Saturday: Price 6d. Fine Edition—Common 3d.
Alſo, juſt publiſhed,
PEACEFUL DISCUSSION, and not TUMULTUARY VIOLENCE, the Means of redreſſing National Grievance: the SPEECH delivered by J. THELWALL, at the General Meeting of the Friends of Parliamentary Reform, called by the *LONDON CORRESPONDING SOCIETY*; and held in the Neighbourhood of
Copenhagen-Houſe,
on Monday, Oct. 26. Price 6d.
Taken in Short-hand, by W. RAMSEY.

201

also made such an impression upon listeners that they became a specific target of the Treasonable Practices Act (Goodwin 1979, pp. 318 and 395). Though essentially a reformer and believer in 'Peaceful Discussion, and not Tumultuary Violence', Thelwall seems to have drawn his rhetoric from fiery spirits like Daniel Eaton and from French Jacobin sources, speaking contemptuously of religion and George III and claiming to be 'a downright sans-culotte' (Goodwin 1979, p. 321). The violence of the imagery and the relative moderation of his political proposals are perhaps reflected in the typography of this pamphlet: the eye-catching title *A Warning Voice* sits oddly with the call for conciliatory measures from the government and radicals.

Radicalism on the margins, 1796–8

JAMES GILLRAY

202 *London Corresponding Society, alarm'd,-Vide. Guilty Consciences*

etching and aquatint, 255 × 173 mm, pub. 20 April 1798 by H. Humphrey
1851-9-1-917; Smith Collection
LITERATURE BMC 9202

Though highly tendentious and grossly caricatured, the grim scene of conspiracy does reflect the change in the

London Corresponding Society in the years after the Two Acts of December 1795, and the withdrawal and disillusionment of middle-class and moderate elements, despite the picture of Horne Tooke as well as Tom Paine, both in *bonnets rouges*, on the wall behind. The caricature types are those used by Gillray to depict the Irish, and the group represents the association between the United Irish, who had assisted the French to gain a foothold in Ireland from December 1796, and the revolutionary English republicans who formed part of what was left by 1798 of the London Corresponding Society. The aim was to set up societies of United Englishmen with a revolutionary programme, which could call upon the support of the French Directory. On 28 February 1798 a party of Irish and English revolutionaries were arrested at Margate, and it is their names – O'Connor, Binns and Quigley (Coigley) – that have alarmed the conspirators in Gillray's etching. Thomas Evans, whose name is also on the list, was the secretary of the LCS and was not arrested until April. His presence implies unfairly that all the executive of the LCS were implicated in treasonable conspiracy.

202

203

204

203 *Token, Liberty and not slavery*

copper, 30 mm, 1796
T6453 (presented by Miss S. S. Banks) and T6454
LITERATURE Bell, *Political Tokens*, no. 115

According to Bell, this token was engraved by Jacobs and issued by Skidmore. The sentiments and style are, however, very close to Spence's tokens (see no. 206s). The obverse shows Pitt (P eye T) hanging beside a cap of liberty, an obelisk inscribed 'PEACE' and a shield bearing the word HOPE and an anchor (as opposed to the constitutional symbol of the crown and anchor). The crown lies, with other emblems of royalty and religion, on the ground below. The reverse inscription, around the initials LCS, reads 'Dedicated to the London Corresponding Society/ may their endeavours meet reward'. MJ

204 *Medal, Greatheads meeting at Warwick*

tin, 36.5 mm, 1797
S. S. Banks, MJC 59
LITERATURE Bell, *Political Tokens*, no. 126

This medal was made by Westwood of Birmingham to commemorate a political meeting at Warwick. It seems that the three central figures, drawn in a donkey cart beneath a bar on which sedition couches and about to be hanged, probably represent Dr Samuel Parr, the Rev. J. H. Williams and another speaker at the meeting. Robert Greathead was the Sheriff of the county. The Wrongheads, presumably radicals, are portrayed as uncouth figures, armed with clubs and axes; the Rightheads as sober citizens.

The reverse legend reads 'As if from Temple Bar [where the heads of traitors were exhibited] some head was cut and on rebelling trunk the face was put'. MJ

Thomas Spence

Thomas Spence was born in Newcastle on 21 June 1750, the son of a poor hardware dealer. He worked first as a clerk and then as a schoolteacher, before opening his own school in Peacock Entry. The Spence family were leading members of the Glassite congregation at the Forster Street Meeting House, who believed in common property.

205 *Countermarked coins* *(illus. p. 56)*

On 8 November 1775 Spence read a paper before the Philosophical Society of Newcastle entitled 'The Real Rights of Man' or 'The True Relations of the People to the land' which he then published as a pamphlet. In this he proposed the suppression of landlords, arguing that all land should be owned by parishes and rented from the parish by its inhabitants.

To publicise his views Spence used a series of punches cut by his friend Thomas Bewick to stamp slogans on to current coins.

a) *Shilling, William III*
NO NO LANDLORDS YOU FOOLS.
SPENCE'S PLAN FOREVER

silver, 25 mm, T6494

b) *Halfpenny*
SPENCE'S PLAN YOU ROGUES

copper, 26 mm, 1855-10-4-374

c) *Irish halfpenny, George II*
SPENCE'S PLAN IS SMALL FARMS

copper, 28 mm, 1760, 1988-11-21-1

d) *Penny, George III*
SPENCE'S PLAN PLENTY/ & EVERY BLESSING

copper, 36 mm, 1797, 1988-11-21-2 MJ

206 *Tokens*

In 1792 Spence left Newcastle for London, where he set up as a book and saloop (hot drink) seller. The following year he started the penny periodical *Pig's Meat or Lessons for the Swinish Multitude*, so called after Burke's phrase in *Reflections on the Revolution in France*, '. . . learning will be cast into the mire and trodden down under the hoofs of a swinish multitude'. After his arrest and detention for seven months in 1794 he took a shop at 8 Little Turnstile, High Holborn, which he called 'The Hive of Liberty'. There he cashed in on the new craze for collecting the privately issued tokens, which had come into being as a result of the chronic shortage of small change, by setting up as a coin dealer. In 1795 he published *The Coin Collector's Companion being a description of modern Political and other copper coins,*

NOTED ADVOCATES FOR THE RIGHTS OF MAN
THOS SPENCE
SIR THOS MORE
THOS PAINE
a
b
1796
c
ARE THE PEOPLE
d
e
f
AMONG
1796
SLAVES
BRINGS
g
h
i
THE END OF OPPRESSION
j

206

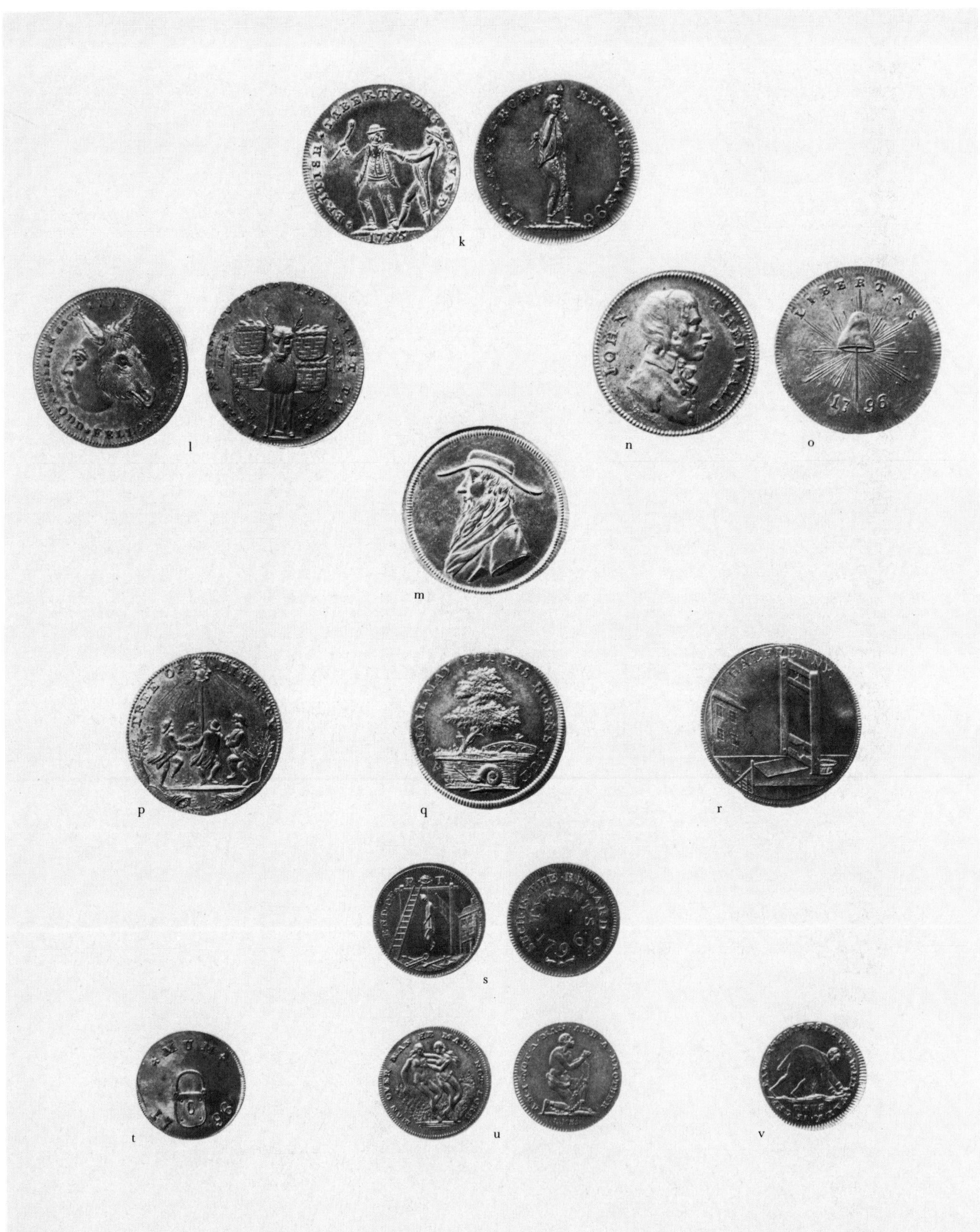
k
l
n
o
m
p
q
r
s
t
u
v
JOHN THELWALL
LIBERTAS
1796
TREE OF LIBERTY
A SNAIL MAY PUT HIS HORNS OUT
HALFPENNY
MUM

which he supplemented by an appendix listing many of his own productions. These seem to have been made in quite large numbers, according to a correspondent of the *Gentleman's Magazine* who wrote in April 1792:

> It is not long since I called at Spence's shop, and saw many thousands of different tokens lying in heaps, and selling at what struck me to be very great prices. These, therefore, could not be considered as struck for limited sale. I confess, considering the number I saw struck, and what the subjects of them were, I thought myself justified in supposing that it was the intention to circulate them very widely.

It may be that the expense of large-scale production overstretched him for at about this time Spence became bankrupt and sold his dies to another coin dealer and publisher of tokens, Peter Skidmore. Skidmore continued Spence's practice of combining dies at random, to produce more varieties for collectors, and he also combined them with his own dies (mainly engraved by Jacobs – Spence's had been engraved by Charles James), thus sometimes making a nonsense of the tokens' political message.

LITERATURE Arthur W. Waters, *Trial of Thomas Spence*, Leamington Spa, 1917. Some information comes from Waters's own, interleaved, copy, now in the British Museum.

a) *Pig's meat*

copper, 28 mm and 29.5 mm
1947-6-7-160 and 1862-9-17-6
LITERATURE Bell, *Political Tokens*, pp. 221, 235

The obverse shows a pig trampling on emblems of royalty and religion. Above the pig is a cap of liberty and a scroll reading 'Pigs meat published by T. Spence London'. Around the edge is inscribed 'SPENCE DEALER IN COINS LONDON', while the reverse bears the inscription 'NOTED ADVOCATES FOR THE RIGHTS OF MAN/THOS SPENCE/SIR THOS MORE/THOS PAINE'. MJ

b) *Red Indian*

copper, 30 mm
1870-5-7-16263
LITERATURE Bell, *Political Tokens*, p. 237

The inscription 'IF RENTS I ONCE CONSENT TO PAY MY LIBERTY IS PAST AWAY' emphasises Spence's vision of the original inhabitants of America as noble savages, whose freedom to use the land without claiming to own it was now threatened by the encroachment of European colonists with their belief that land can belong to an individual. MJ

c) *Only one master grasps the whole domain*

copper, 29.5 mm, 1795
S. S. Banks, p. 5-58, and 1870-5-7-16251
LITERATURE Waters 1917, pp. 16, 23; Bell, *Political Tokens*, p. 226

The obverse shows ruined cottages and dead trees in a desolate landscape, a design taken from Thomas Bewick's illustration of the 1795 edition of Goldsmith's poem 'The Deserted Village'.

> Sweet smiling village, lovliest of the lawn;
> Thy sports are fled and all thy charms withdrawn;
> Amist thy bowers the tyrants hand is seen,
> And desolation saddens all thy green:
> Only one master grasps the whole domain,
> And half a tillage stints thy smiling plain.

Often found as the reverse is a shepherd under a tree, presumably illustrating the rural idyll that would result from Spence's plan. The design seems to have been taken from W. Hawkins's frontispiece to *Shenstone's Works*, dated December 1794. Though dated 1790 it must, like the obverse, date from 1795. MJ

d) *We also are the people*

copper, 28.5 mm, 1796
1947-6-7-179
LITERATURE Bell, *Political Tokens*, p. 231

The scene of a soldier shaking hands with a civilian is a reference to a section of Volney's *Les Ruines*, part of which appeared in translation in *Pig's Meat*, in which soldiers refuse to fire on the crowd with the words 'We also are the people'. MJ

e) *Thomas Spence*

copper, 30.5 mm, 1794
S. S. Banks, p. 5-42, and T6496
LITERATURE Bell, *Political Tokens*, pp. 216, 248

The obverse inscription reads 'T. SPENCE, 7 MONTHS IMPRISONED FOR HIGH TREASON'. The portrait is signed JAMES, under the truncation. The reverse urges 'ROUSE BRITANNIA', and shows the cap of liberty dropping from her spear. MJ

f) *Pig's Meat*

copper, 19.55 mm, 1795
T6811
LITERATURE Bell, *Political Tokens*, p. 229

On the obverse a cat, with the legend 'IN SOCIETY LIVE FREE LIKE ME'; on the reverse a book labelled 'PIGS MEAT' with the legend 'IF LORDS ALL MANKIND ARE/THEN THEY YE RENTS SHOULD SHARE'. MJ

g) *Cat and Dog*

copper, 29 mm, 1796
1870-5-7-16220 and T6502
LITERATURE Bell, *Political Tokens*, pp. 230, 243

This was one of Spence's favourite tokens and was buried with him, at his request. On one side sits a cat saying 'I AMONG SLAVES ENJOY MY FREEDOM', while, of the dog on the other side it is said 'MUCH GRATITUDE BRINGS SERVITUDE'. MJ

h) *The Crow of Liberty*

copper, 28.5 mm, 1795
1938-2-1-3
LITERATURE Bell, *Political Tokens*, p. 228

The British lion slinks away, tail between his legs, as the Gallic cock crows from the top of a dungheap. The legend reads 'LET TYRANTS TREMBLE AT THE CROW OF LIBERTY'. MJ

i) *Before and after the Revolution*

copper, 29 mm, 1795
S. S. Banks, p. 5-28, and 1870-5-7-16218

Before the Revolution a naked and skeletal prisoner sits gnawing a bone, manacled in a prison cell. After the Revolution one man sits eating at a table beneath a shady tree, while three others dance. MJ

j) *The beginning and end of oppression*

copper, 31 mm
S. S. Banks, p. 5-66, and 1870-5-7-1379
LITERATURE Bell, *Political Tokens*, pp. 239, 240

Spence sees oppression as beginning with Cain's murder of Abel. On the reverse he shows it ending when all the documents embodying the ownership of land are burnt. MJ

k) *British Liberty*

copper, 29.5 mm, 1795/6
1870-5-7-16192 and T6498
LITERATURE Bell, *Political Tokens*, pp. 225, 232

On one side a man is press-ganged, under the legend 'BRITISH LIBERTY DISPLAYED'; on the other a man stands bound hand and foot, his tongue padlocked under the legend 'A FREE BORN ENGLISHMAN'. MJ

l) *I was an ass*

copper, 29 mm
S S. Banks, p. 5-82, and 1870-5-7-16169
LITERATURE Bell, *Political Tokens*, p. 227

A Janus-headed creature composed of George III and an ass. The inscription reads 'A GUINEA PIG/A MILLION HOGG/ODD FELLOWS/1795'. Bell suggests that the guinea pig is the king, whose head appeared on guinea coins, and the million hogg (Northumbrian for newly shorn yearling sheep) are the public, who have been fleeced.

On the reverse is a donkey, laden with panniers labelled RENTS (the first pair) and TAXES (the second pair). The inscription reads 'I WAS AN ASS TO BEAR THE FIRST PAIR'. MJ

m) *Lord George Gordon*

copper, 31 mm
S. S. Banks, p. 192-194
LITERATURE Bell, *Political Tokens*, p. 247

The reverse reads 'LORD GEORGE GORDON 1780'. Instigator of the Gordon Riots in 1780, Lord George Gordon was acquitted of treason in 1781 but tried and sentenced for libelling Marie Antoinette in 1788. He died in prison in 1793. MJ

n) *John Thelwall*

copper, 30.5 mm
1870-5-7-16228

The portrait is signed JAMES and seems to be a companion to no. 206e (T. Spence). MJ

o) *Libertas*

copper, 30.5 mm, 1796
S. S. Banks, p. 192-96
LITERATURE Bell, *Political Tokens*, p. 255

Bell suggests that this may have been produced by Skidmore, not Spence. However, given the sentiment, and the fact that Spence was still in business in 1796, this seems unlikely. MJ

p) *Tree of Liberty*

copper, 29 mm
1870-5-7-16183
LITERATURE Bell, *Political Tokens*, p. 241

The tree of Liberty around which four men dance is a maypole topped by William Pitt's severed head. MJ

q) *Snail*

copper, 28 mm
1870-5-7-1385

A snail in a landscape, with the inscription 'A SNAIL MAY PUT HIS HORNS OUT'. MJ

r) *Guillotine*

copper, 29 mm
1870-5-7-16185
LITERATURE Waters 1917, p. 19; Bell, *Political Tokens*, p. 268

Bell suggests that though this is frequently found paired with Spence's dies it was issued by Skidmore. This view of the guillotine seems to have been taken from a print of Louis XVI's execution published by C. Sheppard in March 1793. MJ

s) *End of Pitt*

copper, 21 mm
S. S. Banks, p. 5-22, and T6812
LITERATURE Bell, *Political Tokens*, p. 234

The hanged man is identified as P eye T (see also no. 203) and the reverse reads 'SUCH IS THE REWARD OF TYRANTS 1796'. Fetters, a spear and an executioner's axe on the ground beneath him, and the flag of St George flying from the house behind, emphasise the point.

It is not clear whether this is a reply to the 'End of Pain' token issued by Skidmore or *vice versa*. MJ

t) *Mum*

copper, 20.5 mm, 1796
S. S. Banks, p. 5-84
LITERATURE Bell, *Political Tokens*, p. 233

Like the 'Free born Englishman' this refers to the 'Gagging Acts' of 1795. MJ

u) *Man over man*

copper, 21 mm
1870-5-7-16254 and T6810
LITERATURE Waters 1917, p. 26; Bell, *Political Tokens*, pp. 252, 253

The inscription 'MAN OVER MAN HE MADE NOT LORD', around a depiction of Adam and Eve, implies that the only subjection legitimated by the Bible was that of woman to man. It is derived from Milton's:

> Authority usurp'd from God, not given
> He gave us only over beast, fish, and fowl,
> Dominion absolute. That right we hold
> By his donation: but men over men
> He made not Lords, such title to himself
> Reserving, human left from human free.

The design is taken from a print by J. Richter after H. Richter, published in March 1794.

This obverse is found with a design engraved by James after the seal of the Society for the Abolition of the Slave Trade which shows a manacled slave asking 'AM I NOT A MAN AND A BROTHER?' (see also no. 8). MJ

v) *We will walk thus*

copper, 20 mm
S. S. Banks, p. 5-69

A man on all fours within the inscription 'IF THE LAW REQUIRES IT WE WILL WALK THUS'. MJ

Happy Britannia and Good King George

Caricature was inevitably more effective on the attack than on the defence. Beginning with the Crown and Anchor campaign to counteract radical ideas from November 1792, there is a growing concern to emphasise not only the negative aspects of revolution but also the positive side of British life. The traditional rustic idyll of prosperity and family harmony is increasingly seen as emblematic of Britain under the benign aegis of George III as 'Father to his People'. One can trace in the works in this section the way in which rustic contentment is, with varying degrees of explicitness, contrasted with the horrors of French life under the Jacobins. George III who was the universal butt of satirists, gradually, from about 1794 onwards, ceases to be ridiculed and is frequently depicted as the guarantor of the prosperity of the nation.

JAMES GILLRAY

207 *untitled [England and France contrasted]*

etching and aquatint, unfinished proof, 334 × 489 mm, 1793?
1851-9-1-895; Smith Collection
LITERATURE BMC 8301

A 'contrast' print which, because of its use of the same motif as no. 108 can probably be dated to 1793, though the scene of France appears to show the September Massacres of 1792. It was abandoned unfinished, probably because of Gillray's difficulties with the aquatint process. The contrast is made in terms of a rustic idyll representing England and the murderous disorder of revolutionary France. The idyll is a humorous adaptation of several traditional motifs: the country dance, the festive inn with foaming tankards and the contented mingling of generations, all in a context of productivity, represented by the watermill, and trade, by the ships on the sea. Though the inn-sign has not been etched in, one might expect it to carry a picture of the king. The established order is seen as a guarantor of prosperity and contentment, while radicalism and meddling in politics are implicitly connected with French disorder.

WILLIAM HAMILTON, ENGRAVED BY BARNEY *(illus. p. 64)*

208 *The Happy Cottagers*, from Macklin's Poets' Gallery

stipple engraving, 502 × 407 mm, pub. 1 Jan. 1794 by T. Macklin
1917-12-8-3128; Lucas Collection
INSCRIBED 'What happiness the rural maid attends,
In chearful labour while each day she spends!
No homebred jars her quiet state controul,
Nor watchful jealousy torments her soul;
With secret joy she sees her little race
Hang on her breast, & her small cottage grace;
Still flow her hours with constant peace of mind,
Till age the latest thread of life unwind. Gay'

This print is typical of the type, popular throughout the eighteenth century, which celebrates, often with an undertone of city-dwellers' envy, the contentment enjoyed by the poorest countryman. In the wake of the French Revolution and the continuing threat of popular discontent there is an intensification of such imagery in popular decorative prints, which in this case emphasises the Christian basis of contentment by the conjunction of church and cottage.

HANNAH MORE

209 *The Riot; or Half a Loaf is better than no Bread*

Cheap Repository broadside, 451 × 271 mm, first pub. Aug. 1795
Lent by Bodleian Library, Oxford, John Johnson Collection

LITERATURE W. Roberts (ed.), *Memoirs of the Life and Correspondence of Mrs Hannah More*, 1834, II, pp. 426–30; R. Hole in C. Jones 1983, pp. 64–8

Hannah More's Cheap Repository Tracts, often sold as broadsides as well as pamphlets, were the dominant form of popular loyalist propaganda in the years 1795–8. They were explicitly directed towards the labouring classes, presenting simple moral tales from common experience. Though they rarely mention politics directly, they were conceived primarily to counteract the potential influence of the French Revolution on the common people, and their simplified form and very low price were designed to supplant popular broadsides, which were thought to disseminate immorality and Paine's ideas. *The Riot* points out the need for patience in the face of the grain shortages of 1795 which had helped the growth of popular radicalism. It also proclaims the benefits of the present social order and the essential benevolence of 'The Gentlefolks' who will in the face of distress 'give up their puddings and pies'. Compared with the loyalist propaganda of the Crown and Anchor Society, More and her associates emphasised Christian resignation and the positive side of rural life.

W. WHITLEY *(illus. p. 63)*

210 *Medal, A Philosophical Cure for All Evils*

tin, 48.5 mm, 1795
S. S. Banks, L.M. no. 11
LITERATURE Brown 1980, no. 407

A string of severed heads surrounds a standing corpse whose head is falling to the ground. The devil can be seen in the distance. The inscription above him reads 'A PHILOSOPHICAL CURE FOR ALL EVILS'; that below 'LICENTIOUS LIBERTY IS DESTRUCTION'; and within the circle of heads 'ABHOR EVIL CLEAVE TO THAT WHICH IS GOOD'.

On the reverse, under a crown above the inscription 'GOD SAVE THE KING', a happy family sits outside their home. She spins while he, having laid his spade aside, dandles his children on his knees while quaffing a mug of ale. The legend reads 'THE LAND WE LIVE IN AND MAY THOSE WHO DON'T LIKE IT LEAVE IT'.

Advertisements for this medal recommended it to friends of the constitution for distribution among friends,

211

213

dependants and neighbours. It was sold by B. Laver, a goldsmith of Bruton Street, and A. B. Portal, a wholesale cutler of Castle Street, Holborn, for 1*s*. 6*d*. retail, with a substantial reduction for purchases of a dozen or more. MJ

JAMES GILLRAY

211 *Affability*

etching and aquatint, 339 × 239 mm (cut), coloured, pub. 10 Feb. 1795 by H. Humphrey
1851-9-1-721; Smith Collection
INSCRIBED 'Well, Friend, where a' you going, Hay? – what's your Name, hay?– where d'ye Live, hay? – hay?'
LITERATURE BMC 8616

A classic satire on the attempts in the mid-1790s to capitalise on George III's ordinariness and establish him as the well-loved Father of his People. Here his attempt at simple friendliness towards one of his humble subjects is undercut by his overbearing manner. Though Gillray was a fervent government supporter in his caricatures of this period, he (and also Newton) were extremely reluctant to give up satirising George III and Queen Charlotte. It was apparently one of the conditions of his pension of £200 a year, negotiated with Canning at the end of 1797, that he should cease to caricature the royal family (Hill, *Gillray*, 1965, pp. 67–8, and Jouve 1983, pp. 31–2).

R. LIVESAY, ENGRAVED BY J. MURPHY *(illus. p. 53)*

212 *The Introduction of HRH the Duchess of York to the Royal Family*

mezzotint, 555 × 657 mm, pub. 4 June 1793 by E. Walker
Lent by Her Majesty the Queen

The painting and the mezzotint were no doubt intended to take advantage of the popularity of 'the royal family' as well as the king himself among the middle classes, who evidently admired the unfashionable respectability of his domestic life (Colley 1984, pp. 124–5).

J. WARD AFTER W. BEECHEY

213 *George III with the Prince of Wales and Duke of York reviewing troops*

mezzotint (proof before letters), 610 × 695 mm, pub. 1 June 1799
li 10-31; presented by James Ward

Taken from a large painting now in the Royal Collection, George III is seen in the unlikely role of military leader with his sons, the dissolute Prince of Wales, and the Duke of York who really was a military commander. Such grand public display by the monarch was seen as balancing the domesticity which was at the heart of George III's personal popularity. This image of a warrior king and family man could also be contrasted with the instability of the French Directory and the increasing power of Bonaparte in the months before its collapse.

214

P. DE LOUTHERBOURG

214 *Britannia before a bust of George III*

pen and sepia, 502 × 403 mm
1880-2-14-304

From the same volume celebrating 'Nelson's Victories' as no. 188, it shows George III in a symbolic role as source of the prosperity and naval power of Britain at the end of the eighteenth century, identifying the monarchy completely with patriotism (see Colley 1984, p. 126f.).

215 *Bowl printed in blue with a toast to the king*

pearlware, probably Staffordshire, DIAM. 260 mm
Lent by J. and J. May

The toast reads 'God grant us grace to love the King,/And pray for his long life,/And keep from democratic wolves,/ His children and his wife. A Bumper now my verse shall end./Here goes to Church & State,/And he that will not drink this health,/Shall have it on his Pate'. On the outside are Chinese-style scenes. There is a similar mug in the Victoria and Albert Museum, reg. no. Schreiber II 441. AD

216 *Medal, The happy state of England*

copper and tin, 40.5 mm, 1800
S. S. Banks, p. 11-133, and M5145
LITERATURE Brown 1980, nos 495, 496

Against a backdrop of the Thames at London an allegorical figure shows the genius of History a medal commemorating a British victory. The genius holds a scroll and stands on a book, both of which record similar successes, while a laurel branch rests on the British shield behind him. With her other hand the figure points to the emblems of Science and Art, for they too are flourishing.

On the other side of the medal (which is also found paired with a portrait of George III by the Swedish engraver Bauert) other facets of British prosperity are represented. In the forefront is a mine flanked by a farmer tilling his fields and a canal barge loading up the goods which have been brought in by the ships seen to the right. In the background wind- and water-mills are hard at work, while shepherds shear their sheep. MJ

216

9 The *émigrés*

French *émigrés* in England

About 150,000 people emigrated from France between 1789 and 1800. Some began to leave as early as July 1789 but most left in 1791–2. Among the first to leave were the grandest: the Comte d'Artois, Louis XVI's brother and other princes. Others left in 1790 on the abolition of feudal dues, followed by a great many military officers and priests who refused the Civil Constitution of the Clergy. In response the Convention imposed ever-increasing penalties upon *émigrés* in the form of confiscation and permanent banishment, and refractory priests were effectively ordered out of the country. French *émigrés* went all over Europe, and the centres of military and diplomatic action were Mainz and Coblentz. *Emigrés* often moved from one centre to another, but a fairly settled community began to build up in London, rent as always by political and social differences. Farington mentioned on 21 July 1793 that 'at Richmond, and in the neighboroud [*sic*], there are a great number of French Emigrants, many of them of high fashion. That party spirit rages among them, some being Royalists, others as they call themselves Constitutionalists, which makes it necessary to be cautious not to assemble them together, though they labour under the common grievance of being expelled from their native country'. *Emigrés* were inevitably the object of ambivalent reactions in England, and this is amply reflected in the satire of the period. Though the emigrant clergy in particular received charity from the royal family and others, resentment and a recourse to old stereotypes of the French often surfaced, especially in the difficult economic conditions of 1795–6.

A number of artists and craftsmen came over, not always as long-term *émigrés*, the most prominent of whom was the portrait painter Henri-Pierre Danloux. Apart from the very high quality and interest of his paintings, Danloux kept a journal (Portalis 1910) which describes in detail the circumstances behind his own commissions and gives an insight into the life of a painter caught between the *émigré* community and artistic life in London. Danloux is presented here as the most representative *émigré* painter, though there are many others who surface in contemporary accounts and whose works generally still remain obscure. Some French artists passed through briefly, like Ducreux, a royal portrait painter, who spent time in London in 1791.

ISAAC CRUIKSHANK

217 *A German* [Irish scored through] *Howl or the Emigrant Princes bemoaning the Loss of their Dearest Friend*

etching, coloured, 267 × 381 mm, pub. 15 March 1792 by S. W. Fores
1868-8-8-6164
LITERATURE BMC 8068

Leopold II of Austria, mourned by a group of French *émigrés*, signed the declaration of Pillnitz with Prussia, which pledged the restoration of the French monarchy. His death on 1 March 1792 was perceived as a blow to the militant *émigrés* based on Coblentz under the leadership of the Comte d'Artois, Louis XVI's younger brother and later Charles X, King of France, 1824–30. He lived in Holyrood Palace from 1795 to 1799 and later in London. He is seen in the middle of the group surrounded by his confrères who were notorious for their intrigues across Europe to raise futile expeditions against the French revolutionary governments.

RICHARD NEWTON

218 *Sturdy Beggars collecting for the Emigrant French Clergy*

etching, coloured, 406 × 533 mm, pub. Sept. 1792 by W. Holland
1948-2-14-369

A satire on John Eardley Wilmot's committee of 'Subscribers to a Fund for the Relief of the Suffering Clergy of France in the British Dominions', set up in September 1792 (Weiner 1960, p. 57). The government put Winchester Castle at the disposal of the committee. George III allowed the clergy to preach sermons calling for aid for *émigré* priests, and his and Queen Charlotte's interest in the matter is satirised in this print.

London Pub: Nov 15 1792 by S W Fores No 3 Piccadilly
Emigrant Clergy Reading the late Decree, that all who returns shall be put to Death.

218

Caricature Drawings and Prints. Admit.ce One Shilling.
Your Offerings in the honor of God!
Pity the poor French Clergy—
Open your Purses and give liberally—
Be bountiful like your Great Master
feed the hungry and clouth the
Winter!
will be of great use to them!
your back upon me for Pity's sake, for
It is so melancholy a piece of affliction! Let me
conjure you to assist these poor Foreigners!
consider they are in a strange land without
a house or a home! while all the poor of this
land of milk and honey sing dance and
enjoy every blessing under heaven!
two thousand a year, out of
which I pay an exhorbitant
Curate thirty pounds for
doing duty for me only
Three times every Sunday
Refugee Box
Sturdy Beggars collecting for the Emigrant French Clergy

219

ISAAC CRUIKSHANK

219 *Emigrant Clergy Reading the late Decree, that all who returns shall be put to Death*

etching, 212 × 326 mm, pub. 15 Nov. 1792 by S. W. Fores
1861-10-12-44; H. W. Martin Collection
LITERATURE BMC 8130

A cruel caricature satirising the *émigré* clergy who had come to England after refusing to agree to the Civil Constitution of the Clergy. The decree referred to was one of a number of harsh laws promulgated in France against *émigrés* after the establishment of the Republic in September 1792.

WILLIAM SHELTON AFTER H-P. DANLOUX

220 *Jean François Lamarche, Bishop St Pol de Leon*

engraving, 647 × 478 mm, pub. March 1797 by H-P. Danloux
E e 2-146
LITERATURE Weiner 1960, p. 64f.; Portalis 1910, p. 200f.

The Bishop Saint Pol de Leon administered the Wilmot Fund (see no. 218), and was effectively in charge of distributing relief to the French *émigré* clergy in England. He had arrived in London in late 1791 and was painted by Danloux in September 1792 (Louvre). This engraving was made from the painting in 1797 and distributed by subscription to supporters of the aims of the Fund. The Bishop is shown in his lodgings in Queen Street, Bloomsbury, engaged in the work of raising money from subscribers. At the head of the 'List of Subscribers to the [relief] of the suffering clergy of France' John Wilmot's name is most prominent, followed by the Duke of Portland. The screen shows Winchester Castle which had been given for the accommodation of the clergy.

220

H-P. DANLOUX

221 *Bishop St Pol de Leon*(?)

chalk drawing, 376 × 263 mm
1910-2-18-9; presented by Mrs Robert Low

There is some doubt as to whether this superb drawing, apparently drawn from life, is of the Bishop Saint Pol de Leon, but he is known to have been rather burlier than is suggested in the portrait above.

221

222

224

H-P. DANLOUX

222 *The Foster Children*

oil on canvas, 1156 × 952 mm
Private Collection by courtesy of H. Fritz-Denneville Fine Arts Ltd, London
LITERATURE Portalis 1910, p. 99

This portrait was exhibited at the Royal Academy in 1792 and is one of a group of portraits of the family of Richard Foster, made by Danloux after his arrival in England. Richard Foster, the father of the boys, had a lucrative position as a customs official and was particularly interested in collecting Dutch and Flemish paintings. The painting is a fine example of the incisive handling Danloux brought with him from France, which was gradually tempered by a broader handling and greater informality under the influence of British portrait painting in his later years in England. Danloux apparently became acquainted with the Foster family through his landlord Greenwood, the auctioneer, and his journal records several visits to the family in their house at Vauxhall.

H-P. DANLOUX

223 *Portrait of a girl holding a dog*

pencil drawing with watercolour, 263 × 178 mm, dated 22 Oct. 1795
1887-10-10-5

Nothing is known of the identity of the sitter. According to Aileen Ribiero the head-dress appears to be French and is perhaps appropriate to a servant.

J. DUCREUX

224 *Three etchings of expressions*

etchings, all 295 × 213 mm (approx.), pub. 21 Feb. 1791 by the Author
1876-10-14-70, 71, 72
INSCRIBED (on all three etchings) 'Invented & Engraved by J. Ducreux Painter to the King of France, to his Imperial Majesty, & Principal Painter to the Queen of France.'
LITERATURE *French Printmaking*, 1984–5, p. 296

Ducreux was a painter of considerable standing in France who had been appointed as painter to the royal family by Marie Antoinette. His stay in England was a brief one: according to Victor Carlson (in *French Printmaking*, 1984–5) he left Paris for London on 12 January 1791 and returned on 15 August of the same year. Even so he exhibited five works at the Royal Academy that year including paintings entitled *Surprise* and *Surprise Mixed with Terror*, and published this suite of *têtes d'expression*, all of which exist in painted versions. Though they are evidently self-portraits, they are principally studies of expression developed from the famous examples of Charles Le Brun, used as a textbook for painters. Any attempt to connect their emotions with the fate of the *émigré* artist in a strange land should be resisted.

10 Retrospect: the view from the nineteenth century

The view of the French Revolution as achieving its essential expression in the Terror of 1793–4 was reinforced in nineteenth-century Britain in different kinds of spectacle. In Madame Tussaud's waxworks grisly relics were exhibited in an atmospheric setting evoking the height of the Terror, becoming known as the 'Chamber of Horrors'. *A Tale of Two Cities* owes much to such a narrow conception of the Revolution, but Dickens was equally conscious of the ghastly cruelty associated with the Bastille.

If Madame Tussaud's exhibition concentrated upon the horror of the Revolution, a number of paintings exhibited in the 1850s and 60s concentrated upon the pathetic last days of the French royal family and of Charlotte Corday. E. M. Ward made something of a speciality of this genre, as did the little-known artist W. H. Fisk, whose paintings occasionally take as their subject the ordinary people of Paris under the Revolution. By the 1860s with the rise of international publishers like Goupil a number of French engravings of revolutionary scenes were issued in London as well as in Paris, and these also had the effect of reinforcing a hostile view of the Revolution.

Madame Tussaud

(illus. p. 75)

225 *Two wax heads of Robespierre and Fouquier-Tinville*

Lent by Madame Tussaud's, London

These grim objects have been cast from the moulds apparently brought over by Madame Tussaud from Paris in 1802, along with heads of Carrier and Hébert. Despite Madame Tussaud's claims to have cast them from the heads of the victims immediately after they were guillotined, under threat of death herself, their origins may have been less dramatic. They were undoubtedly made in the period after the fall of Robespierre and the execution of Fouquier-Tinville on 7 May 1795, and under the Thermidor government and the Directory it was not unusual to exhibit ghastly reminders of the Terror and the fate of its perpetrators. They were evidently exhibited in Paris in a separate room in the waxworks, in trunks which could be opened for inspection (Delécluze 1983, pp. 344–5), and they remained an important element in the grisly separate room of relics in Madame Tussaud's in Baker Street, which became known as the Chamber of Horrors in 1846.

226 *Key to Bastille, formerly on stone from Bastille*

180 mm
Lent by Madame Tussaud's, London
LITERATURE Wheeler, p. 58

There are a great many keys in existence which purport to come from the Bastille, but there is some evidence to support this one's claim to authenticity. Before the Tussaud's fire in 1925 which destroyed the great Napoleon collection and other relics, this key was attached to a carved stone (609 × 406 mm) from the Bastille with an inscription stating that it was presented to Moreau de Saint-Méry (deputy from Martinique) in the year IV by 'le patriote Palloy', who had the contract for the demolition of the Bastille. It seems therefore to be a typical presentation stone put together by Palloy, and apparently it was originally given to Bailly, the first Mayor of Paris, a letter from whom authenticating the stone was attached to it, in addition to a more dubious item, a note from the Man in the Iron Mask, which Palloy claimed to have found under the floor of his cell. The stone with key attached was one of the star items in a sale at Chinnock and Galsworthy on 18 June 1860 of 'the founder of the Napoleon Museum' which was exhibited at the Egyptian Hall in 1843. It was bought at the sale by Madame Tussaud's and was regarded in the later nineteenth century as a great attraction. Another key to the Bastille was presented to George Washington by Lafayette and taken to the United States by Tom Paine (Conway 1909, p. 109). It now hangs in Mount Vernon.

227 *Guillotine blade, from Sanson family*

Madame Tussaud's, London (not exhibited)
LITERATURE Wheeler, pp. 59–60

There are many claimants for the title of the very guillotine blade which 'severed Marie Antoinette's lovely head from her body, and which did the same cruel office

A Mr MOREAU St MÉRY; PRÉSIDENT DES
ÉLECTEURS 1789, PAR LE PATRIOTE PALLOY, L'AN 4e
CETTE PIERRE VIENT DES CACHOTS DE LA BASTILLE, DONNÉE
Monument élevé a la gloire des Électeurs de 1789

226

for her husband, Louis XVI', but this has one excellent circumstance in its favour: it was bought from the family of the executioner Sanson, as is confirmed by a bill in the Tussaud archives, dated 27 March 1854, for the immense sum of £110. Sanson's son and grandson kept a small museum of relics of the guillotine in Paris which was visited by Alexandre Dumas (see article 'Ce Qu'on Voit Chez Madame Tussaud', in *Causeries*, 1860). It was badly damaged in the fire of 1925, and was at that time accompanied by a wooden lunette to hold the victim's head but this seems to have perished in the fire.

228

ATTRIBUTED TO JOHN THEODORE TUSSAUD

228 *Madame Tussaud in Prison forced to make wax heads*

watercolour, 245 × 354 mm
Lent by Madame Tussaud's, London

John Theodore was the great-grandson of Madame Tussaud who took over the business in 1885. This appears to be a design for a tableau which existed in a slightly different form until the 1960s. It shows an undoubtedly fictional scene of Madame Tussaud forced to model the heads of decapitated victims.

PAUL FISCHER

229 *Madame Tussaud*

pen drawing, 301 × 239 mm
Lent by Madame Tussaud's, London

This a study for the celebrated watercolour of 1845 (Madame Tussaud's, London) of Madame Tussaud in old age presiding over her exhibition rooms. Part of the famous group of the French royal family, made before the Revolution and still in existence, can be seen in the background.

229

230 *Madame Tussaud posters*

(a) *1810 Edinburgh, Leith Walk*
(b) *1864 London, Baker Street*

(a) 523 × 204 mm; (b) 217 × 134 mm
Lent by Madame Tussaud's, London

These two posters show the transition of Madame Tussaud's from a travelling show to a permanent installation in Baker Street in 1835. Many of the French Revolution waxes in the present exhibition can be seen on show in (a) near the bottom of the poster and they remain in (b) but this time in what is now called the Chamber of Horrors.

Victorian images of the Revolution

ALFRED ELMORE *(illus. p. 218)*

231 *The Tuileries, June 20, 1792*

oil on canvas, 350 × 370 mm
Lent by The Makins Collection

The following extract is quoted from the Royal Academy catalogue, 1860:

'They brought the Queen's children to her, in order that their presence, by softening the mob, might serve as a buckler to their mother. They placed them in the depth of the window. They wheeled in front of this the Council table. Preserving a noble and becoming demeanour in this dreadful situation, she held the Dauphin before her, seated upon the table. Madame was at her side.

'A young girl, of pleasing appearance, and respectably attired, came forward and bitterly reviled in the coarsest terms *L'Autrichienne*. The Queen, struck by the contrast between the rage of this young girl and the gentleness of her face, said to her in a kind tone, "Why do you hate me? Have I ever done you any injury?" "No, not to me," replied the pretty patriot, "but it is you who cause the misery of the nation." "Poor child!" replied the Queen, "someone has told you so and deceived you. What interest can I have in making the people miserable? The wife of the King, mother of the Dauphin, I am a Frenchwoman in all the feelings of my heart as a wife and mother. I shall never again see my own country. I can only be happy or unhappy in France. I was happy when you loved me." This gentle reproach affected the heart of the young girl, and her anger was effaced. She asked the Queen's pardon, saying, "I did not know you, but I see that you are good."'

Probably a small version of the painting exhibited at the Royal Academy, 1860, no. 153. The painting was an immense success and was discussed at length in the *Art Journal* (1 June 1860, p. 165, and 1 July 1862, p. 152) and elsewhere. For the events of 20 June 1792 when the Tuileries were invaded and Louis XVI humiliated, see no. 43.

FREDERICK GOODALL

232 *The Arrest of a Peasant Royalist, Brittany, 1793*

oil on canvas, 838 × 1219 mm, 1855
Lent by Atkinson Art Gallery, Southport
EXHIBITED Royal Academy, 1755 (no. 402); Manchester, 1857 (no. 45)
LITERATURE *Art Journal*, 1855; *A Selection of Victorian Oil Paintings*, Atkinson Art Gallery, Southport, 1978, no. 20

Goodall was not a specialist in historical subjects, and this subject seems to have derived from several visits he made to Brittany in the 1840s and in 1854. The painting is Royalist in sympathy, showing the arrest of a Breton peasant during the harsh campaign against the counter-revolution in north-western France in 1793. The Convention's levy of 300,000 men on 24 February 1793 sparked off riots in Brittany in which the peasantry often demanded that nobles take the lead in a revolt against conscription, calling for a restoration of the *ancien régime*. By early April the government had regained control in

232

Brittany, though the Vendée continued to be ungovernable. Goodall's painting presumably refers to the suppression of royalism in Brittany in the early months of 1793, and it inevitably shows the Royalist peasantry in an heroic light.

E. M. WARD

233 *The Royal Family of France in the Prison of the Temple – Louis XVI., Queen Marie Antoinette, the Dauphin, Dauphiness, and Madame Elizabeth, the King's Sister*

pen and watercolour, with body colour, 243 × 310 mm, ?1851
Private Collection by courtesy of Quint-Harris Fine Art
LITERATURE *Art Journal*, 1855, p. 45; Dafforne 1874, pp. 26–9

A small version of the most famous and admired Victorian painting of a French Revolution subject, painted in 1851, now in the Harris Museum and Art Gallery, Preston. It was also acclaimed at the Paris exhibition of 1855, where it was noted by Charles Dickens (L. Ormond in *The Dickensian*, 1984, no. 402, p. 18). Its success led E. M. Ward to become a specialist in French Revolution subjects, and Queen Victoria herself was thought to be interested in acquiring it. The subject derives from a passage in Lamartine's *History of the Girondins*: 'The Queen was obliged to mend the King's coat while he was asleep, in order that he might not be obliged to wear a vest in holes.' According to a pamphlet published by Gambart in 1859 (quoted in Dafforne 1874, p. 27): 'In no history – of whatever people, period, or class – is summed up more pathos than in this chamber of the Temple, tenanted by a family who – whatever their faults or failings – loved each other deeply and truly, and left the world a memorable example of suffering borne with resignation, and of life laid down with dignity and Christian courage.

'When, in 1855, this picture was at Paris, in the Great Exhibition of Industry and the Arts, it was surrounded by a crowd, among which might often be seen eyes wet with tears. Those who wept before it were, perhaps, as often the sons of parents who had bawled execrations against "Monsieur Veto", or shouted "A bas l'Autrichienne", as of those who had crowded the upper windows round the Temple to offer to its prisoners their tribute of unavailing loyalty, or had treasured relics of Louis XVI, and Marie Antoinette, as of saints and martyrs'. Dafforne also quotes an interesting French discussion of the painting when it was in Paris (pp. 28–9 and Introduction, p. 77).

235

236

PRINCESS ALICE

234 *The Separation of the Dauphin from Marie Antoinette in the Temple (composition)*

watercolour on card, 392 × 330 mm, 1858
Lent by Her Majesty the Queen
SIGNED 'Alice fecit et inv. Dec. 24 1858'

Painted by Princess Alice (1843–78), the third daughter of Queen Victoria and Albert, as a Christmas present for her parents. A study for the watercolour is in an album at Wolfsgarten and is inscribed 'for Papa and Mama 1858'.

CH. L. MULLER, ENGRAVED BY PAUL GIRARDET

235 *Dernières Victimes de la Terreur: Appel des condamnés, 9 Thermidor 1794*

engraving, 535 × 1070 mm, pub. 1 April 1866 by Goupil, Paris, Londres, Bruxelles, La Haye
Lent by Musée de la Révolution Française, Vizille

By the 1850s it was common for publishers like Goupil to publish large prints in several capitals, always including Paris and London. This meant that a number of Paris Salon paintings of French Revolution subjects of a Royalist tendency, most notably by Delaroche whose *Marie Antoinette* was published by Goupil in 1857, became almost as familiar to British audiences as they were to French. This engraving, though very rarely seen in its original form, remains one of the defining images of the Terror, showing all the conditions of humanity at the moment they realise their death is imminent. As Bordes (*Premières Collections*, Vizille, 1985, p. 104) has pointed out, it is a classic Salon composition in which a great variety of different responses to the news are revealed in the physiognomy of the victims. The scene is supposedly the last act of the 'Grand Terreur', the mass guillotining that marked the last days of Robespierre's regime, and the figure seated alone in the centre is the poet André Chénier, in reality executed on 7 Thermidor, three days before Robespierre himself was executed.

W. H. FISK

236 *Awaiting publication of Le Moniteur for News of the Arrest of Robespierre*

oil on canvas, 635 × 762 mm, 1866
Lent by Harris Museum and Art Gallery, Preston
EXHIBITED Royal Academy, 1866

William Henry Fisk (1827–84) is a little-known painter who exhibited fairly regularly at the Royal Academy and elsewhere without achieving a great reputation. Perhaps following the lead of E. M. Ward he exhibited some French Revolution subjects but tended to concentrate on the period of the Terror. This painting, which tells of the events of 9–10 Thermidor, when Robespierre was wounded in the Hôtel de Ville and executed the next morning (see no. 152), is notable for its sympathetic view of the common people of Paris who are shown not as sans-culottes but as ordinary human beings outside the horrific events. At the Royal Academy in 1863 the same artist exhibited *Robespierre receiving letters from the friends of his Victims which threaten him with Assassination.*

H. K. BROWNE (PHIZ.) *(illus. p. 41)*

237 Illustrations to *A Tale of Two Cities*

(a) 2 on mount, frontispiece and title-page; (b) 4 on mount; all 132 × 214 mm (approx.), 1859
Lent by Victoria and Albert Museum, E. 776-767-1972; E. 776-779-1972
EXHIBITED *Dickens*, Victoria and Albert Museum, 1970, no. L5

A Tale of Two Cities was originally serialised in Dickens's weekly magazine *All the Year Round*, commencing on 30 April 1859. It appears he was not happy with the illustrations and ended his connection with Browne afterwards. For a discussion of the origins of the character of Dr Manette, who was imprisoned in the Bastille, see Introduction, pp. 38–41.

GEORGE CRUIKSHANK

238 *The Leader of the Parisian Blood Red Republic, or the Infernal Fiend!*

etching, coloured, 383 × 280 mm, pub. June 1871 by G. Cruikshank
Lent by Victoria and Albert Museum, 9449.1
LITERATURE *George Cruikshank*, exh. cat., Arts Council, 1974, no. 405

A late work of the artist done at the age of seventy-eight, it is an attack on the Paris Commune of 1870 connecting it with a tradition of bloodshed and massacre going back to the French Revolution of 1789. The 'Leader of the Parisian Blood Red Republic' is a demon based upon stereotypes of the sans-culotte originating in the work of Gillray and his own father Isaac Cruikshank in the early 1790s. The skull on the pike the demon carries has a *bonnet rouge* inscribed 'The Blood Red cap of Liberty Manufactured in 1789 and made *Red* with *Blood* in 1790–91–92 & 93'.

231

Notes

'This monstrous tragi-comic scene': British reactions to the French Revolution

1. Quoted in Roy Porter, '"Under the Influence": Mesmerism in England', *History Today*, September 1985, pp. 22–9.
2. A fuller account of Matthews can be found in John Haslam, *Illustrations of Madness* (ed. Roy Porter), Routledge, 1988, *passim*.
3. For an excellent discussion of these developments see Lynn Hunt, *Politics, Culture, & Class in the French Revolution*, London, 1986, pp. 93–119.
4. Quoted ibid., p. 29.
5. See Dickinson 1985, pp. 1–24.
6. Quoted in Paulson 1983, p. 43.
7. See Paulson 1983 for a brilliant discussion of these themes.
8. Burke's motives and vehemence have been the subject of much interesting discussion. See especially Conor Cruise O'Brien's introduction to the Penguin edition of the *Reflections*, London, 1968; Isaac Kramnick's *The Rage of Edmund Burke: Portrait of an Ambivalent Conservative*, New York, 1977; and Paulson 1983.
9. R. Hole in C. Jones 1983, pp. 55–69.
10. Quoted in Thompson 1963, p. 57.
11. See Brewer 1986, p. 31.
12. Quoted in Paulson 1983, p. 66.
13. Quoted by R. Hole in C. Jones 1983, pp. 57, 60.
14. Hannah More, 'Village Politics', *Works* (11 vols, London, 1852), vol. 2, p. 222.
15. Ibid., p. 227.

Introduction

1. Wordsworth, *Prelude*, Book IX, 50.
2. Blanning 1986, p. 133.
3. Farington, 26 November 1795, vol. II, p. 414.
4. Wordsworth, *Prelude*, Book XI, 1.
5. Farington, 28 October 1795, vol. II, p. 392.
6. See no. 197 and Brewer 1986, nos 116–19.
7. *Letter Addressed to the Addressers*, 1792, 26. Quoted in Thompson 1980, p. 101.
8. *An Historical and Moral View . . . of the French Revolution*, 1794. Quoted in *Wollstonecraft Anthology*, p. 137.
9. Dickinson 1985, p. 7.
10. Goodwin 1979, pp. 318–20.
11. Goodwin 1979, p. 321. Thelwall on one occasion claimed to be 'a downright *sans-culotte*'.
12. Webster, *Zoffany*, 1976, p. 14. Zoffany had been forced by lack of success to make his career in India from 1783 to 1789. On his return to England he was never able to regain his early reputation.
13. See *Discourse*, IV: 'Strictly speaking, indeed, no subject can be of universal, hardly can it be of general, concern; but there are events and characters so popularly known in those countries where our Art is in request, that they may be considered as sufficiently general for all our purposes. Such are the great events of Greek and Roman fable and history, which early education and the usual course of reading, have made familiar and interesting to all Europe, without being degraded by the vulgarism of ordinary life in any country.'
14. See the section in this Introduction entitled *Revolution as myth: public art and private dissent*.
15. See Newman 1987, p. 126f.
16. See Webster, *Wheatley*, 1970, and E. D. H. Johnson, *Painters of the English Social Scene*, London, 1986, especially chapter 3. See also Barrell 1980, pp. 89–131.
17. See Klingender 1944, p. 13 and no. 100 (Gillray's *Cymon and Iphigenia*, 1798).
18. Dated 21 April 1788, but was offered as a pair with the Northcote print in the *London Gazette*, 26 June 1790 (Hill, *Gillray*, 1965, p. 42).
19. For an excellent account of this phenomenon see D. Alexander and R. T. Godfrey, *Painters and Engraving: The Reproductive Print from Hogarth to Wilkie*, Yale, 1980.
20. See Hill, *Gillray*, 1965, p. 20, and especially his great caricature *Titianus Redivivus* (BMC 9085).
21. George 1959, pp. 205–6.
22. Surprisingly few popular broadsides of a Painite or revolutionary tendency are known before 1794, and not all that many later, despite the alarms of loyalists like Beilby Porteus and Hannah More. The works of Hawes (see no. 70) and Citizen Lee (nos 198, 199) are exceptional, and Porteus's idea that the popular literature available on the streets 'would form the best *sans culotte* library in Europe' (Roberts 1834, vol. II, p. 426) makes sense only if one assumes that he is talking about any broadsides of a secular tendency.
23. Hill, *Gillray*, 1965, p. 95f.
24. Hill, *Gillray*, 1965, pp. 67–8.
25. R. Hole in C. Jones 1983, pp. 57–61.
26. Anon., *Proceedings of the Association for Preserving Liberty and Property against Republicans and Levellers*, 1792, number I, 9.
27. There are examples in the British Museum's Print Room, Foreign History Series, 1793.
28. Thompson 1980, p. 122.
29. Hill, *Gillray*, 1965, chapters 6 and 7.
30. Simon Linguet's *Memoirs of the Bastille* was reprinted several times since its first publication in London in 1783.
31. Godechot 1970, p. 94f.
32. Mark Jones 1977, p. 1 and fig. 2.
33. Laurence Sterne, *A Sentimental Journey*, chapters entitled 'The Passport: the hotel at Paris' and 'The Captive'.

34. William Cowper, *The Task*, Book v, ll. 379–93.
35. The inscription is to be found in a letter accompanying a model of the Bastille made from 'des vestiges de la Bastille' and sent in 1790 to the *département* of Isère. It is now on loan to the Musée de la Révolution Française, Vizille (*Une Dynastie Bourgeoise dans la Révolution: Les Perier*, exh. cat. Vizille, 1984, no. 178).
36. The British Museum has a small number of medals made by Palloy supposedly from manacles found in the Bastille.
37. J. L. Carra, *Le Comte de Lorges, prisonnier à la Bastille pendant trente-deux ans, enfermé en 1757, du temps de Damien, et mis en liberté le 14 juillet, 1789*. This pamphlet appeared as early as September 1789, and was repeated in the same author's *Mémoires Historiques et authentiques sur la Bastille* later in the same year under the events of the year 1757. The author claims to have heard the whole story of the Comte's dispute with Madame de Pompadour from the prisoner on the way to the Hôtel de Ville after his release from detention: 'Quel étoit mon crime? L'élan d'une âme Républicaine, qui souffre de voir le vice triompher.' Carra was a minor author who made a great deal of noise to little effect in the Club des Jacobins. Though strongly Montagnard in spirit, his association in 1791 with Brissot in advocating war led to his execution with the Girondin leaders on 31 October 1793.
38. Godechot 1970, p. 92, where he is described as an Irishman born in Dublin.
39. See de V 1642.
40. For the full text see Keynes, *Blake*, pp. 134–48. The only known copy, probably page proofs for an abandoned edition, is in the Huntington Library (R. Essick, *The Works of William Blake in the Huntington Collections*, San Marino, 1985, pp. 178–9). For the fullest discussion of this work see Erdman 1969, pp. 162–7.
41. Manchester catalogue, 1822, p. 38 (copy in Madame Tussaud's, London).
42. Charles Dickens, *All the Year Round*, 7 January 1860, p. 252.
43. Tussaud 1838, p. 94. See also Godechot 1970, pp. 263–4: 'A toothed wheel was presented as having served to torture prisoners: it was actually a printing press, confiscated in 1786.'
44. Newman 1987, especially chapter 1. See also Paulson 1983, who was the first to raise many of the issues discussed in this section in his chapter 'The view from England: Stereotypes', pp. 37–57.
45. Paulson 1983, p. 134, and Bindman in *Kunst um 1800*, 1988, pp. 87–94.
46. See Horace Walpole's comment quoted in Bindman in *Kunst um 1800*, 1988, p. 89.
47. This remarkable painting has not been fully published as it was rediscovered only after the Zoffany exhibition of 1976. Despite the initial identification of the painting as of the Massacre of the Champ de Mars in 1791, it is reasonably certain that Farington (1 August 1794) is referring to this painting in Zoffany's studio as 'the women [*sic*] & Sans Culottes, dancing &c over the dead bodies of the Swiss Soldiers', and not the *Plundering the King's Cellar*, as Webster suggests (*Zoffany*, 1976, no. 108).
48. D. Jarrett, *Pitt the Younger*, London, 1974, pp. 166 and 174.
49. See J-P. Bertand, *Camille et Lucile Desmoulins*, Paris, 1986.
50. With a few changes of wording this version of events seems to have held from early broadsides, through Carlyle's *The French Revolution*, 1837, to J. M. Thompson's account in *The French Revolution*, Oxford, 1943, p. 333.
51. Reproduced in *Wordsworth*, 1987, fig. 17. For another engraving of the subject, without attribution but probably English, see de V 5160.
52. According to E. Bénézit, *Dictionnaire des Peintres*, Benazech was born in London and worked with Greuze after a period of study in Rome. His father, Peter-Paul Benazech, was an engraver who worked in London and Paris.
53. Portalis 1910, p. 87.
54. See Walzer 1974, especially chapter 2.
55. This is generally so despite Colley's observation of 'the conflation of royal and patriotic with religious terminology' in this period (Colley 1984, pp. 120–1).
56. In the sense used by Abie Warburg. See E. H. Gombrich, *Aby Warburg: An Intellectual Biography*, London, 1970, pp. 177–85.
57. British Museum, 1917-12-8-998 (Foreign History Series, 1793).
58. See *Louis XVI et son image*, exh. cat., Paris, October 1986.
59. British Museum, 1917-12-6-1895. See also no. 140 in the present catalogue.
60. Colley 1984, pp. 94–129.
61. Colley 1984, p. 125.
62. See note 54 above.
63. Thompson 1980, p. 111f.
64. Goodwin 1979, p. 220.
65. Goodwin 1979, pp. 478–92.
66. Burke 1790 (World's Classics edn, p. 86).
67. Goodwin 1979, p. 319.
68. For Thomas Spence see G. I. Gallop (ed.), *Pig's Meat: Selected Writings of Thomas Spence*, Nottingham, 1982, and H. T. Dickinson (ed.), *The Political Works of Thomas Spence*, Newcastle upon Tyne, 1982.
69. Goodwin 1979, p. 320.
70. Dickinson 1985, p. 17.
71. Goodwin 1979, p. 392.
72. Williams 1968, p. 103.
73. E. K. Chambers, *Samuel Taylor Coleridge*, Oxford, 1938, pp. 30–8.
74. Webster, *Zoffany*, exh. cat., 1976, no. 108.
75. Bindman in *Kunst um 1800*, pp. 93–4.
76. Hill, *Gillray*, 1965, p. 74.
77. Hill, *Gillray*, 1965, p. 67.
78. Hill, *Gillray*, 1965, p. 69.
79. Hill, *Gillray*, 1965, p. 74.
80. Quoted in Thompson 1980, p. 61. The Duke of York, however, appears to have been worried that too much emphasis upon the benefits of peace and prosperity might undermine the fighting spirit of British soldiers (see Deuchar 1988, pp. 157–60, and note 83 below).
81. Barrell 1980, p. 35f.
82. Colley 1984, p. 111.
83. For an example of the suspicion of disloyalty that could be aroused by works of art see the case of William Hodges's two paintings of *The Effects of Peace* and *The Effects of War* exhibited in 1794–5. The Duke of York closed down the exhibition on the grounds that they portrayed the horrors of war in such a way as to encourage hostility to the war against France. For a fascinating discussion of this incident see Deuchar 1988, pp. 157–9.
84. Farington, 28 December 1799, vol. IV, p. 1334.
85. Farington, 23 April 1794, vol. I, p. 182.
86. Farington, 5–6 May 1794, vol. I, pp. 186–7.
87. Bell 1938, p. 99. Banks appeared before the Privy Council on 14 June 1794 and claimed to have joined the SCI 'for the instruction he hoped to derive from it'. He seemed to have

persuaded the Privy Council that he was not involved in an active way with the Society and was dismissed without further charges.

88. W. L. Pressly (ed.), *Facts and Recollections of the XVIIIth Century in a Memoir of John Francis Rigaud Esq., R.A.*, *Walpole Society*, vol. L, 1984, p. 87. J. F. Rigaud claimed to have been one of the first to have enrolled as a member of Reeves's Crown and Anchor Society in November 1792.
89. Farington, 16 November 1795, vol. II, pp. 403–4.
90. See no. 171 and Girtin and Loshak 1954, p. 112.
91. Jaffé 1977, pp. 52–3.
92. Bindman 1982, pp. 10–14.
93. First published in F. W. Hilles, *Portraits by Sir Joshua Reynolds*, London, 1952, Appendix II, p. 123.
94. *Analytical Review*, December 1789, pp. 463–4. Quoted in *Fuseli* cat., 1975, p. 41.
95. Bindman 1982, p. 16f.
96. Erdman 1969, pp. 173–4.
97. Bindman, *Graphic Works*, 1978, no. 153.
98. Bindman, *Graphic Works*, 1978, no. 181.
99. Bell 1938, p. 83.
100. See his comments on the British Constitution as a 'sepulchre of precedents' and a kind of 'Political Popery', quoted in Thompson, 1980, p. 99.
101. Bindman, *Graphic Works*, 1978, no. 150.
102. Keynes, *Blake*, p. 149f.
103. Keynes, *Blake*, p. 150.
104. Essick, *Separate Plates*, 1983, p. 42, and Erdman 1969, p. 213.
105. Schiff 1963, pp. 12–13.
106. For a chronological catalogue of the *Milton Gallery* paintings, see Schiff 1963, p. 162.
107. Quoted in *Fuseli* cat., 1975.
108. Schiff 1963, pp. 162–3.
109. Tomalin 1974, p. 269.
110. Schiff 1973, vol. I, pp. 160–1.
111. 'Annotations to Reynolds'. Keynes, *Blake*, p. 446.
112. Pressly 1981, p. 100.
113. Pressly 1981, pp. 152–3.
114. Jaffé 1977, pp. 52–3.
115. *Prelude*, Book IX, 288–552.
116. According to Thomas Clio Rickman (*The Life of Tom Paine*, 1819, quoted in Jaffé 1977, p. 57) they were 'Lord Edward Fitzgerald; the French and American Ambassadors, Mr Sharp the engraver, Romney the painter, [and] Mrs Wolstonecroft [*sic*].
117. Jaffé 1977, p. 53, and nos 94–100.
118. Jaffé 1977, pp. 66–7.
119. Jaffé 1977, p. 67.
120. Keynes, *Blake*, pp. 383–96. Hannah More told Bishop Watson, referring to this book, 'that a shilling poison like Paine's should not have had a four shilling antidote' (Roberts 1834, vol. II, p. 446).
121. Keynes, *Blake*, p. 396.
122. Leslie and Chapman 1978, pp. 174–5.
123. Leslie and Chapman 1978, pp. 42–3.
124. Tussaud 1838.
125. There is a copy in the library of the Victoria and Albert Museum.
126. Copy at Madame Tussaud's, London.
127. Manchester catalogue, 1822, pp. 35–8.
128. See Dafforne 1879.
129. It first appeared in England in translation in 1847–8.
130. Dafforne 1879, pp. 26–8.
131. Dafforne 1879, p. 27.
132. 'Robespierre, Danton, and Camille Desmoulins had placed themselves on her passage to gaze on her; for all those who anticipated assassination were anxious to study in her features the expression of that fanaticism which might threaten them on the morrow . . . Hordes of savage furies followed her with imprecations to the scaffold' (quoted in Dafforne 1879, pp. 31–2).
133. Susan P. Casteras, *the Edward J. and Suzanne McCormick Collection*, Yale Center for British Art, 1984, no. 39.
134. Engraved by Alphonse François. There is an impression in the Musée de la Révolution Française, Vizille.

Abbreviated references and bibliography

Barrell 1980 J. Barrell, *The dark side of the landscape: The rural poor in English painting 1730–1840*, Cambridge, 1980

Bell 1938 C. F. Bell, *Annals of Thomas Banks*, Cambridge, 1938

Bell, *Political Tokens* R. C. Bell, *Political and commemorative pieces simulating tradesmens' tokens 1770–1802*, n.d.

Bennett 1988 Shelley Bennett, *Thomas Stothard: The Mechanisms of Art Patronage in England circa 1800*, Columbia, 1988

Bentley, *Blake Books*, 1977 G. E. Bentley jun., *Blake Books*, Oxford, 1977

Bindman 1977 D. Bindman, *Blake as an Artist*, Oxford, 1977

Bindman 1982 D. Bindman, *William Blake: His Art and Times*, exh. cat., Yale Center for British Art and Art Gallery of Ontario, 1982–3

Bindman, *Graphic Works*, 1978 D. Bindman, assisted by D. Toomey, *The Complete Graphic Works of William Blake*, London, 1978

Binyon 1902 L. Binyon, *Catalogue of Drawings by British Artists and Artists of Foreign Origin working in Great Britain preserved in the Department of Prints and Drawings in the British Museum*, London, 1898

Blanning 1986 T. C. W. Blanning, *The Origins of the French revolutionary Wars*, London, 1986

Brewer 1986 J. Brewer, *The Common People and Politics 1750–1790s*, Cambridge, 1986

Brown 1980 Laurence Brown, *A Catalogue of British Historical Medals*, vol. I, London, 1980

Butler 1982 Marilyn Butler, *Romantics, Rebels and Reactionaries*, Oxford, 1982

Butlin 1981 M. Butlin, *The Paintings and Drawings of William Blake*, 2 vols, New Haven and London, 1981

Carnavalet 1977 *L'Art de l'Estampe et la Révolution Française*, exh. cat., Musée Carnavalet, Paris, 1977

Causeries Alexandre Dumas, *Causeries*, 1860

Chambers 1938 E. K. Chambers, *Samuel Taylor Coleridge*, Oxford, 1938

Colley 1984 Linda Colley, 'The apotheosis of George III: loyalty, royalty and the British nation 1760–1820', *Past and Present*, no. 102, Feb. 1984, pp. 94–129

Conway, *Paine*, 1909 M. D. Conway, *The Life of Thomas Paine*, London, 1909

Dafforne 1879 J. Dafforne, *E. M. Ward, R.A.*, London, 1879

Dawson 1984 Aileen Dawson, *Masterpieces of Wedgwood in the British Museum*, London, 1984

Delécluze 1983 E J. Delécluze, *David, son école et son temps*, Paris, 1983 (reprint of 1855 edn)

Deuchar 1988 S. Deuchar, *Sporting Art in Eighteenth-Century England: A Social and Political History*, New Haven and London, 1988

Dickens, Victoria and Albert Museum, 1970 *Charles Dickens*, exh. cat., Victoria and Albert Museum, 1970

Dickinson 1985 H. T. Dickinson, *British Radicalism and the French Revolution 1789–1815*, Oxford, 1985

Dickinson 1986 H. T. Dickinson, *Caricatures and the Constitution 1760–1832*, Cambridge, 1986

Duffy 1986 M. Duffy, *The Englishman and the Foreigner*, Cambridge, 1986

Erdman 1969 D. V. Erdman, *Blake: Prophet against Empire*, rev. edn, 1969

Essick, *Separate Plates*, 1983 R. N. Essick, *The Separate Plates of William Blake: A Catalogue*, Princeton, 1983

Farington Diary K. Garlick and A. Macintyre, *The Diary of Joseph Farington*, New Haven and London, 1978–

Flaxman, R. A. D. Bindman (ed.), *John Flaxman, R. A.*, exh. cat., Royal Academy, 1979 (pottery section written by Bruce Tattersall)

Fonds Français *Inventaire des Fonds Français: Gravures du XVIIIe siècle*, Bibliothèque Nationale, Paris, 1931

French Printmaking, 1984–5 *Regency to Empire: French Printmaking, 1715–1814*, exh. cat., Baltimore and Minneapolis, 1984–5

Furet and Richet 1970 F. Furet and D. Richet, *The French Revolution*, London, 1970

Garlick 1964 K. Garlick, *A Catalogue of Paintings, Drawings and Pastels of Sir Thomas Lawrence, Walpole Society*, 1962–4

George 1959 M. Dorothy George, *English Political Caricature*, 2 vols., Oxford, 1959 and 1960

Girtin and Loshak 1954 T. Girtin and D. Loshak, *The Art of Thomas Girtin*, London, 1954

Godechot 1970 J. Godechot, *The taking of the Bastille*, London, 1970

Godfrey 1984 R. Godfrey (and L. Lambourne), *English Caricature 1620 to the present*, exh. cat., Victoria and Albert Museum, 1984

Goodwin 1979 A. Goodwin, *The Friends of Liberty: The English Democratic Movement in the age of the French Revolution*, London, 1979

Goya, Hamburg, 1980 Werner Hofmann (ed.), *Goya: Das Zeitalter der Revolutionen, 1789–1830*, exh. cat., Kunsthalle, Hamburg, 1980

Hennin, 1877 M. Hennin, *Inventaire de la Collection d'estampes . . . à la Bibliothèque Nationale*, Paris, 1877

Hill, *Gillray*, 1965 Draper Hill, *Mr Gillray The Caricaturist*, London, 1965

Hill 1976 Draper Hill (ed.), *The Satirical Etchings of James Gillray*, New York, 1976

Jaffé 1977 Patricia Jaffé, *Drawings by George Romney*, exh. cat., Fitzwilliam Museum, Cambridge, 1977

C. Jones 1983 C. Jones (ed.), *Britain and Revolutionary France: conflict, subversion and propaganda*, Exeter, 1983

Mark Jones 1977 Mark Jones, *Medals of the French Revolution*, London, 1977

Joppien 1973 R. Joppien, *Philippe Jacques de Loutherbourg, RA*, exh. cat., Kenwood, 1973

Jouve 1983 Michael Jouve, *L'Age d'Or de la Caricature Anglaise*, Paris, 1983

Keynes, *Blake* G. Keynes, *Blake: Complete Writings*, Oxford, 1957 and subsequent edns

Klingender 1944 F. D. Klingender, *Hogarth and English Caricature*, London, 1944
Kunst um 1800, 1988 C. Beutler, P-K. Schuster and M. Warnke (eds), *Kunst um 1800 und die Folgen: Werner Hofmann zu Ehren*, Munich, 1988
Leslie and Chapman 1978 A. Leslie and P. Chapman, *Madame Tussaud Waxworker Extraordinary*, London, 1978
Lewis 1984 J. and G. Lewis, *Pratt Ware*, Woodbridge, 1984
Lugt F. Lugt, *Les Marques de Collections de Dessins et D'Estampes*, Amsterdam, 1921
Marshall 1984 P. H. Marshall, *William Godwin*, New Haven and London, 1984
Newman 1987 G. Newman, *The Rise of English Nationalism: a cultural history*, London, 1987
Nicolson 1968 B. Nicolson, *Joseph Wright of Derby*, London, 1968
Paulson 1983 R. Paulson, *Representations of Revolution (1789–1820)*, New Haven and London, 1983
Pollard 1970 J. G. Pollard, 'Matthew Boulton and Conrad Heinrich Küchler', *Numismatic Chronicle*, 1970, pp. 259–318
Portalis 1910 R. Portalis, *Henri-Pierre Danloux Peintre de portraits et son journal durant l'emigration (1753–1809)*, Paris, 1910
Pot. Cat. R. L. Hobson, *Catalogue of English Pottery*, London, 1903
Pressly 1981 W. L. Pressly, *The Life and Art of James Barry*, New Haven and London, 1981
Pressly, *Barry* cat., 1983 W. L. Pressly, *James Barry: The Artist as Hero*, exh. cat., Tate Gallery, 1983
Priestley in Birmingham, 1980 J. Tann, S. Price and D. McCulla, *Joseph Priestley in Birmingham*, exh. cat., Birmingham Museums and Art Gallery, Birmingham, 1980
Reilly and Savage 1973 R. Reilly and G. Savage, *Wedgwood: The Portrait Medallions*, London, 1973
Roberts 1834 W. Roberts (ed.), *Memoirs of the Life and Correspondence of Mrs Hannah More*, 1834
Schiff 1963 Gert Schiff, *Johann Heinrich Füsslis Milton-Galerie*, Zurich, 1963
Schiff 1973 Gert Schiff, *Johann Heinrich Füssli: oeuvrekatalog*, Zurich, 1973
Fuseli cat., 1975 Gert Schiff, *Henry Fuseli 1741–1825*, exh. cat., Tate Gallery, 1975
Spence 1795 T. Spence, *The Coin Collector's Companion being a description of modern Political and other copper coins*, London, 1795
Thompson 1980 E. P. Thompson, *The Making of the English Working Class*, London, 1980
Tomalin 1985 Claire Tomalin, *The Life and Death of Mary Wollstonecraft*, London, 1974
Tussaud 1838 F. Hervé (ed.), *Madame Tussaud's Memoirs and Reminiscences of France, forming an abridged history of the French Revolution*, London, 1838
Vovelle 1986 M. Vovelle, *La Révolution Française: Images et Récit*, 5 vols, Paris, 1986
Vovelle 1988 M. Vovelle (ed.), *Les Images de la Révolution Française*, Paris, 1988
Walker, *Regency Portraits*, 1985 Richard Walker, *Regency Portraits*, National Portrait Gallery, London, 1985
Walzer 1974 M. Walzer, *Regicide and Revolution: Speeches at the trial of Louis XVI*, Cambridge, 1974
Waterhouse 1981 E. Waterhouse, *Dictionary of British 18th century painters in oils and crayons*, London, 1981
Waters 1917 Arthur W. Waters, *Trial of Thomas Spence*, Leamington Spa, 1917
Webster, *Wheatley*, 1970 M. Webster, *Francis Wheatley*, London, 1970
Webster, *Zoffany*, 1976 M. Webster, *Johan Zoffany 1733–1810*, exh. cat., National Portrait Gallery, London, 1976
Weiner 1960 M. Weiner, *The French Exiles, 1789–1815*, London, 1960
Wheeler W. Wheeler, *Catalogue of Pictures and Historical Relics in Madame Tussaud & Sons' Exhibition*, London, n.d. (but *c.* 1900)
Willett cat., 1899 *Catalogue of a Collection of Pottery and Porcelain illustrating Popular British History lent by Henry Willett esq., of Brighton*, Bethnal Green Branch of the Victoria and Albert Museum, South Kensington, London, 1899
Williams 1968 Gwyn A. Williams, *Artisans and Sans-Culottes: Popular movements in France and Britain during the French Revolution*, London, 1968
Wollstonecraft Anthology J. M. Todd (ed.), *A Wollstonecraft Anthology*, Bloomington, 1977
Wordsworth, 1987 J. Wordsworth, M. C. Jaye, R. Woof and P. Funnell (eds), *William Wordsworth and the Age of English Romanticism*, exh. cat., New York Public Library, 1987

Other works used

D. Bindman, 'Blake und die Französische Revolution', *Bildende Kunst*, Heft 12, 1983, pp. 594–8
J. Black, *Natural and Necessary Enemies*, London, 1986
J-C. Bonnet, *La Carmagnole des Muses: L'homme de lettres et l'artiste dans la Révolution*, Paris, 1988
P. A. Brown, *The French Revolution in English History*, London, 1918
R. Cobb and C. Jones, *The French Revolution: Voices from a momentous epoch*, London, 1988
T. E. Crow, *Painters and Public Life in 18th century France*, New Haven and London, 1985
O. Dann and J. Dinwiddy, *Nationalism in the Age of the French Revolution*, London, 1988
W. Doyle, *Origins of the French Revolution*, Oxford, 1980
Droits de l'Homme & Conquête des Libertés, Musée de la Révolution Française, Vizille, 1986
C. Emsley, *British Society and the French Wars 1793–1815*, London, 1979
E. H. Gombrich, 'The Dream of Reason: Symbolism in the French Revolution', *British Journal for Eighteenth-Century Studies*, Autumn, 1979, pp. 187–205
La Guillotine dans la Révolution, exh. cat., Vizille, 1987
L. Hunt, *Politics, Culture and Class in the French Revolution*, London, 1986
P. Jouve, 'L'image du sans-culotte dans la caricature politique anglaise', *Gazette des Beaux Arts*, vol. 92, 1978, p. 196
F. M. Kircheisen, *The Grim Bastille*, London, n.d.
I. Kramnick, *The Rage of Edmund Burke*, New York, 1977
Richard Margolis, 'Matthew Boulton's French ventures of 1791 and 1792: Tokens for the Monneron Brothers of Paris', *British Numismatic Journal*, vol. 58, 1988
Premières Collections, Musée de la Révolution Française, Vizille, 1985
G. Rudé, *The Crowd in the French Revolution*, Oxford, 1967
Charles Saunier, *Augustin Dupré*, Paris, 1894
D. M. G. Sutherland, *France 1789–1815: Revolution and Counterrevolution*, London, 1985
J. Tulard, J-F. Fayard and A. Fierro, *Histoire et dictionnaire de la Révolution française*, Paris, 1987
L. Werkmeister, *A Newspaper History of England 1792–3*, Lincoln, 1967
D. G. Wright, *Revolution and Terror in France 1789–1795*, London, 1974

Chronology

1776 American Declaration of Independence; publication of Thomas Paine's *Common Sense*

1780 JUNE Gordon Riots; foundation of Society for Constitutional Information

1783 Pitt the Younger's first ministry

1788 Centenary celebrations of 'Glorious Revolution' of 1688; Anglo–French Trade Treaty

1789 5 MAY Meeting of Estates-General
17 JUNE Tiers Etat becomes National Assembly in defiance of the king
20 JUNE Oath of Tennis Court, taken by deputies who agree to sit until they have established a Constitution
11 JULY Dismissal of the finance minister Necker
14 JULY Fall of the Bastille
4 AUGUST National Assembly agrees to abolish feudal privileges
26 AUGUST National Assembly adopts Declaration of the Rights of Man and the Citizen
5–6 OCTOBER March to Versailles by women of Paris and National Guard under Lafayette; French king brought to Paris
10 OCTOBER Dr Guillotin proposes novel and humane method of execution
2 NOVEMBER Nationalisation of church property

1790 MARCH Reform of Test and Corporation Acts defeated finally in Commons
19 JUNE Formal abolition of nobility and all hereditary titles
12 JULY Civil Constitution of the Clergy adopted by Assembly
14 JULY Fête de la Fédération at Champ de Mars in Paris
DECEMBER Publication of Burke's *Reflections on the Revolution in France*

1791 FEBRUARY Publication of Paine's *The Rights of Man*, part I; organisation of *émigré* army under prince de Condé at Worms
20–1 JUNE Royal family's flight and capture at Varennes
14 JULY Birmingham Riots and destruction of Priestley's house
17 JULY Massacre at the Champ de Mars of members of the crowd calling for the impeachment of the king
27 AUGUST Declaration of Pillnitz by Emperor of Austria and King of Prussia affirming their intention to return the King of France to his former power
14 SEPTEMBER King formally accepts Constitution before the National Assembly
9 NOVEMBER *Emigrés* ordered by Assembly to return to France on pain of confiscation or death, but king exercises Veto

1792 JANUARY Foundation of London Corresponding Society
FEBRUARY Publication of Paine's *The Rights of Man*, part II
APRIL Foundation of Association of the Friends of the People
28 APRIL France at war with Austria
21 MAY George III's proclamation against 'tumultuous meetings and seditious writings'
20 JUNE On the anniversary of the king's flight a crowd invades the Tuileries and humiliates Louis XVI by forcing him to wear a *bonnet rouge*
11 JULY Proclamation by the Assembly of 'la patrie en danger'; arrival of *fédérés* from the south of France
28 JULY the Duke of Brunswick's manifesto published, which threatens the people of Paris with punishment if they do not submit to the king
10 AUGUST One of the great revolutionary *journées* in which the Tuileries are captured and the king suspended. The Assembly agrees to set up a Convention to work out a new Constitution
13 AUGUST Royal family imprisoned in Temple
19 AUGUST Desertion of Lafayette to the Austrians
2 SEPTEMBER September Massacres begin of suspects kept in prisons
20 SEPTEMBER Battle of Valmy, a surprising victory for the French army over the Prussians, which effectively secures the Revolution at its most threatened moment
21 SEPTEMBER Formal abolition of the French monarchy

22 SEPTEMBER The first day of 'l'an I de la République française'
6 NOVEMBER Defeat of the Austrians by the French army at Jemappes; foundation of Association for Preserving Liberty and Property against Republicans and Levellers
19 NOVEMBER The Convention offers assistance to peoples seeking to regain their liberty
20 NOVEMBER Discovery of incriminating iron chest in the Tuileries
20 DECEMBER Trial of king opens

1793 17 JANUARY King condemned to death
21 JANUARY Execution of Louis XVI
1 FEBRUARY War declared by France upon England and Holland
MARCH Outbreak of Royalist insurrection in Brittany and Vendée, provoked by conscription
6 APRIL Establishment of Committee of Public Safety
2 JUNE *Journée* in which the Convention is forced to expel 29 Girondin deputies effectively putting the Montagnards in power
13 JULY Assassination of Marat by Charlotte Corday
28 JULY Capture of Valenciennes by Duke of York
2 AUGUST Marie Antoinette transferred from Temple to prison of Conciergerie
10 AUGUST *Fête révolutionnaire* on site of Bastille to commemorate *journée* of 10 August 1792 and promulgation of new Constitution
17 SEPTEMBER Law of suspects voted by Convention – effective beginning of the Terror
22 SEPTEMBER Beginning of l'an II and inauguration of Revolutionary Calendar
16 OCTOBER Execution of Marie Antoinette
31 OCTOBER Execution of Girondin deputies
7 NOVEMBER Execution of Philippe Egalité
10 NOVEMBER Fête de la Raison in deconsecrated cathedral of Notre-Dame

1794 24 MARCH Execution of Hébertists, radical opponents of Robespierre
5 APRIL Execution of Danton
10 MAY Execution of Madame Elizabeth, the king's sister
1 JUNE Naval victory of 'Glorious 1st of June'
8 JUNE Fête de l'Etre Suprême, the last great *fête révolutionnaire* under Robespierre
27–8 JULY Arrest and execution of Robespierre
5 AUGUST Release of suspects imprisoned under the Terror
OCTOBER–NOVEMBER Treason Trials with acquittal of Thomas Hardy, Horne Tooke and Thelwall
16 DECEMBER Execution of Carrier, the most brutal of the Terrorists

1795 7 MAY Execution of Fouquier-Tinville, *accusateur public* under the Terror
20 MAY Invasion of Convention by sans-culottes and assassination of Deputy Féraud: the last major intervention by the sans-culottes. Insurrection crushed in the next few days
8 JUNE Death of Dauphin in Temple. The Comte de Provence becomes Louis XVIII
31 OCTOBER Election of new Directory and end of Convention
NOVEMBER–DECEMBER Seditious Meetings and Treasonable Practices Act
18 DECEMBER Release of Louis XVI's daughter Marie-Thérèse Charlotte

1796 10 APRIL Beginning of Bonaparte's Italian campaign
10 MAY Bonaparte's victory over the Austrians at Lodi
20 JULY Hoche commander of army to invade Ireland
15–17 DECEMBER Beginning of abortive French attempt to invade Ireland under Hoche

1797 APRIL Naval mutinies, Spithead and the Nore; *The Anti-Jacobin* founded
19 SEPTEMBER Death of Hoche

1798 12 JANUARY Bonaparte presents plan for invasion of England to Directory
23 MAY Beginning of revolt in Ireland in expectation of help from Bonaparte
14 JULY Irish rebellion crushed by British army
1 AUGUST Nelson's decisive victory over French fleet in battle of the Nile: landing of French expeditionary force in Ireland, defeated in mid-September

1799 9–10 NOVEMBER Bonaparte's *coup d'état* removes Directory and Council of Five Hundred and establishes a Consulate with himself as First Consul; suppression of London Corresponding Society

Glossary

ancien régime The name subsequently given to the French monarchical system, the regime previous to the revolution of 1789.

bonnet rouge A red cap worn by revolutionaries, supposedly in emulation of freed slaves in antiquity.

Brissotins Followers of J. P. Brissot, a deputy and leader of the Girondins in the Assembly. They dominated the Convention from mid-1792 until their fall in June 1793. The leaders were imprisoned and executed on 30 October 1793. (See *Girondins*.)

Church and King Clubs Formed in 1791–2 in many towns by loyalists to combat the spread of Paine's ideas. (See *Crown and Anchor Society*.)

Civil Constitution of the Clergy (*Constitution Civile du Clergé*) In 1790 the Assembly voted to reorganise the clergy and demand from them an oath of allegiance to the Nation, King and Constitution, as well as to take over the assets of the French Church. The Pope's opposition in 1791 to these threats to his spiritual authority led to a sharp division between the 'Constitutional' clergy who accepted the oath and those who refused and were often forced into exile.

Committee of Public Safety (*Comité de Salut Public*) The Committee began as a link between the Convention and ministers in April 1793 but evolved into a dominant group of twelve men who took all the executive decisions of government and were responsible for instituting the Terror.

Convention The Convention replaced the Assembly on the demise of the French monarchy in September 1792. Its brief was to devise a new constitution for the Republic, while continuing to act as the governing assembly.

Council of Elders See *Directory*.

Council of Five Hundred See *Directory*.

Crown and Anchor Society Founded in November 1792 by John Reeves as the Association for Preserving Liberty and Property against Republicans and Levellers to provide propaganda material, for distribution among the labouring classes, in defence of the British constitution against 'French' ideas.

Dauphin The eldest son and heir of the French king.

Democrat Term of abuse used by English loyalists to denote sympathy with the French Revolution.

départements The 1789 Revolution allowed for a new division of France based on rational principles rather than ancient rights. In 1790 the country was divided into eighty-three *départements*, and the number increased as other territories were absorbed into France.

Directory (*Directoire*) The system set up to govern France from 26 October 1795 (4 Brumaire, l'an IV) until Bonaparte's *coup* of 10 November 1799 (19 Brumaire, l'an VIII). Legislative power was given to two chambers, the Council of Five Hundred and the Council of Elders, and executive power to five directors elected by them.

Fédération, Fête de la Spectacular ceremony held on 14 July 1790 on the Champ de Mars in Paris to celebrate national unity on the first anniversary of the fall of the Bastille.

fédérés National Guardsmen and others who came to Paris for the Fête de la Fédération of 14 July 1790. They represented a powerful revolutionary force especially in late 1792. Wordsworth accompanied groups of them returning home from Paris after Fédération in 1790.

fêtes révolutionnaires Quasi-religious ceremonies on an immense scale to consolidate national unity under the Revolution by re-enacting symbolically its ideals.

'Gagging Acts' The name given to the Acts of November 1795 against Treasonable Practices and Seditious Meetings, intended to curb radicals and supporters of peace with France.

Girondins The deputies, many of whom came from the Gironde, who dominated the Assembly and then the Convention from early 1792 until their fall in June 1793. Though humane and idealistic in most respects, they believed in aggressive war. Their more radical enemies, the Montagnards, with the support of the Parisian sections, had them arrested and eventually guillotined on 31 October 1793. (See *Brissotins*.)

Gordon Riots An anti-Catholic demonstration outside Parliament in 1780, led by Lord George Gordon, which was followed by several days of uncontrolled rioting and destruction of property.

Jacobins, the Jacobin Club A revolutionary club established in the Jacobin convent in Paris. Its membership reflected the growing popular intervention in political life in the years 1789–94. It ended under the control of Robespierre and his supporters and did not long survive his fall. 'Jacobin' became a term of derision in England like 'sans-culotte'.

journée Literally a day, but under the Revolution it denoted a popular uprising worthy of annual commemoration. The *journée* of 10 August 1792, for example, was celebrated for the decisive attack on the Tuileries which led to the formation of the first French Republic.

lettre de cachet An order for imprisonment, usually in the Bastille, which could be given on the sole authority of the king. Though in practice not used for political purposes by Louis XVI, the existence of such powers was perceived as one of the great symbolic injustices of the *ancien régime*.

London Corresponding Society (LCS) The society was founded in 1792 to campaign throughout the country for parliamentary reform. By contrast with the SCI it had more support among artisans. Despite periods of great success it suffered increasingly from government hostility and fragmentation, and in 1799 it was finally wound up.

loyalist General name for supporters of the British government who feared the spread of French revolutionary ideas.

Montagnards The Montagnards were the more radical members of the Assembly, and later the Convention, who grouped together on the higher benches. The more moderate deputies sat below in what was called the Plain. The Montagnards triumphed over their opponents after the *journée* of 2 June 1793.

National Assembly (*Assemblée Nationale*) On 17 June 1789 the Estates-General proclaimed itself a National Assembly in defiance of the king. After the Revolution it established itself in the Manège, by the Tuileries palace in Paris. It became a legislative assembly by the September 1791 Constitution and was replaced by the Convention in September 1792.

National Guard (*Garde Nationale*) It was formed on 13 July 1789 as a citizen's militia to restore order in Paris and remained a revolutionary force until after the fall of Robespierre.

poissardes The fishwives of northern France who were often caricatured as coarse and brawny. In British caricature the female equivalent of the sans-culotte.

sans-culotte Literally without the knee-breeches worn by the aristocracy, but a title adopted by artisans and popular revolutionaries, and those who claimed to speak for them, in the years 1792–4. The term was used indiscriminately and unfairly in Britain to denote a violent revolutionary.

September Massacres The first major atrocities of the Revolution, they took place in early September 1792 in the period of panic which followed the Duke of Brunswick's declaration that he would destroy Paris and reinstate Louis XVI. A great many priests and aristocrats were murdered as suspected traitors.

septembriseurs Derisive name given to those involved in the Massacres of early September 1792. (See *September Massacres*.)

Society for Constitutional Information (SCI) The SCI was founded originally in 1780 in support of Wilkes's campaign for parliamentary reform. It was revived in 1792 and became the voice of intellectual middle-class reformers like Horne Tooke.

Temple The Temple was a monastery in Paris, suppressed in 1790, the tower of which was used as a prison for the French royal family after August 1792.

Terror The name given to the system of public order, under the Committee of Public Safety, in the period from June 1793 to July 1794. It involved widespread surveillance and powers of denunciation, with extensive use of the guillotine to eliminate those suspected of treason.

Test and Corporation Acts Seventeenth-century acts which remained in force throughout the eighteenth century in England. They effectively barred all non-members of the Church of England from political life, and their repeal was the cornerstone of all parliamentary reform campaigns.

Thermidor Government The government which came to power on the fall of Robespierre on the *journée* of 9 Thermidor, l'an II (27 July 1794). It was replaced by the Directory on 26 October 1795 (4 Brumaire, l'an IV).

Vendée A *département* in western France which was the centre of the strongest counter-revolutionary movements, especially during the period of the Terror.

The Revolutionary Calendar

On 5 October 1793 the Convention, as part of its programme of inaugurating a new era of rationality, abolished the Gregorian calendar in favour of a new Republican one, which started from the foundation of the Republic on 22 September 1792. L'an I thus began on that date, l'an II on 22 September 1793, and so on. The year was divided into twelve months of thirty days each, plus five complementary days, or 'Sans-culottides'. The months themselves were divided not into weeks but into three *décades* of ten days each. The Republican calendar was finally abolished in 1806.

Because the Revolutionary months did not begin at the same time as the Gregorian months it is perhaps easier to see them not as equivalents of our months but, as they were originally conceived, as aspects of the character of the seasons in which they occurred. Thus Brumaire, i.e. the foggy month, corresponds to late October to late November, while Thermidor, the warm month, is late July to late August. They are laid out below according to their seasons:

Autumn: Vendémiaire, Brumaire, Frimaire

Winter: Nivôse, Pluviôse, Ventôse

Spring: Germinal, Floréal, Prairial

Summer: Messidor, Thermidor, Fructidor

Index